Unlocking the Digital Realm: An Introduction to Operating Systems

Table of Content

Chapter 1: The Foundation of Operating Systems

- Define the concept of operating systems and their fundamental role in computing.
- Explore the core functions performed by operating systems.
- Differentiate between various types of operating systems, including single-user, multi-user, real-time, and network operating systems.
- Explore the role of the kernel as the core component of an operating system.
- Explain the concepts of processes and threads in the context of operating systems.
- Discuss how operating systems manage memory resources.
- Explore the role of file systems in organizing and managing data.
- Explain the importance of device drivers in facilitating communication between hardware and software.
- Introduce the concept of system calls and application programming interfaces (APIs).
- Trace the historical development of key operating system concepts.

Chapter 2: Evolution of Operating Systems: Past to Present

- Explore the evolution of operating systems from the early days of computing.
- Discuss the emergence of time-sharing systems and their impact on user interaction.
- Compare and contrast single-user and multi-user operating systems.
- Explore the role of operating systems in the personal computer revolution.
- Discuss the evolution of operating systems to support networking capabilities.
- Explore how operating systems adapted to support client-server architectures.
- Discuss the challenges and benefits of distributed operating systems.
- Explore the impact of virtualization on operating system architecture.
- Discuss the evolution of operating systems for mobile devices.
- Discuss the role of operating systems in the internet age.

Chapter 3: Key Components and Functions of Modern Operating Systems

- Define the key components that constitute a modern operating system.
- Explore the evolution of GUIs in modern operating systems.
- Discuss various process scheduling algorithms used in modern operating systems.
- Explore advanced memory management techniques in modern operating systems.
- Discuss modern file system design principles.
- Discuss how modern operating systems handle device management.
- Explore the networking capabilities of modern operating systems.
- Discuss security measures implemented in modern operating systems.
- Discuss how modern operating systems optimize power consumption.
- Discuss user account control mechanisms in modern operating systems.

Chapter 4: Operating System Architectures: Unveiling the Framework

- Define the concept of operating system architectures.
- Explore the monolithic kernel architecture and its characteristics.
- Discuss the microkernel architecture and its approach to system design.
- Explore the hybrid kernel architecture, combining elements of monolithic and microkernel designs.
- Discuss the exokernel architecture and its focus on flexibility and resource management.
- Discuss operating system architectures that support virtualization.
- Discuss the client-server model as an architectural choice in operating systems.
- Discuss architectural considerations in distributed operating systems.
- Explore architectures designed for fault tolerance and reliability.
- Discuss the challenges of scalability in operating system design.

Chapter 5: User Interfaces and Interaction in Operating Systems

- Trace the historical development of user interfaces in operating systems.
- Explore key design principles of modern GUIs.
- Discuss different user interaction models in operating systems.
- Discuss how operating systems incorporate accessibility features.
- Explore the integration of gesture and touch interfaces in modern operating systems.
- Discuss the role of voice recognition and natural language processing in user interfaces.
- Discuss features that allow users to customize their operating system experience.
- Discuss how modern operating systems facilitate multitasking.
- Explore emerging interfaces in virtual and augmented reality environments.
- Discuss current trends in user experience design for operating systems.

Chapter 6: Security Measures and Challenges in Operating Systems

- Discuss the critical role of security in operating systems.
- Discuss methods of user authentication and authorization in operating systems.
- Discuss the role of firewalls in protecting operating systems from network-based threats.
- Discuss strategies for protecting operating systems from malware.
- Discuss the importance of timely security patching.
- Explore encryption mechanisms for protecting data at rest and in transit.
- Discuss technologies such as secure boot and trusted computing.
- Discuss the role of security auditing and logging in operating systems.
- Emphasize the role of user awareness in maintaining operating system security.
- Discuss common challenges and complexities in securing operating systems.

Chapter 7: Operating Systems in the Mobile Era: From Smartphones to IoT

- Define mobile operating systems and their role in powering smartphones and mobile devices.
- Trace the evolution of mobile operating systems from early handheld devices to smartphones.
- Explore the architecture of smartphones and how mobile operating systems integrate with hardware.
- Discuss the app-centric nature of mobile operating systems.
- Discuss the design principles of user interfaces in mobile operating systems.
- Discuss security challenges specific to mobile operating systems.
- Explore the role of operating systems in the context of IoT devices.
- Discuss how operating systems power wearable devices.
- Explore how mobile operating systems extend to tablets and hybrid devices.
- Discuss current and future trends in mobile operating systems.

Chapter 8: Future Horizons: Innovations and Trends in Operating Systems

- Discuss the dynamic nature of technology and its impact on the future of operating systems.
- Discuss the integration of artificial intelligence (AI) in operating systems.
- Explore the role of operating systems in edge computing environments.
- Discuss the potential integration of blockchain technology in operating systems.
- Explore the impact of quantum computing on operating system design.
- Discuss the concept of ephemeral operating systems that adapt to user behavior.
- Explore innovations in human-computer interaction within operating systems.
- Discuss the role of operating systems in promoting sustainability and green computing.
- Discuss how operating systems integrate with augmented and virtual reality environments.
- Discuss the concept of collaborative and decentralized operating systems.

Introduction

In the ever-evolving landscape of computing, operating systems stand as the cornerstone, orchestrating the intricate dance between hardware and software. Chapter 1, "The Foundation of Operating Systems," embarks on a journey to unravel the fundamental principles that underpin these systems. Through a comprehensive exploration of resource management, user interactions, and application execution, this chapter aims to provide a solid grounding for readers in the realm of operating systems.

Moving forward, Chapter 2, "Evolution of Operating Systems: Past to Present," invites readers on a captivating historical voyage. Tracing the trajectory from early batch processing systems to the sophisticated operating systems of the present era, this chapter highlights pivotal milestones, paradigm shifts, and the transformative influence these systems have had on the course of computing history.

As we venture deeper into the intricacies of modern computing, Chapter 3, "Key Components and Functions of Modern Operating Systems," takes center stage. This chapter intricately dissects the myriad components that constitute contemporary operating systems, shedding light on their nuanced functionalities and the synergies that enable a seamless user experience. It is a voyage into the heart of operating systems as they navigate the complexities of today's computing landscape.

With a robust understanding of operating system fundamentals and evolution, we pivot to Chapter 4, "Operating System Architectures: Unveiling the Framework." This chapter delves into the structural blueprints that define the architecture of operating systems. From monolithic kernels to microkernel designs, hybrid architectures, and beyond, readers will explore the frameworks shaping the functionalities and performances of these intricate systems.

As computing interfaces transitioned from command lines to graphical user interfaces (GUIs), Chapter 5, "User Interfaces and Interaction in Operating Systems," unfolds. This chapter explores the evolution of user interfaces, the principles of GUI design, and the diverse modes of interaction that have become integral to the user experience. It offers insights into the user-centric aspects of operating systems, reflecting the evolution towards more intuitive and responsive interfaces.

Security takes center stage in Chapter 6, "Security Measures and Challenges in Operating Systems." Operating systems are not just functional platforms; they are guardians of data integrity and user privacy. This chapter delves into the critical realm of cybersecurity, addressing authentication, authorization, malware protection, and the ongoing challenges of safeguarding operating systems from an ever-evolving threat landscape.

The narrative then shifts to Chapter 7, "Operating Systems in the Mobile Era: From Smartphones to IoT." This chapter navigates the transformational shift brought about by mobile operating systems. From the rise of iOS and Android to the integration of operating systems in Internet of Things (IoT) devices, readers will uncover the mobile-centric innovations reshaping the technological landscape.

Our exploration culminates in Chapter 8, "Future Horizons: Innovations and Trends in Operating Systems." As we gaze into the crystal ball of computing, this chapter unpacks emerging trends. From artificial intelligence integration to edge computing, blockchain, and quantum computing, readers will embark on a speculative journey into the potential future trajectories of operating systems.

This comprehensive guide aims not only to impart knowledge but to spark curiosity about the dynamic field of operating systems, inviting readers to contemplate their integral role in shaping the past, present, and future of computing.

Chapter 1: The Foundation of Operating Systems

Define the concept of operating systems and their fundamental role in computing.

The concept of operating systems (OS) lies at the heart of modern computing, serving as a foundational layer that orchestrates and manages the interaction between hardware and software components. An operating system is a crucial piece of software that acts as an intermediary between users and the computer hardware, providing a platform for executing applications and facilitating efficient utilization of system resources. Its multifaceted role encompasses tasks ranging from process management, memory allocation, and file system organization to device management, security enforcement, and user interface provision. The fundamental purpose of an operating system is to abstract the complexities of hardware interfaces, offering a standardized environment that empowers users and application developers to interact with computer systems in a streamlined and efficient manner.

At its core, the operating system acts as a supervisor, overseeing the execution of various processes and ensuring the orderly sharing of the system's resources. Process management is a key aspect, involving the creation, scheduling, and termination of processes – the individual units of program execution. The OS allocates processor time, manages communication between processes, and enforces synchronization to prevent conflicts. By providing a controlled execution environment, the operating system facilitates the illusion of multitasking, allowing users to run multiple applications concurrently without interference.

Memory management is another critical function of operating systems, responsible for allocating and deallocating memory to processes. This involves the creation of a virtual memory space that enables efficient utilization of RAM and storage devices. The OS employs techniques like paging and segmentation to optimize memory usage, ensuring that each process has the necessary space without encroaching on others. Memory protection mechanisms prevent unauthorized access, contributing to the stability and security of the overall system.

File systems, integral components of operating systems, organize and manage data storage. They provide a structured hierarchy for data storage and retrieval, enabling users to organize, access, and modify files. The OS abstracts the underlying complexities of storage devices, presenting a unified interface for interacting with diverse storage media. This abstraction layer enhances user convenience and shields applications from intricacies related to specific storage hardware.

Device management is fundamental to the operating system's ability to interface with a diverse range of hardware components. From input and output devices like keyboards and printers to storage devices and network interfaces, the OS acts as an intermediary, enabling seamless communication between applications and hardware peripherals. Device drivers, specialized modules within the operating system, facilitate this communication by translating generic commands from the OS into instructions understood by specific hardware.

Security is a paramount concern in modern computing environments, and operating systems play a pivotal role in enforcing security measures. Through user authentication, access control mechanisms, and encryption, the OS safeguards sensitive data and ensures that only authorized users can access specific resources. Furthermore, the operating system acts as a barrier against external threats, implementing firewalls, intrusion detection systems, and other security measures to fortify the system against malicious activities.

The user interface provided by the operating system serves as the primary means of interaction between users and the computer. Whether through command-line interfaces (CLI) or graphical user interfaces (GUI), the OS offers a platform for users to initiate commands, launch applications, and manage files effortlessly. The user interface contributes significantly to the overall user experience, making computing accessible to a broader audience by abstracting the complexities of underlying processes.

The concept of operating systems extends beyond traditional desktop and server environments to encompass diverse computing paradigms. Mobile operating systems, tailored for smartphones and tablets, bring the principles of OS to handheld devices, managing processes, memory, and security in a mobile context. Real-time operating systems (RTOS) prioritize responsiveness and predictability, making them suitable for applications where timing constraints are critical, such as in industrial automation and embedded systems.

As computing continues to evolve, operating systems evolve in tandem, adapting to emerging technologies and paradigms. The advent of cloud computing has led to the development of cloud operating systems, orchestrating virtualized resources in distributed environments. Containerization technologies, exemplified by Docker and Kubernetes, introduce a new layer of abstraction, enabling efficient deployment and management of applications across diverse computing environments.

In conclusion, the concept of operating systems represents a foundational pillar in the realm of computing, providing an essential framework for the seamless execution of applications and the efficient management of hardware resources. From process and memory management to file systems, security, and user interfaces, operating systems encapsulate a diverse array of functionalities that underpin the modern computing experience. As technology advances, the role of operating systems continues to evolve, adapting to new challenges and opportunities while maintaining their fundamental role as orchestrators of the intricate dance between software and hardware in the digital landscape.

Explore the core functions performed by operating systems.

Operating systems (OS) serve as the backbone of computer systems, performing a myriad of core functions that are essential for the efficient operation and management of hardware and software resources. At the heart of these functions is process management, a critical aspect that involves the creation, scheduling, and termination of processes—individual units of program execution. Operating systems allocate processor time, manage interprocess communication, and enforce synchronization to ensure that multiple processes can run concurrently without conflicts. This functionality is fundamental to the illusion of multitasking, allowing users to interact with diverse applications simultaneously while the operating system orchestrates the sharing of CPU resources.

Memory management stands as another cornerstone function, addressing the challenge of allocating and deallocating memory to processes. The OS creates a virtual memory space, providing an abstraction layer that enables efficient utilization of Random Access Memory (RAM) and storage devices. Techniques like paging and segmentation are employed to optimize memory usage, ensuring that each process has the necessary space for execution. Memory protection mechanisms prevent unauthorized access, contributing to the stability and security of the overall system.

File systems, a vital component of operating systems, manage the organization and storage of data. They provide a structured hierarchy for data storage and retrieval, enabling users to organize, access, and modify files. The OS abstracts the complexities of storage devices, presenting a unified interface for interacting with diverse storage media. This abstraction enhances user convenience and shields applications from intricacies related to specific storage hardware, facilitating a seamless and standardized approach to data management.

Device management is instrumental in the operating system's ability to interface with a diverse array of hardware components. From input and output devices like keyboards and printers to storage devices and network interfaces, the OS acts as an intermediary, facilitating communication between applications and hardware peripherals. Device drivers, specialized modules within the operating system, translate generic commands from the OS into instructions understood by specific hardware, ensuring compatibility and interoperability across a wide range of devices.

Security is paramount in modern computing, and operating systems play a pivotal role in enforcing security measures. Through user authentication, access control mechanisms, and encryption, the OS safeguards sensitive data and ensures that only authorized users can access specific resources. Beyond user-level security, the operating system acts as a barrier against external threats by implementing firewalls, intrusion detection systems, and other security measures to fortify the system against malicious activities and unauthorized access.

The user interface provided by the operating system serves as the primary means of interaction between users and the computer. Whether through command-line interfaces (CLI) or graphical user interfaces (GUI), the OS offers a platform for users to initiate commands, launch applications, and manage files effortlessly. The user interface contributes significantly to the overall user experience, making computing accessible to a broader audience by abstracting the complexities of underlying processes and providing an intuitive means of interaction.

Operating systems also play a crucial role in managing the input and output (I/O) operations of a computer system. This includes handling data transfers between the central processing unit (CPU) and peripherals such as disks, keyboards, and displays. I/O management encompasses buffering, caching, and scheduling mechanisms to optimize the flow of data, ensuring efficient communication between the CPU and various external devices. This function is vital for overall system efficiency and responsiveness.

Concurrency control and multithreading are integral functions that address the challenges of managing multiple tasks concurrently. Operating systems facilitate the creation and execution of threads, allowing for parallelism and efficient resource utilization. Synchronization mechanisms, such as locks and semaphores, are employed to prevent conflicts and ensure the orderly execution of threads. Multithreading enhances system responsiveness, enabling applications to perform multiple tasks concurrently and efficiently utilize multicore processors.

In addition to managing ongoing processes, operating systems also play a crucial role in initiating and overseeing the boot process. The bootstrapping process, commonly known as booting, involves loading the operating system into memory and initializing the hardware components of the computer. The OS handles tasks such as loading the kernel, initializing device drivers, and establishing the initial system state. The successful execution of the boot process is essential for bringing the computer system to a usable state.

Beyond these core functions, operating systems also extend their capabilities to include networking support. Networking functions enable communication between computers, facilitating tasks such as file sharing, printing, and internet connectivity. The OS manages network protocols, handles data transmission, and provides the necessary infrastructure for applications to communicate over local area networks (LANs) or the broader internet. Network support is integral for modern computing environments, enabling seamless connectivity and collaboration.

As technology evolves, operating systems adapt to emerging trends and paradigms. The rise of cloud computing has led to the development of cloud operating systems, orchestrating virtualized resources in distributed environments. Containerization technologies, exemplified by Docker and Kubernetes, introduce a new layer of abstraction, enabling efficient deployment and management of applications across diverse computing environments. These advancements highlight the adaptability and continual evolution of operating systems to meet the changing needs of contemporary computing.

In conclusion, the core functions performed by operating systems form the bedrock of modern computing, providing a comprehensive framework for managing processes, memory, files, devices, security, and user interactions. Operating systems act as orchestrators, seamlessly coordinating the intricate dance between hardware and software to deliver a cohesive and efficient computing experience. From the basic functions of process and memory management to the sophisticated aspects of security enforcement and network support, operating systems play a pivotal role in shaping the functionality and usability of computer systems across diverse computing environments.

Differentiate between various types of operating systems, including single-user, multi-user, real-time, and network operating systems.

Operating systems come in diverse types, each tailored to specific computing environments and user requirements. One fundamental categorization is based on the number of users the operating system can support simultaneously. In the realm of single-user operating systems, the primary focus is on providing a computing environment dedicated to a solitary user. These systems are commonplace in personal computers, laptops, and other devices used by individuals. Operating systems like Microsoft Windows, macOS, and various Linux distributions are prominent examples. They offer user-friendly interfaces, application management, and file systems, catering to the needs of a single user at a time.

Conversely, multi-user operating systems are designed to support concurrent interactions from multiple users. In these environments, several users can access the system and its resources simultaneously, making them well-suited for scenarios where collaboration and resource sharing are essential. Unix and its derivatives, such as Linux, are notable examples of multi-user operating systems. They provide robust user authentication, access control mechanisms, and facilitate concurrent execution of processes from multiple users. Multi-user systems are prevalent in enterprise environments, server deployments, and research institutions where shared access to computing resources is paramount.

Real-time operating systems (RTOS) represent another distinct category, characterized by their ability to meet stringent timing constraints for task execution. Real-time systems are employed in applications where tasks must be completed within precise deadlines to ensure system reliability and performance. Examples include industrial automation, aerospace systems, and medical devices. RTOS prioritize predictability and responsiveness, often employing scheduling algorithms that guarantee timely execution of critical tasks. VxWorks and FreeRTOS are examples of real-time operating systems widely used in embedded systems and critical applications where timing accuracy is crucial.

Network operating systems (NOS) are tailored for managing and coordinating network resources and services. These systems facilitate communication and resource sharing across interconnected computers within a network. Network operating systems are particularly relevant in environments where collaboration and information exchange are central, such as corporate networks. Novell NetWare, Windows Server, and Linux-based servers configured for network services exemplify NOS. These systems provide functionalities like file sharing, printer management, and user authentication, enhancing the collaborative potential of networked computing environments.

Another dimension of operating system classification considers the scope and purpose of the system. General-purpose operating systems cater to a broad spectrum of applications and user needs. Examples include Windows, macOS, and various Linux distributions, which offer comprehensive environments suitable for a wide range of computing tasks. Special-purpose operating systems, on the other hand, are designed for specific applications or hardware platforms. For instance, embedded operating systems are tailored to the constraints of embedded systems, such as those found in smart appliances, automotive control systems, and IoT devices. They prioritize efficiency, resource conservation, and customization to meet the unique demands of embedded applications.

Further classification arises from the architecture and design philosophy of operating systems. Microkernel and monolithic kernel architectures represent two distinct approaches. Monolithic kernels, as seen in traditional Unix-like operating systems, integrate most of the essential operating system functions into a single monolithic piece of software. In contrast, microkernel architectures modularize the operating system, keeping a minimal kernel that handles core functionalities, while additional services run as separate modules or user-space processes. This design enhances flexibility, maintainability, and adaptability in microkernel systems.

Another innovative class is the distributed operating system, designed for interconnected systems that collaborate to achieve a common goal. In a distributed operating system, multiple independent computers function as a unified system, sharing resources and coordinating tasks seamlessly. This is particularly relevant in cloud computing environments where resources are distributed across servers and data centers. Examples include Google's Chrome OS and various cloud-based operating systems that leverage distributed architectures to provide scalable and resilient computing resources.

Mobile operating systems constitute a specialized category designed for mobile devices such as smartphones and tablets. These systems prioritize power efficiency, touch interfaces, and mobility. iOS, developed by Apple for its mobile devices, Android, used by a multitude of smartphone manufacturers, and Windows Mobile are prominent examples of mobile operating systems. They offer app ecosystems, touch-friendly interfaces, and optimizations for portable and resource-constrained devices.

In summary, the differentiation between various types of operating systems is nuanced, reflecting the diverse needs and contexts in which computers operate. From single-user environments to real-time systems, networked environments, and specialized architectures, operating systems exhibit versatility to cater to an array of computing scenarios. As technology evolves, the boundaries between these classifications continue to blur, giving rise to hybrid and adaptive operating systems that blend features from different categories to meet the evolving demands of modern computing.

Explore the role of the kernel as the core component of an operating system.

At the heart of every operating system resides the kernel, a core component that plays a pivotal role in managing and controlling the computer's hardware resources. The kernel acts as the bridge between the hardware and the higher-level software layers, serving as the nucleus that orchestrates and regulates system operations. It is, in essence, the essential layer responsible for ensuring the seamless functioning of the entire operating system. In understanding the role of the kernel, one delves into the intricate details of how it interacts with various hardware components, facilitates process execution, manages memory, handles input and output operations, and enforces security policies.

The kernel's primary responsibility lies in managing processes, the dynamic entities that execute programs. It oversees the creation, scheduling, and termination of processes, allocating processor time and system resources efficiently. The kernel ensures that processes run cohesively, preventing conflicts and providing a controlled environment for the execution of diverse applications. Through process management, the kernel enables multitasking, allowing users to run multiple programs simultaneously without interference. This ability to juggle concurrent tasks lies at the core of the user experience, whether on a personal computer or within a complex server environment.

Memory management is another critical function of the kernel, addressing the complexities of allocating and deallocating memory for processes. The kernel creates a virtual memory space that abstracts the physical RAM and storage devices, optimizing the use of available memory resources. Techniques such as paging and segmentation are employed to efficiently manage memory, ensuring that each process has the necessary space for execution. Memory protection mechanisms prevent unauthorized access and contribute to the overall stability and security of the system.

Input and output (I/O) operations are fundamental to the functioning of any computer system, and the kernel takes a central role in managing these operations. From interacting with storage devices to handling user input and output to peripherals, the kernel facilitates seamless communication between the software and hardware layers. Device drivers, specialized modules within the kernel, enable the translation of generic commands from the operating system into instructions understood by specific hardware components. This abstraction allows for compatibility with a wide range of devices and peripherals.

Security is a paramount concern in modern computing environments, and the kernel serves as the guardian of system integrity. It enforces security policies, manages user authentication, and controls access to system resources. The kernel acts as a barrier against unauthorized access and malicious activities, implementing measures such as access control lists, encryption, and intrusion detection. By safeguarding the system's security, the kernel ensures the confidentiality, integrity, and availability of sensitive data and resources.

The kernel also oversees the system's bootstrapping process, commonly known as the boot sequence. During booting, the kernel is loaded into memory, initializing the essential components of the computer system. This includes loading the operating system's core functionalities, initializing device drivers, and establishing the initial system state. The successful execution of the boot process is critical for bringing the computer system to a usable state, making the kernel an integral component of the system's startup sequence.

In the realm of communication and synchronization, the kernel facilitates interprocess communication (IPC) and ensures coordination between concurrent processes. Mechanisms such as semaphores, mutexes, and message passing allow processes to communicate and synchronize their activities. The kernel's role in IPC is crucial for applications that require collaboration, data exchange, or coordination of tasks, contributing to the overall efficiency and reliability of the system.

The design and architecture of the kernel play a significant role in shaping the overall performance and stability of the operating system. Kernels come in different architectures, with monolithic and microkernel being two prominent models. In a monolithic kernel, most of the operating system's functionalities are integrated into a single, large piece of software. This design, exemplified by traditional Unix-like operating systems, facilitates efficient communication between components but may lack the modularity and flexibility offered by other architectures.

Microkernel architectures, on the other hand, modularize the kernel, keeping a minimal core that handles essential functions, while additional services run as separate modules or user-space processes. This design promotes modularity, making it easier to update or replace specific components without affecting the entire system. Microkernels are known for their adaptability and maintainability, allowing for greater flexibility in tailoring the operating system to specific needs.

As technology continues to evolve, the role of the kernel adapts to new challenges and opportunities. The emergence of virtualization technologies and containerization has influenced the design of kernels to support the efficient sharing of resources among multiple virtualized environments. Kernels in modern operating systems are also increasingly designed to support features like power management, ensuring energy efficiency in devices ranging from smartphones to servers.

Moreover, the kernel's role extends to real-time operating systems (RTOS), where timely execution of tasks is crucial. RTOS kernels prioritize predictability and responsiveness, employing scheduling algorithms that guarantee tasks are completed within precise deadlines. Such kernels find applications in critical systems like industrial automation, aerospace, and medical devices where timing accuracy is paramount.

In conclusion, the kernel stands as the core and critical component of an operating system, serving as the orchestrator that bridges the gap between hardware and software layers. Its multifaceted role encompasses process management, memory allocation, I/O operations, security enforcement, and system coordination. As the driving force behind the operating system, the kernel's design, functionality, and adaptability shape the overall performance, stability, and efficiency of modern computing environments. The evolution of technology continues to influence the kernel's role, as it adapts to meet the demands of contemporary computing paradigms and contributes to the seamless functioning of computer systems across diverse applications.

Explain the concepts of processes and threads in the context of operating systems.

In the realm of operating systems, the concepts of processes and threads are fundamental to the orchestration and execution of tasks. A process, in its broadest sense, encapsulates the execution environment for a program, providing the necessary resources and structure for its execution. It is a dynamic entity, representing the program in execution, along with its associated resources, such as memory, files, and devices. A process is characterized by its address space, which includes the program code, data, and stack, along with other attributes like process identifier (PID) and status information. Operating systems use processes as a means to isolate and manage the execution of multiple programs concurrently, fostering an illusion of multitasking and allowing users to interact with various applications simultaneously.

Within the context of processes, the concept of a thread emerges as a more granular unit of execution. A thread represents the smallest sequence of programmed instructions that can be managed independently by the operating system's scheduler. Threads within a process share the same address space, file descriptors, and other process-related resources, providing a lightweight and efficient means of achieving concurrency. Threads are often referred to as the "lightweight processes" as they exist within the context of a process and share its resources. The division of a process into multiple threads enables parallel execution of tasks, enhancing overall system responsiveness and performance.

The management of processes and threads is a complex undertaking handled by the operating system's kernel. The kernel oversees the creation, scheduling, and termination of processes and threads, ensuring a cohesive and controlled execution environment. When a program is executed, the operating system creates a new process for it, allocating the necessary resources, initializing the program counter, and establishing the initial state. Processes transition through various states such as ready, running, blocked, and terminated, depending on their execution status and interactions with the system.

The scheduling of processes and threads is a critical aspect of operating system functionality. The scheduler, a component within the kernel, determines the order in which processes and threads are allocated processor time. Various scheduling algorithms, such as First-Come-First-Serve (FCFS), Round Robin, and Priority Scheduling, dictate the order in which processes are given access to the CPU. Threads within a process share the same scheduling context, allowing the operating system to efficiently manage their execution.

Interprocess communication (IPC) is a vital consideration when multiple processes or threads coexist within a system. IPC mechanisms enable communication and coordination between processes and threads, facilitating the exchange of data and synchronization of activities. Common IPC techniques include shared memory, message passing, and semaphores. These mechanisms are essential for scenarios where collaboration, data exchange, or coordination between concurrently executing tasks is required.

The distinction between processes and threads lies in the level of isolation and resource sharing they exhibit. Processes provide a high level of isolation, with each process having its own address space, file descriptors, and resources. While this isolation enhances security and stability, it also incurs higher overhead due to the need for separate memory spaces. In contrast, threads share the same address space, making them more lightweight and efficient in terms of resource utilization. However, this shared space introduces the potential for conflicts, necessitating synchronization mechanisms to manage access to shared resources.

Multithreading, the concurrent execution of multiple threads within a single process, leverages the benefits of both isolation and resource sharing. Multithreaded applications exploit parallelism to enhance performance, as threads can execute independently and share data seamlessly. However, the design and implementation of multithreaded applications demand careful consideration of synchronization to avoid issues such as data races and deadlocks. The use of synchronization primitives like locks, mutexes, and semaphores ensures that threads coordinate their activities effectively.

Operating systems offer support for both user-level threads and kernel-level threads. User-level threads are managed entirely by user-space libraries, without kernel intervention. While lightweight, user-level threads lack the ability to exploit parallelism on multiprocessor systems efficiently. Kernel-level threads, managed by the operating system's kernel, offer more flexibility and can be scheduled independently, taking full advantage of multiple processors. However, the overhead associated with kernel-level thread management is higher compared to user-level threads.

The concepts of processes and threads are integral to the design and functionality of modern operating systems, shaping how programs are executed and resources are managed. The balance between isolation and efficiency, the orchestration of concurrency, and the intricacies of synchronization define the landscape of processes and threads within operating systems. Whether facilitating the execution of a single program or managing the parallelism within a complex application, processes and threads are the foundational elements that contribute to the dynamic and responsive nature of contemporary computing environments.

Discuss how operating systems manage memory resources.

Memory management is a critical aspect of operating systems, ensuring efficient utilization of a computer system's memory resources. The operating system's role in managing memory encompasses tasks such as allocation, deallocation, protection, and virtualization, all aimed at providing a seamless and secure environment for program execution. In understanding how operating systems manage memory, one delves into the complexities of physical and virtual memory, memory hierarchy, and the mechanisms employed to meet the diverse demands of applications running concurrently on a system.

At the heart of memory management lies the concept of physical memory, the actual hardware space where data and instructions reside. Physical memory, often referred to as RAM (Random Access Memory), serves as the working space for currently executing programs. The operating system is responsible for efficiently allocating portions of this physical memory to different processes, ensuring that each process has sufficient space for its data and code.

One of the key challenges in memory management is dealing with the limited physical memory available in a system. To overcome this limitation, operating systems employ techniques such as virtual memory, a layer of abstraction that allows processes to access more memory than is physically available. Virtual memory creates the illusion of a vast, contiguous address space for each process, enabling the efficient sharing of resources and enhancing the system's overall flexibility.

The concept of paging is integral to virtual memory management. Operating systems divide physical memory into fixed-size blocks called pages and extend this concept to the virtual address space of processes. When a process needs more memory than is physically available, the operating system swaps out unused pages to disk, making room for pages that are actively in use. This swapping, managed by the memory manager, ensures that processes can execute without being constrained by the limitations of physical memory.

Another technique employed in memory management is segmentation, which divides the address space of a process into logically meaningful segments, such as code, data, and stack. Each segment is managed independently, providing a flexible and structured approach to memory organization. Segmentation allows for the dynamic growth of data structures and facilitates protection mechanisms by assigning access permissions to different segments.

In addition to managing the allocation and deallocation of memory, operating systems play a crucial role in protecting the integrity of memory spaces. Memory protection mechanisms prevent unauthorized access to memory regions, ensuring that each process can only access the portions of memory allocated to it. Unauthorized access attempts result in exceptions or segmentation faults, preserving the stability and security of the overall system.

Address translation is a pivotal aspect of memory management, enabling the mapping of virtual addresses to physical addresses. The Memory Management Unit (MMU), a hardware component closely tied to the operating system, performs this translation. Through techniques such as page tables, the MMU translates virtual addresses used by processes into corresponding physical addresses in the actual memory. This translation ensures that each process operates within its allocated memory space, contributing to the isolation and security of processes.

Operating systems also engage in demand paging, a strategy that loads only the necessary portions of a program into memory when they are actively required. This approach minimizes the initial loading time of programs and optimizes memory usage by fetching pages from disk on-demand. Demand paging is particularly beneficial in scenarios where not all portions of a program are utilized during its execution, conserving physical memory for actively used code and data.

Memory fragmentation poses a challenge to efficient memory utilization. Fragmentation can occur in two forms: external fragmentation, where free memory is scattered in small chunks, and internal fragmentation, where allocated memory is not fully utilized. To address fragmentation, operating systems employ techniques such as compaction, which rearranges the allocated memory to create larger contiguous blocks, and memory allocation algorithms that aim to minimize both forms of fragmentation.

The choice of memory allocation algorithm significantly impacts system performance. First-Fit, Best-Fit, and Worst-Fit algorithms determine how free memory is allocated to processes. These algorithms strike a balance between simplicity and efficiency, with each having its advantages and trade-offs. First-Fit is straightforward but may lead to fragmentation, Best-Fit aims to minimize waste by selecting the smallest available block, and Worst-Fit attempts to optimize for larger allocations.

Shared memory is a concept in memory management that facilitates communication and collaboration between processes. Operating systems provide mechanisms for processes to share portions of their address spaces, allowing them to exchange data without the need for complex interprocess communication mechanisms. Shared memory is particularly useful in scenarios where multiple processes need to collaborate or communicate efficiently.

In multiprogramming environments, where multiple processes execute concurrently, the operating system must allocate processor time and memory resources judiciously. Scheduling algorithms, a crucial component of memory management, determine the order in which processes are given access to the CPU. The scheduler selects processes based on factors such as priority, execution history, and responsiveness, contributing to fair resource distribution and system responsiveness.

In conclusion, memory management is a multifaceted aspect of operating systems, encompassing the efficient allocation, protection, and utilization of memory resources. From the abstraction of virtual memory to the intricacies of paging, segmentation, and address translation, operating systems navigate the complexities of memory organization to provide a cohesive and secure environment for program execution. As technology evolves, memory management techniques continue to adapt to meet the demands of increasingly sophisticated applications and diverse computing environments. The delicate balance between physical and virtual memory, coupled with the optimization of allocation algorithms, ensures that modern operating systems can effectively harness memory resources to deliver responsive and efficient computing experiences.

Explore the role of file systems in organizing and managing data.

File systems serve as the backbone of modern computing, providing the organizational framework for storing, retrieving, and managing data on storage devices. At the core of their functionality is the fundamental concept of files, which represent discrete units of data ranging from documents and images to executable programs. The role of file systems extends beyond a mere container for data; it encompasses a complex set of structures, protocols, and algorithms designed to facilitate efficient data storage, retrieval, and maintenance. Understanding the intricate mechanisms of file systems involves delving into concepts such as directory structures, file naming conventions, access controls, and the various strategies employed to ensure data integrity and reliability.

Central to the organization of data within file systems is the concept of directories or folders. Directories provide a hierarchical structure, allowing users to organize files into meaningful and logical groupings. This hierarchical arrangement not only simplifies the management of data but also aids in locating and accessing files efficiently. Directories can contain both files and subdirectories, enabling users to create a well-organized and navigable hierarchy that mirrors the logical structure of their data.

File naming conventions play a crucial role in file systems, providing a means to uniquely identify and differentiate files. These conventions typically include rules for permissible characters, length restrictions, and case sensitivity. A well-defined naming scheme contributes to the orderliness of file systems, making it easier for users to recognize and locate specific files amidst a potentially vast and diverse collection. Additionally, file extensions are often employed to denote the type or format of a file, aiding both users and the operating system in understanding how to interpret and handle the data.

Access controls are essential components of file systems, ensuring that only authorized users or processes can read, write, or execute specific files. File permissions, assigned based on user roles or groups, dictate the level of access granted to individuals. By enforcing access controls, file systems contribute to data security, protecting sensitive information from unauthorized modification or disclosure. This aspect becomes particularly crucial in multi-user environments and shared storage systems.

One of the key features of file systems is their ability to manage the physical storage of data on storage devices. The organization of data on disk involves the use of data structures such as file allocation tables (FAT), master file tables (MFT), or indexed allocation methods. These structures maintain metadata about files, including their location, size, and attributes. Through these mechanisms, file systems optimize storage space, reduce fragmentation, and enable efficient data retrieval.

File allocation strategies determine how space is allocated on storage devices to accommodate files. Common allocation methods include contiguous allocation, where files occupy consecutive blocks of storage, and linked allocation, where each file points to the next block in a chain-like structure. Additionally, indexed allocation employs index structures to map file blocks, allowing for random access and efficient retrieval. The choice of allocation strategy impacts factors such as file access speed, storage efficiency, and fragmentation.

In the pursuit of enhanced reliability and data integrity, file systems often incorporate features such as journaling and versioning. Journaling maintains a log of file system transactions, facilitating recovery in the event of unexpected system failures or crashes. Versioning, on the other hand, keeps track of multiple versions of a file, allowing users to revert to previous states or recover data from specific points in time. These features contribute to the resilience of file systems, safeguarding data against accidental loss or corruption.

File systems must contend with the challenge of data storage on various types of storage devices, including hard disk drives (HDDs), solid-state drives (SSDs), and network-attached storage (NAS). Each type of storage device comes with its unique characteristics, influencing factors such as access speed, durability, and cost. Modern file systems are designed to adapt to the specific traits of these devices, optimizing performance and ensuring compatibility across a diverse range of storage technologies.

The concept of file systems extends beyond local storage to networked environments, where distributed file systems enable collaborative work and data sharing among multiple users or systems. Network file systems (NFS) and distributed file systems (DFS) facilitate seamless access to files and directories over a network, allowing users to collaborate and share resources irrespective of physical location. The complexities of distributed file systems involve addressing issues such as latency, synchronization, and data consistency across interconnected nodes.

Data redundancy and backup mechanisms are critical aspects of file systems, addressing the need for data preservation and recovery. Redundancy involves creating duplicate copies of important files or employing techniques such as RAID (Redundant Array of Independent Disks) to enhance data resilience. Backup strategies, including periodic backups to external storage or cloud-based solutions, provide an additional layer of protection against data loss due to hardware failures, accidental deletions, or other unforeseen events.

The evolution of file systems has been influenced by the advent of cloud computing, ushering in cloud-based file systems that provide scalable and distributed storage solutions. Cloud file systems offer the flexibility to store and access data across geographically dispersed servers, catering to the dynamic demands of modern applications and services. These file systems integrate with cloud platforms, enabling seamless data migration, synchronization, and collaboration in a virtualized and scalable environment.

As technology advances, file systems continue to evolve to meet the demands of an increasingly digital and interconnected world. Concepts such as object storage, which organizes data as discrete objects with unique identifiers, and file systems designed for specialized workloads, such as those used in high-performance computing (HPC) or big data analytics, showcase the adaptability and versatility of file system architectures. The pursuit of improved performance, scalability, and resilience remains at the forefront of file system development.

In conclusion, the role of file systems in organizing and managing data is multifaceted, encompassing organizational structures, naming conventions, access controls, storage optimization, and features designed to enhance reliability and resilience. File systems form the bedrock of data management in computing environments, providing users with an intuitive and efficient means of interacting with their data. Whether navigating the hierarchical structures of local directories or leveraging distributed file systems in networked environments, users and applications rely on file systems to organize, protect, and access the vast array of digital information that defines the modern computing experience.

Explain the importance of device drivers in facilitating communication between hardware and software.

Device drivers play a pivotal role in the intricate interplay between hardware and software, serving as the essential conduits that enable communication and collaboration within a computing system. At the core of their significance lies the fundamental challenge of bridging the abstraction divide between the high-level instructions executed by software and the intricate, specialized operations performed by hardware components. These drivers act as indispensable translators, converting generic software commands into precise instructions that hardware devices can comprehend and execute. This translation layer is crucial for the seamless functioning of the diverse array of hardware peripherals and components that constitute a modern computer system.

In essence, a device driver serves as the intermediary between the operating system and a specific hardware device. It encapsulates the intricacies of hardware communication protocols, device-specific functionalities, and low-level operations, shielding higher-level software layers from the complexities of hardware interactions. By abstracting the hardware details, device drivers provide a standardized interface through which software applications can communicate with a variety of hardware devices, ranging from basic input/output devices like keyboards and mice to more complex components such as graphics cards, network adapters, and storage devices.

One of the primary functions of device drivers is to facilitate the initialization and configuration of hardware components during the system's bootstrapping process. As the operating system initializes, device drivers are loaded to establish communication with critical hardware elements. This initialization involves configuring hardware settings, allocating resources, and ensuring that the hardware is in a state ready for interaction with software components. Without this foundational role, the seamless integration of hardware into the computing environment would be compromised, leading to system instability and the inability to leverage the full potential of hardware capabilities.

Furthermore, device drivers are instrumental in implementing a standardized and consistent interface for software applications to interact with various hardware devices. This standardization is essential for software developers, as it abstracts the specific intricacies of each hardware device, allowing them to write code that can be executed across a broad spectrum of systems without the need for device-specific modifications. This abstraction layer is particularly crucial in heterogeneous computing environments, where diverse hardware configurations are prevalent, ensuring that software remains hardware-agnostic and compatible across a range of devices.

Device drivers contribute significantly to the efficiency and performance of a computing system by optimizing the communication between software and hardware. Through efficient data transfer mechanisms, optimized algorithms, and streamlined command execution, device drivers enhance the overall responsiveness of hardware devices. In the realm of graphics processing units (GPUs), for example, specialized graphics drivers are pivotal for rendering complex visuals in applications such as video games and graphic design software. These drivers implement optimized algorithms that exploit the parallel processing capabilities of GPUs, ensuring smooth and responsive graphics rendering.

In the context of network adapters, device drivers are critical for enabling communication between a computer and a network. Network interface card (NIC) drivers implement protocols and algorithms for data packet transmission and reception, as well as for error detection and correction. The efficiency of these drivers directly influences network performance, affecting data transfer speeds, latency, and overall network responsiveness. In scenarios where high-performance networking is crucial, such as data centers or real-time communication applications, the role of well-optimized network drivers becomes paramount.

Device drivers also play a pivotal role in power management and energy efficiency. Modern computing systems often feature advanced power management capabilities to optimize energy consumption and extend battery life in mobile devices. Power management drivers interact with hardware components to dynamically adjust power states, clock frequencies, and voltage levels based on system workload and user activity. Through these interactions, device drivers contribute to the balance between system performance and energy efficiency, particularly in laptops, tablets, and other portable devices.

Moreover, device drivers are indispensable for the proper functioning of peripheral devices such as printers, scanners, and external storage devices. Printer drivers, for instance, interpret print job commands from software applications and translate them into printer-specific language for accurate and efficient printing. Without the printer driver acting as the intermediary, the software would lack the means to communicate the precise instructions needed for the diverse array of printers available in the market.

Storage device drivers, including those for hard disk drives (HDDs) and solid-state drives (SSDs), play a critical role in managing data storage and retrieval. These drivers implement file system interactions, manage data caching, and optimize read and write operations. The efficiency of storage device drivers directly impacts system responsiveness, application loading times, and overall data access speeds. In the rapidly evolving landscape of storage technologies, drivers also play a role in leveraging new features such as advanced encryption, wear leveling, and error correction mechanisms.

The significance of device drivers extends beyond traditional computing environments to encompass embedded systems, IoT (Internet of Things) devices, and specialized hardware configurations. Embedded systems, ranging from smart appliances to industrial control systems, rely on device drivers to facilitate communication with sensors, actuators, and other embedded components. The adaptability of device drivers allows them to accommodate the diverse requirements of specialized hardware configurations, ensuring that software applications can seamlessly interface with custom or proprietary devices.

In the realm of audio processing, sound card drivers are crucial for enabling the translation of digital audio signals into analog signals for output through speakers or headphones. These drivers implement audio processing algorithms, manage audio buffers, and ensure synchronization between audio playback and system timing. The quality and efficiency of audio drivers directly impact the fidelity and responsiveness of audio playback in multimedia applications, gaming, and content creation.

The dynamic landscape of device drivers is influenced by ongoing developments in hardware technology, operating system advancements, and the evolution of software applications. Manufacturers regularly release updated drivers to address compatibility issues, enhance performance, and introduce support for new features. The seamless integration of hardware advancements, such as new graphics rendering techniques or networking protocols, often relies on the availability of corresponding device driver updates that unlock the full potential of these innovations.

In conclusion, the importance of device drivers in facilitating communication between hardware and software cannot be overstated. These drivers serve as indispensable intermediaries, translating high-level software commands into precise instructions that hardware devices can execute. By abstracting the intricacies of hardware communication, device drivers provide a standardized interface for software applications to interact with a diverse array of hardware peripherals and components. Their role encompasses initialization, configuration, optimization, and standardization, contributing to the efficiency, performance, and reliability of computing systems across a broad spectrum of devices and applications. As technology continues to advance, the role of device drivers remains pivotal in ensuring seamless interoperability and unlocking the full potential of emerging hardware innovations.

Introduce the concept of system calls and application programming interfaces (APIs).

The concept of system calls and application programming interfaces (APIs) lies at the heart of modern computing, serving as crucial mechanisms that facilitate communication and interaction between software applications and the underlying operating system. These foundational concepts form the bridge between the high-level abstractions of software and the low-level functionalities of the operating system, enabling developers to harness the power of the underlying hardware while abstracting complexities for efficient and standardized software development.

System calls represent a fundamental interface through which user-level programs or applications communicate with the kernel of an operating system. The kernel, as the core component of the operating system, manages essential tasks such as process scheduling, memory management, file system operations, and device interaction. However, direct access to the kernel by user-level applications is restricted for security and stability reasons. System calls provide a controlled and well-defined mechanism for applications to request specific services or functionalities from the operating system.

When a program requires a service that involves privileged operations, such as reading from or writing to a file, allocating memory, or interacting with hardware devices, it initiates a system call. This entails a transition from user mode, where regular application code runs, to kernel mode, where the operating system kernel executes. The system call acts as a gatekeeper, mediating the interaction between user-level applications and the underlying operating system, ensuring that sensitive operations are performed with the necessary permissions and controls.

System calls cover a diverse range of functionalities, each associated with specific operations and services provided by the operating system. For instance, file-related system calls allow applications to open, read, write, and close files, while process-related system calls govern aspects such as process creation, termination, and communication. Other categories of system calls include those related to memory management, networking, interprocess communication, and device interaction. Each system call has a unique identifier or number associated with it, and the operating system kernel dispatches the appropriate service based on the provided identifier.

In addition to system calls, APIs play a pivotal role in facilitating software development by providing a set of interfaces, protocols, and tools for building applications. An API acts as an abstraction layer that shields developers from the complexities of underlying implementations, allowing them to interact with software components, libraries, or services in a standardized and efficient manner. APIs serve as a contract between different software modules or layers, defining how they can communicate and interoperate.

Application Programming Interfaces encompass a broad spectrum of interfaces, ranging from low-level APIs that interact with hardware or operating system services to high-level APIs that provide abstractions for specific functionalities or services. System APIs, closely related to system calls, expose a set of functions that applications can use to interact with the underlying operating system. These functions often encapsulate common system call patterns, making it more convenient for developers to incorporate operating system services into their applications.

A notable example of a system API is the POSIX API, which provides a standardized interface for interacting with operating systems that adhere to the POSIX (Portable Operating System Interface) standard. POSIX-compliant systems, including various Unix-like operating systems, share a common set of system calls and API functions, enabling developers to write portable and platform-independent code. This standardization simplifies the process of porting applications across different operating systems, fostering compatibility and interoperability.

Higher-level APIs, often associated with specific programming languages or libraries, abstract lower-level functionalities, providing developers with ready-made tools and building blocks to expedite application development. For instance, graphical user interface (GUI) APIs, such as the Windows API for Microsoft Windows or the Cocoa API for macOS, offer developers pre-built components and functions for creating interactive and visually appealing user interfaces. These APIs encapsulate complex operations related to window management, event handling, and graphical rendering, allowing developers to focus on application logic rather than low-level implementation details.

Web APIs, a prevalent category in modern software development, facilitate communication and data exchange between web-based applications. Web APIs define protocols and conventions for making requests and receiving responses over the internet. Representational State Transfer (REST) and GraphQL are common architectural styles for designing web APIs, providing standardized approaches for building scalable and interoperable web services. Web APIs enable diverse applications to interact, share data, and provide services in a distributed and interconnected digital landscape.

The concept of system calls and APIs intertwines at various levels of software development. System calls serve as the foundational mechanism for applications to access operating system services, while APIs, both at the system and application levels, offer developers the means to build robust, scalable, and interoperable software solutions. The relationship between system calls and APIs exemplifies the abstraction hierarchy in computing, allowing developers to navigate between different layers of the software stack while adhering to established standards and conventions.

The evolution of computing has seen the proliferation of APIs in diverse domains, reflecting the growing complexity and interconnectedness of modern software ecosystems. Cloud computing platforms leverage APIs to provide scalable and programmable infrastructure services, allowing developers to provision resources, manage data, and deploy applications through standardized interfaces. In the context of microservices architecture, APIs play a central role in facilitating communication and coordination between independently deployable services, contributing to the agility and scalability of distributed systems.

The symbiotic relationship between system calls and APIs underscores their collective impact on the efficiency, portability, and extensibility of software applications. Developers leverage system calls to harness the capabilities of the operating system, while APIs empower them to interact with a multitude of software components, services, and platforms. The adherence to standardized APIs fosters a collaborative and interoperable ecosystem, enabling the seamless integration of diverse technologies and promoting innovation in software development. As computing continues to advance, the concepts of system calls and APIs remain foundational, shaping the landscape of software development and influencing the design principles of modern, interconnected applications.

Trace the historical development of key operating system concepts.

The historical development of key operating system concepts is a fascinating journey that reflects the evolution of computing from its nascent stages to the complex, interconnected digital ecosystems of the present day. The roots of operating systems trace back to the early days of mainframe computers and batch processing systems, where the need for efficient resource utilization and task management became apparent. In the 1950s, systems like the UNIVAC I and IBM's OS/360 laid the groundwork for essential operating system functions. These early systems focused on managing hardware resources such as the central processing unit (CPU) and introduced the concept of job scheduling to optimize the utilization of expensive computing resources.

The advent of time-sharing systems in the 1960s marked a significant milestone in operating system development. MIT's CTSS (Compatible Time-Sharing System) and the later MULTICS (Multiplexed Information and Computing Service) project pioneered the idea of allowing multiple users to interact with a computer simultaneously. Time-sharing systems introduced the concept of virtualization, allowing users to have the illusion of dedicated access to the computer's resources while sharing them efficiently. This era also saw the emergence of the first file systems, enabling users to store and retrieve data in a more organized and accessible manner.

The 1970s witnessed the birth of UNIX, a landmark operating system developed at Bell Labs by Ken Thompson, Dennis Ritchie, and others. UNIX introduced several key concepts that have become foundational in the world of operating systems. The hierarchical file system structure, the notion of processes, and the idea of a shell for interacting with the operating system were pivotal innovations. UNIX's design principles emphasized simplicity, modularity, and portability, making it highly influential and eventually leading to the development of various UNIX-like operating systems.

Simultaneously, the concept of microkernels started gaining attention. The idea behind microkernels was to minimize the kernel's functionality and move non-essential services, such as file systems and device drivers, to user space. This approach aimed to enhance the system's reliability and maintainability. The Mach microkernel, developed at Carnegie Mellon University, was a prominent example that influenced subsequent operating system designs, including the development of Apple's macOS.

The 1980s witnessed the rise of personal computers, and with them, the popularization of graphical user interfaces (GUIs). Operating systems like Apple's Macintosh System Software and Microsoft's Windows introduced a more intuitive way for users to interact with computers. GUIs relied on window managers, which allowed users to work with multiple applications simultaneously, introducing concepts like multitasking and windowing systems. Concurrently, the concept of a graphical desktop environment, exemplified by the X Window System, provided a standardized way to create graphical interfaces across different UNIX systems.

In the realm of real-time operating systems (RTOS), the 1980s saw the development of operating systems designed to meet stringent timing constraints. RTOS found applications in embedded systems, aerospace, and industrial control systems, where timely and predictable responses are critical. QNX, a real-time UNIX-like operating system, emerged as a notable player in this domain, showcasing the adaptability of operating system concepts to diverse application domains.

The 1990s witnessed the ascendance of Microsoft Windows as a dominant desktop operating system. Windows 95 introduced a 32-bit architecture, preemptive multitasking, and a more user-friendly interface. This era also marked the emergence of Linux, an open-source UNIX-like operating system kernel. Linux, coupled with the GNU userland utilities, offered a free and highly customizable alternative to proprietary UNIX and Windows operating systems. The collaborative nature of open-source development contributed to the rapid evolution and widespread adoption of Linux.

The concept of distributed operating systems gained prominence in the 1990s as networks became more prevalent. Distributed systems aimed to provide a seamless experience for users accessing resources across interconnected computers. Operating systems like Novell NetWare and Microsoft Windows NT introduced features for managing distributed file systems and network resources. The rise of the internet further fueled the need for operating systems that could support distributed computing on a global scale.

As the 21st century unfolded, the proliferation of mobile devices brought new challenges and opportunities for operating system design. The development of smartphones and tablets necessitated operating systems optimized for touchscreens, energy efficiency, and seamless connectivity. Apple's iOS and Google's Android emerged as dominant players in the mobile operating system landscape, each bringing unique concepts such as app stores, mobile application sandboxes, and gesture-based interfaces.

Virtualization, a concept rooted in the early days of time-sharing systems, experienced a renaissance in the 2000s. Virtualization technologies allowed multiple operating system instances to run on a single physical machine, leading to the development of hypervisors like VMware, Xen, and KVM. Virtualization revolutionized server management, enabling more efficient resource utilization, easier software deployment, and improved system isolation.

Security became an increasingly critical aspect of operating system design in the 21st century. Concepts like access control, encryption, and secure boot mechanisms became integral to modern operating systems. Operating systems like Apple's macOS and Microsoft

Windows implemented security features to protect users from malware, unauthorized access, and other cyber threats. The importance of security was further underscored by the development of security-focused operating systems, such as Qubes OS and Tails, designed with a strong emphasis on isolation and privacy.

In recent years, the rise of containerization technologies, notably Docker, has influenced how applications are packaged and deployed. Containers encapsulate an application and its dependencies in a lightweight, portable environment, streamlining the deployment process and enhancing consistency across different computing environments. Container orchestration platforms like Kubernetes have further propelled the adoption of containerized applications, reshaping the landscape of modern application deployment and management.

The development of key operating system concepts is an ongoing and dynamic process. Concepts like virtualization, distributed systems, and security continue to evolve to meet the demands of emerging technologies. The integration of artificial intelligence (AI) and machine learning (ML) into operating systems, as seen in features like predictive text input and intelligent voice assistants, represents a contemporary convergence of computing paradigms.

In conclusion, the historical development of key operating system concepts mirrors the transformative journey of computing from its early stages to the intricate, interconnected systems of today. Each era has contributed foundational ideas, design principles, and innovations that have shaped the evolution of operating systems. From the simplicity of early batch processing systems to the complexity of modern distributed and mobile operating systems, the concepts born in the crucible of computing history continue to influence how we interact with technology and navigate the digital landscape. As technology advances, the ongoing refinement and adaptation of these concepts underscore their enduring relevance in shaping the future of operating systems.

Chapter 2: Evolution of Operating Systems: Past to Present

Explore the evolution of operating systems from the early days of computing.

The evolution of operating systems from the early days of computing is a fascinating journey that traces the growth of technology, the changing paradigms of computing, and the increasing complexity of user interactions with machines. In the embryonic stages of computing, the absence of operating systems as we know them today characterized the landscape. In the 1940s and 1950s, mainframe computers operated in a batch processing mode, where users submitted their tasks on punched cards, and the computer processed them sequentially. The lack of an operating system meant that users had to manually oversee the execution of their programs and contend with inefficiencies in resource utilization.

The advent of the 1950s marked a pivotal period with the introduction of early operating systems. One such example is the UNIVAC I (Universal Automatic Computer I), designed by J. Presper Eckert and John Mauchly. UNIVAC I, which became operational in 1951, featured a rudimentary operating system that handled various tasks such as input/output control, job scheduling, and memory management. Similarly, IBM's OS/360, introduced in the 1960s, represented a leap forward by providing a more comprehensive operating system for the IBM System/360 mainframe series. OS/360 introduced the concept of job control language (JCL) for submitting and managing batch jobs, marking a significant step towards the modern operating system.

The 1960s saw the emergence of time-sharing systems, a transformative concept that revolutionized user interactions with computers. MIT's Compatible Time-Sharing System (CTSS), developed by a team led by Fernando Corbató, was a pioneer in this domain. CTSS allowed multiple users to access a computer simultaneously, enabling interactive computing. This marked a paradigm shift from batch processing to time-sharing, where users could share the computing resources dynamically. The success of time-sharing systems paved the way for the evolution of multitasking, a concept that would become fundamental in future operating systems.

The 1970s brought about groundbreaking developments with the creation of UNIX, a seminal operating system that has left an indelible mark on the computing landscape. Developed at Bell Labs by Ken Thompson, Dennis Ritchie, and others, UNIX introduced several revolutionary concepts. The hierarchical file system structure provided a more organized way to store and retrieve data, while the introduction of processes allowed for concurrent execution of tasks. UNIX's design principles emphasized simplicity, modularity, and portability, making it highly influential and eventually leading to the development of various UNIX-like operating systems.

Simultaneously, the concept of microkernels began to gain attention. The idea behind microkernels was to minimize the kernel's functionality and move non-essential services, such as file systems and device drivers, to user space. This approach aimed to enhance the system's reliability and maintainability. The Mach microkernel, developed at Carnegie Mellon University, was a notable example that influenced subsequent operating system designs, including the development of Apple's macOS.

The 1980s witnessed the rise of personal computers and the popularization of graphical user interfaces (GUIs). Operating systems like Apple's Macintosh System Software and Microsoft's Windows introduced a more intuitive way for users to interact with computers. GUIs relied on window managers, which allowed users to work with multiple applications simultaneously, introducing concepts like multitasking and windowing systems. Concurrently, the concept of a graphical desktop environment, exemplified by the X Window System, provided a standardized way to create graphical interfaces across different UNIX systems.

The 1990s saw a proliferation of operating systems with the rise of Microsoft Windows as a dominant desktop platform. Windows 95 introduced a 32-bit architecture, preemptive multitasking, and a more user-friendly interface. This era also marked the emergence of Linux, an open-source UNIX-like operating system kernel. Linux, coupled with the GNU userland utilities, offered a free and highly customizable alternative to proprietary UNIX and Windows operating systems. The collaborative nature of open-source development contributed to the rapid evolution and widespread adoption of Linux.

Real-time operating systems (RTOS) also gained prominence in the 1990s, designed to meet stringent timing constraints. RTOS found applications in embedded systems, aerospace, and industrial control systems, where timely and predictable responses are critical. QNX, a real-time UNIX-like operating system, emerged as a notable player in this domain, showcasing the adaptability of operating system concepts to diverse application domains.

The 21st century ushered in new challenges and opportunities for operating system design, particularly with the proliferation of mobile devices. The development of smartphones and tablets necessitated operating systems optimized for touchscreens, energy efficiency, and seamless connectivity. Apple's iOS and Google's Android emerged as dominant players in the mobile operating system landscape, each bringing unique concepts such as app stores, mobile application sandboxes, and gesture-based interfaces.

Virtualization, a concept rooted in the early days of time-sharing systems, experienced a renaissance in the 2000s. Virtualization technologies allowed multiple operating system instances to run on a single physical machine, leading to the development of hypervisors like

VMware, Xen, and KVM. Virtualization revolutionized server management, enabling more efficient resource utilization, easier software deployment, and improved system isolation.

Security became an increasingly critical aspect of operating system design in the 21st century. Concepts like access control, encryption, and secure boot mechanisms became integral to modern operating systems. Operating systems like Apple's macOS and Microsoft Windows implemented security features to protect users from malware, unauthorized access, and other cyber threats. The importance of security was further underscored by the development of security-focused operating systems, such as Qubes OS and Tails, designed with a strong emphasis on isolation and privacy.

In recent years, the rise of containerization technologies, notably Docker, has influenced how applications are packaged and deployed. Containers encapsulate an application and its dependencies in a lightweight, portable environment, streamlining the deployment process and enhancing consistency across different computing environments. Container orchestration platforms like Kubernetes have further propelled the adoption of containerized applications, reshaping the landscape of modern application deployment and management.

The evolution of operating systems from the early days of computing underscores the dynamic nature of technology. From the simplicity of early batch processing systems to the complexity of modern distributed and mobile operating systems, each era has contributed foundational ideas, design principles, and innovations that have shaped the evolution of operating systems. The ongoing refinement and adaptation of these concepts underscore their enduring relevance in shaping the future of operating systems as technology continues to advance.

Discuss the emergence of time-sharing systems and their impact on user interaction.

The emergence of time-sharing systems in the 1960s marked a paradigm shift in the landscape of computing, transforming the way users interacted with computers and laying the foundation for modern interactive computing environments. Time-sharing systems were a response to the growing demand for more efficient and interactive use of computing resources, particularly in academic and research institutions where access to mainframe computers was limited and the need for shared resource utilization was evident.

MIT's Compatible Time-Sharing System (CTSS) is often considered the pioneer in the development of time-sharing systems. CTSS, initiated in the early 1960s under the leadership of Fernando Corbató and his team, was designed to allow multiple users to simultaneously access a single computer. This departure from the prevailing batch processing systems, where users submitted their jobs on punched cards and waited for the entire batch to be processed, represented a groundbreaking innovation.

The core idea behind time-sharing systems was to divide the computing resources, particularly the central processing unit (CPU), into time slots or slices and allocate these slices to different users. Each user would have the illusion of dedicated access to the computer during their allotted time slice, allowing them to interact with the system in real-time. This approach dramatically increased the efficiency of resource utilization, enabling a more dynamic and responsive computing experience.

CTSS introduced the concept of interactive computing, where users could submit commands, receive immediate feedback, and iteratively refine their instructions. The system's ability to provide a shared environment for users to work concurrently was revolutionary, fostering collaboration and enabling a broader user base to benefit from computing resources. This interactive model laid the groundwork for the principles of user interface design, system responsiveness, and the concept of a timesharing operating system.

The impact of time-sharing systems extended beyond MIT, influencing the development of similar systems at other institutions. One notable example is the development of the Berkeley Time-Sharing System (BTS) at the University of California, Berkeley. BTS, initiated in the mid-1960s, further advanced the capabilities of time-sharing systems, introducing features such as file systems, hierarchical directory structures, and program libraries. These enhancements contributed to the evolving notion of a user-friendly computing environment.

Another influential time-sharing system of this era was the Dartmouth Time-Sharing System (DTSS), developed at Dartmouth College. DTSS, operational from the mid-1960s, aimed to make computing accessible to a broader audience, including non-computer science students. It introduced the BASIC programming language, providing a user-friendly interface for writing and executing programs. This democratization of access to computing resources paved the way for increased interdisciplinary use and contributed to the integration of computing into various academic disciplines.

The impact of time-sharing systems on user interaction was profound in several dimensions. Firstly, the introduction of interactive computing meant that users could submit commands, receive immediate feedback, and iterate on their instructions in real-time. This departure from the batch processing model not only increased the efficiency of computing resource utilization but also empowered users to have more direct control over the computation process. The interactive nature of these systems facilitated a closer and more dynamic relationship between users and the computer.

Secondly, time-sharing systems democratized access to computing resources. Prior to the advent of time-sharing, access to computers was limited, and users had to contend with lengthy queues and wait times for their jobs to be processed in batch mode. Time-sharing systems allowed multiple users to share the same machine concurrently, providing each user with dedicated time slices for their computations. This democratization broadened access to computing resources, enabling a more diverse user base, including researchers, scientists, and students, to leverage computational power for their work.

Thirdly, the collaborative potential of time-sharing systems fostered a sense of community among users. The shared environment created by time-sharing systems allowed users to collaborate, share insights, and collectively benefit from the computing resources. This collaborative ethos was particularly pronounced in academic and research settings, where multiple users with diverse backgrounds and research interests could interact with the same system. The communal aspect of time-sharing systems contributed to the development of a computing culture that emphasized cooperation, knowledge exchange, and interdisciplinary collaboration.

The interactive and collaborative nature of time-sharing systems also had a profound impact on software development practices. Users could experiment with and debug their programs interactively, leading to a more iterative and exploratory approach to programming. This shift in programming paradigms influenced the development of programming languages and tools that supported interactive and incremental development, laying the groundwork for modern software engineering practices.

Furthermore, the emergence of time-sharing systems paved the way for the development of graphical user interfaces (GUIs) and the concept of windowing systems. The ability of users to interact with the computer in real-time necessitated more intuitive and user-friendly interfaces. Research conducted at institutions like Stanford, including the development of the Engelbart's oN-Line System (NLS), explored graphical interfaces, pointing devices, and the concept of "windows" for organizing and managing multiple tasks simultaneously. These early experiments laid the foundation for the graphical interfaces that became ubiquitous in personal computing.

The legacy of time-sharing systems endured as these concepts influenced subsequent developments in computing environments. Time-sharing laid the groundwork for the development of modern operating systems that prioritize user interaction, multitasking, and resource sharing. The principles of time-sharing evolved into the concepts of multitasking operating systems, where multiple processes can run concurrently, and time-sharing schedulers allocate CPU time slices to various tasks.

In conclusion, the emergence of time-sharing systems in the 1960s marked a transformative period in the history of computing, fundamentally altering the way users interacted with computers. These systems introduced the concept of interactive computing, democratized access to computing resources, fostered collaboration among users, and influenced the development of graphical user interfaces. The impact of time-sharing systems reverberates in contemporary computing environments, shaping the principles of user-centered design, collaborative software development, and the dynamic allocation of computing resources. As technology continues to advance, the legacy of time-sharing systems remains integral to the evolving nature of user interaction in computing.

Compare and contrast single-user and multi-user operating systems.

A single-user operating system is designed to support the needs of a single individual on a computing device, such as a personal computer or a workstation. In this environment, the operating system serves as an intermediary between the user and the computer hardware, managing resources, providing a user interface, and facilitating the execution of applications. Single-user operating systems are often intuitive and user-friendly, emphasizing simplicity and ease of use. Examples include Microsoft Windows, macOS, and various Linux distributions with desktop environments. These operating systems prioritize personalization and customization, allowing users to configure settings and preferences tailored to their specific requirements. Additionally, single-user systems typically provide a straightforward file management system, enabling users to organize and access their data efficiently.

On the other hand, multi-user operating systems are designed to accommodate the needs of multiple users concurrently, enabling them to share resources and work collaboratively on a network. These systems are commonly found in enterprise environments, data centers, and servers where numerous users may require access to the same set of resources. Examples include various Unix and Linux server distributions, such as Ubuntu Server and Red Hat Enterprise Linux. Multi-user operating systems prioritize security and resource allocation, employing authentication mechanisms to control user access and permissions. They often feature robust networking capabilities, allowing users to connect remotely and collaborate on projects in real-time. Additionally, these operating systems implement advanced file and process management systems to ensure efficient utilization of shared resources among multiple users.

One key differentiator between single-user and multi-user operating systems lies in their resource management strategies. Single-user systems primarily focus on providing a responsive and seamless experience for a solitary user, allocating resources based on the demands of a single individual. In contrast, multi-user systems must carefully manage resources to ensure fair distribution among multiple users, preventing one user from monopolizing the system's capacity and degrading the overall performance for others. This requires sophisticated scheduling algorithms, efficient memory management, and robust process prioritization to maintain a balance between responsiveness and fairness in a multi-user environment.

Security considerations also distinguish single-user and multi-user operating systems. In a single-user environment, security concerns are often centered around protecting the individual user's data and ensuring the integrity of the system from external threats. User accounts on single-user systems typically have administrative privileges, granting full control over the system's configuration. In contrast, multi-user systems employ more granular access controls, restricting user privileges based on defined roles and responsibilities. Authentication mechanisms, such as username-password combinations or more advanced methods like public key authentication, play a crucial role in safeguarding the system from unauthorized access in multi-user environments.

Furthermore, the user interfaces of single-user and multi-user operating systems cater to the specific needs of their respective user bases. Single-user systems prioritize graphical interfaces and interactive desktop environments, providing a visually intuitive experience for individual users. These interfaces are designed to be user-friendly, with point-and-click interactions and visually appealing elements. In contrast, multi-user systems often rely on command-line interfaces, emphasizing efficiency and scalability for remote administration and automation. Command-line interfaces allow system administrators to execute tasks quickly and script complex operations, which is essential for managing large-scale deployments and maintaining consistency across multiple users.

File and storage management also differ between single-user and multi-user operating systems. Single-user systems typically offer a straightforward file hierarchy, where users can organize their personal files and documents with relative simplicity. Multi-user systems, especially in enterprise settings, implement more advanced file systems that support features like access control lists (ACLs) and quotas. These features enable administrators to define fine-grained permissions for files and directories, ensuring that sensitive information is protected and that users only have access to the resources necessary for their roles.

Another critical aspect of comparison is the approach to system maintenance and updates. Single-user systems often allow users to manage software updates and installations individually, with the user having control over when and how updates are applied. In multi-user environments, system administrators typically oversee updates centrally to ensure consistency and security across the network. This centralized approach allows administrators to deploy updates in a controlled manner, minimizing disruptions and ensuring that all users are working with the same set of software versions.

In conclusion, single-user and multi-user operating systems cater to distinct user scenarios and have evolved to meet the diverse needs of individual users and collaborative environments. Single-user systems prioritize simplicity, personalization, and user-friendly interfaces, while multi-user systems emphasize resource management, security, and scalability in shared computing environments. Both types of operating systems play crucial roles in the broader computing landscape, serving the varied requirements of individual users, businesses, and organizations. Understanding the nuances and trade-offs between single-user and multi-user operating systems is essential for choosing the most suitable platform based on specific use cases and requirements.

Explore the role of operating systems in the personal computer revolution.

The personal computer revolution, a transformative era that began in the late 20th century, witnessed the widespread adoption of personal computers (PCs) and was fundamentally shaped by the role of operating systems. Operating systems played a pivotal role in democratizing computing, making it accessible to individuals in homes and small businesses. Prior to this revolution, computers were largely the domain of large corporations, research institutions, and government entities due to their high costs and complexity. However, with the advent of the personal computer, operating systems became the bridge that connected users to the underlying hardware, enabling them to interact with the machine in a more user-friendly and intuitive manner.

In the early days of the personal computer revolution, the operating systems were rudimentary, often limited to command-line interfaces that required users to input text commands to execute tasks. One of the pioneering operating systems of this era was MS-DOS (Microsoft Disk Operating System), which became a standard for early IBM-compatible personal computers. MS-DOS provided a command-line interface and basic file management capabilities, laying the groundwork for subsequent developments in personal computing. However, the real breakthrough came with the introduction of graphical user interfaces (GUIs), which revolutionized the way individuals interacted with computers.

The graphical user interface was popularized by Apple's Macintosh operating system and later by Microsoft Windows. These GUI-based operating systems introduced the concept of point-and-click interactions, making computers more accessible to a broader audience. The graphical interface, characterized by icons, windows, and a mouse-driven cursor, transformed computing into a visual and intuitive experience. Users could now navigate through files and applications, open programs, and perform tasks with a level of simplicity that was unprecedented. This shift from command-line interfaces to graphical interfaces was instrumental in making personal computers more user-friendly and appealing to a non-technical audience.

Windows 95, released by Microsoft in 1995, marked a significant milestone in the personal computer revolution. It brought further refinements to the graphical user interface and introduced features like the Start menu and taskbar, providing users with a more organized and streamlined experience. Windows 95 also incorporated preemptive multitasking, allowing multiple applications to run simultaneously without causing system instability. This improved the overall efficiency and productivity of personal computers, laying the foundation for the multitasking capabilities we take for granted in modern operating systems.

Simultaneously, the rise of the internet during the late 20th century had a profound impact on personal computing. Operating systems played a crucial role in facilitating internet connectivity and enhancing the user experience. Internet Explorer, bundled with Microsoft Windows, became one of the most widely used web browsers, enabling users to explore the vast resources of the World Wide Web. The integration of networking capabilities into operating systems allowed individuals to connect their personal computers to local area networks (LANs) and, eventually, to the global network of the internet, transforming personal computing into a gateway to information, communication, and collaboration.

As personal computers became more prevalent, operating systems evolved to support a growing ecosystem of software applications. The availability of a diverse range of applications—from word processors to multimedia tools—contributed to the versatility of personal computers. Operating systems provided a standardized platform for software developers, allowing them to create applications that could run seamlessly across a variety of hardware configurations. This standardization fostered a thriving software industry, further fueling the popularity of personal computers.

The personal computer revolution also witnessed the emergence of open-source operating systems, with Linux being a prominent example. Linux, inspired by Unix principles, offered a robust and stable alternative to commercial operating systems. Its open-source nature allowed users to customize and modify the operating system to suit their needs, fostering a community-driven approach to software development. Linux became a preferred choice for servers and power users who sought reliability, security, and flexibility in their computing environments.

Security became an increasingly important aspect of operating systems as personal computers became interconnected and more vulnerable to threats. Operating systems incorporated security features such as user account controls, firewalls, and encryption to protect users from malicious software and unauthorized access. The awareness of security issues led to regular updates and patches being released by operating system vendors to address vulnerabilities, highlighting the ongoing commitment to enhancing the resilience of personal computing environments.

The personal computer revolution also saw the integration of multimedia capabilities into operating systems, transforming PCs into versatile entertainment hubs. Operating systems began to support audio and video playback, graphics-intensive applications, and gaming. This shift expanded the role of personal computers beyond traditional productivity tools, turning them into multimedia consumption and creation devices.

Mobile computing marked another significant phase in the evolution of personal computing, and operating systems played a central role in this transition. The development of operating systems specifically designed for mobile devices, such as iOS for Apple's iPhones and iPads and Android for a myriad of smartphones and tablets, revolutionized the way people accessed information and communicated on the go. These mobile operating systems introduced touch-based interfaces, app ecosystems, and optimized power management, setting new standards for user experience and mobility.

In conclusion, the personal computer revolution was shaped by the continuous evolution of operating systems, from the early command-line interfaces to the graphical user interfaces that made computing accessible to a broader audience. Operating systems played a crucial role in standardizing platforms, supporting a vast array of applications, facilitating internet connectivity, and adapting to the changing needs of users. As personal computers became an integral part of daily life, operating systems evolved to meet the challenges of security, multimedia integration, and mobile computing, contributing to the transformative impact of the personal computer revolution on society, communication, and information access.

Discuss the evolution of operating systems to support networking capabilities.

The evolution of operating systems to support networking capabilities has been a transformative journey, fundamentally altering the way computers communicate and collaborate. In the early days of computing, operating systems were primarily designed for stand-alone machines, with little consideration for networking. As the need for sharing resources and information among multiple computers emerged, the evolution of operating systems took a decisive turn towards incorporating networking features.

One of the pioneering steps in this evolution was the development of Unix, a powerful and versatile operating system created at Bell Labs in the late 1960s. Unix introduced fundamental concepts such as time-sharing and multi-user capabilities, laying the groundwork for networked computing. The adoption of Unix in academic and research institutions facilitated collaboration among users on different terminals, marking an early example of operating systems supporting networking.

The 1980s saw the emergence of local area networks (LANs) and the need for operating systems to facilitate communication between computers within a confined geographic area. Novell NetWare, introduced in 1983, was among the first operating systems dedicated to networking. NetWare provided file and print sharing services, enabling users to access resources on a networked server. Its success highlighted the growing importance of networking capabilities in operating systems and set the stage for future developments in the field.

Microsoft's foray into networking began with the introduction of LAN Manager in the late 1980s. LAN Manager, initially a separate product, was later integrated into Microsoft's operating systems, including OS/2 and Windows NT. This integration marked a significant step in the evolution of Windows operating systems towards networking support. With the release of Windows 3.11 for Workgroups in 1993, Microsoft incorporated peer-to-peer networking capabilities, allowing users to share files and printers in a workgroup environment.

However, it was Windows 95, released in 1995, that represented a watershed moment in the integration of networking features into mainstream operating systems. Windows 95 introduced built-in networking support, including the NetBIOS protocol and the ability to connect to networks using Microsoft's implementation of the Server Message Block (SMB) protocol. The inclusion of networking capabilities in the consumer-oriented Windows 95 marked a significant shift, making networking more accessible to individual users and further popularizing the concept of connected computing.

Simultaneously, Novell NetWare continued to evolve, maintaining its dominance in the networking arena. Novell's NetWare 3.x and 4.x versions introduced advanced features such as directory services and improved scalability. NetWare's success underscored the growing demand for operating systems that could effectively manage and optimize network resources, paving the way for subsequent advancements in the networking capabilities of operating systems.

The late 1990s witnessed the ascendancy of the internet, and operating systems adapted to facilitate seamless connectivity. The integration of TCP/IP (Transmission Control Protocol/Internet Protocol) into operating systems became a standard, enabling computers to communicate over the global network. Windows 95, Windows

NT, and Unix-based systems embraced TCP/IP, solidifying its status as the foundation of internet communication. This shift marked a departure from proprietary networking protocols, fostering interoperability and global connectivity.

The advent of Windows 2000 in 2000 marked another significant milestone in Microsoft's networking evolution. Windows 2000 introduced Active Directory, a directory service that centralizes network management and authentication. Active Directory enhanced the scalability and security of Windows-based networks, providing a centralized repository for user accounts, computers, and other network resources. This innovation reflected a growing emphasis on the role of operating systems in simplifying network administration and enhancing the overall efficiency of networked environments.

Linux, as an open-source operating system, also played a vital role in the evolution of networking capabilities. The flexibility and modularity of Linux allowed developers to customize and extend its networking features. Linux distributions like Red Hat and Debian became popular choices for servers, leveraging the operating system's stability and networking capabilities to support a wide range of applications and services.

The release of Windows XP in 2001 marked a consumer-focused refinement of Microsoft's networking capabilities. Windows XP featured improved support for wireless networking, reflecting the growing popularity of Wi-Fi technology. The inclusion of features like the Network Setup Wizard made it easier for users to set up and configure home networks, contributing to the proliferation of residential networking.

As networking technologies continued to advance, operating systems adapted to support emerging standards and protocols. The rise of wireless networking, exemplified by the widespread adoption of Wi-Fi, prompted operating systems to incorporate native support for wireless connectivity. Windows Vista, released in 2007, introduced enhancements to wireless networking, including improved security features and simplified configuration options.

The proliferation of mobile devices and the advent of smartphones brought new challenges and opportunities for operating systems in terms of networking. Mobile operating systems like iOS and Android were designed with a strong focus on connectivity, leveraging technologies such as 3G and later 4G/LTE to enable mobile data access. The integration of mobile operating systems with cloud services further expanded the scope of networking, allowing seamless synchronization of data and applications across multiple devices.

Cloud computing marked another paradigm shift in networking, and operating systems adapted to harness the potential of distributed computing environments. Operating systems increasingly incorporated features to facilitate seamless integration with cloud services, enabling users to access and store data remotely. This shift reflected a broader trend towards decentralization, where computing resources were distributed across networks rather than being concentrated on individual devices.

The advent of Windows 7 in 2009 continued Microsoft's trajectory towards optimizing networking capabilities. Windows 7 featured improved home networking options, enhanced support for IPv6 (Internet Protocol version 6), and advancements in file and printer sharing. The operating system also introduced the Home-Group feature, simplifying the process of sharing resources on home networks.

The subsequent release of Windows 8 in 2012 brought a significant departure in terms of the user interface but continued to build upon networking capabilities. Windows 8 emphasized cloud integration, with a strong focus on Microsoft's cloud platform, OneDrive. The operating system aimed to provide a seamless experience where users could access their files and settings across different devices through cloud synchronization.

With the release of Windows 10 in 2015, Microsoft further emphasized the importance of networking in modern computing. Windows 10 introduced a range of features designed to enhance connectivity, including the integration of the Microsoft Edge browser with Cortana, the voice-activated digital assistant. The operating system also featured the Windows Subsystem for Linux (WSL), allowing users to run Linux commands and tools natively within Windows, showcasing a commitment to cross-platform compatibility.

In the realm of server operating systems, Windows Server editions continued to evolve to meet the demands of enterprise networking. Windows Server 2003, for instance, introduced improvements in Active Directory, security, and scalability. Subsequent releases, such as Windows Server 2008, Windows Server 2012, and Windows Server 2016, continued to refine networking features, offering enhanced support for virtualization, network security, and cloud integration.

Linux, being a versatile and open-source platform, saw continuous enhancements to its networking capabilities. The adoption of Linux in server environments and networking devices further solidified its role as a robust and scalable operating system for diverse networking scenarios. Projects like OpenStack, an open-source cloud computing platform, leveraged Linux to build scalable and flexible cloud infrastructures.

As networking technologies continued to advance, the concept of the Internet of Things (IoT) emerged, introducing a new dimension to the networking capabilities of operating systems. IoT devices, ranging from smart thermostats to industrial sensors, required operating systems that could efficiently manage large-scale networks of interconnected devices. Operating systems adapted to support the unique requirements of IoT, emphasizing low-power consumption, real-time processing, and secure communication.

The evolution of operating systems in supporting networking capabilities has been characterized by a continuous drive towards greater connectivity, interoperability, and efficiency. From the early days of standalone machines to the present era of cloud computing and IoT, operating systems have played a pivotal role in shaping the landscape of networked computing. The integration of networking features, standards, and protocols has not only facilitated communication between computers but has also transformed the way individuals, businesses, and societies access and share information. As we look towards the future, operating systems will likely continue to evolve in response to emerging technologies, ensuring that networking capabilities remain at the forefront of computing innovation.

Explore how operating systems adapted to support client-server architectures.

The evolution of operating systems to support client-server architectures has been a transformative journey, fundamentally altering the landscape of distributed computing and collaboration. The concept of client-server architecture emerged as a response to the growing need for efficient resource sharing, centralized management, and collaborative computing. Operating systems played a pivotal role in adapting to and facilitating this paradigm shift, enabling the development and deployment of complex, networked applications.

In the early days of computing, the predominant model was centered around standalone systems, where a single computer performed all tasks, including processing data, managing storage, and handling user interfaces. However, as the demand for scalable and collaborative computing solutions increased, the limitations of this model became apparent. Operating systems needed to evolve to accommodate a more distributed approach where multiple computers, serving distinct roles as clients and servers, could work together seamlessly.

The emergence of local area networks (LANs) in the 1980s marked a significant catalyst for the adoption of client-server architectures. LANs provided a means for computers to communicate and share resources within a confined geographic area, and operating systems had to adapt to this new networking environment. Novell NetWare, one of the pioneering operating systems dedicated to networking, played a crucial role in popularizing the client-server model. NetWare facilitated file and print sharing among networked computers, laying the groundwork for the distributed computing landscape.

Microsoft's Windows operating systems also evolved to embrace the client-server architecture. With the release of Windows NT in 1993, Microsoft introduced a powerful and scalable operating system designed to support client-server computing. Windows NT incorporated a preemptive multitasking kernel, advanced security features, and built-in networking capabilities. It provided a foundation for subsequent Windows operating systems, including Windows 2000, Windows XP, and their successors, to seamlessly integrate into client-server environments.

The client-server model is characterized by the division of labor between client machines, which request services or resources, and server machines, which fulfill those requests. Operating systems needed to support the development of applications that adhered to this model. This shift led to the creation of software frameworks and protocols that allowed seamless communication between clients and servers. Operating systems became responsible for managing the intricacies of networking, ensuring efficient data transfer, and handling user authentication and access controls in distributed environments.

The development of networking protocols played a crucial role in the successful implementation of client-server architectures. The Transmission Control Protocol/Internet Protocol (TCP/IP), which became the standard for internet communication, was integral to the evolution of operating systems in this context. Operating systems began to natively support TCP/IP, enabling them to communicate across heterogeneous networks and forming the basis for the global connectivity we experience today.

The advent of the World Wide Web further underscored the importance of client-server architectures. Web browsers, acting as clients, needed to interact with web servers to retrieve and display information. Operating systems adapted to accommodate the requirements of web browsing, supporting protocols like Hypertext Transfer Protocol (HTTP) and providing a platform for the development of server-side applications.

Database management systems (DBMS) also played a pivotal role in the client-server model, and operating systems had to evolve to support their integration. The server-side component of a DBMS manages the storage and retrieval of data, while client applications interact with the database through a user-friendly interface. Operating systems needed to provide a robust foundation for the seamless interaction between client applications and database servers, facilitating efficient data processing and retrieval in distributed environments.

The integration of graphical user interfaces (GUIs) into operating systems contributed significantly to the user experience in client-server architectures. GUIs provided a visual and intuitive means for users to interact with both client and server applications. The evolution of GUIs in operating systems, exemplified by Microsoft Windows and various Unix-based systems, facilitated the development of user-friendly client applications that could communicate with server counterparts over networks.

The concept of middleware emerged as a critical component in the client-server architecture, and operating systems adapted to support these intermediary software layers. Middleware facilitates communication and data exchange between clients and servers, abstracting the complexities of networking protocols and enabling interoperability between diverse systems. Operating systems needed to ensure seamless integration with middleware solutions to support the development and deployment of distributed applications.

Security considerations became paramount in client-server architectures, and operating systems had to evolve to address the challenges of securing communication and data exchange over networks. Authentication mechanisms, encryption protocols, and access control features became integral parts of operating systems, safeguarding sensitive information and ensuring that only authorized clients could access server resources. The evolution of secure sockets layer (SSL) and its successor, transport layer security (TLS), further enhanced the security of client-server communication.

Virtualization technologies also made a significant impact on client-server architectures, influencing how operating systems manage resources in distributed environments. Virtualization allows multiple operating system instances to run on a single physical machine, enabling more efficient resource utilization and scalability. Operating systems had to adapt to support virtualization, providing features like hypervisors and virtual machine management tools to optimize the deployment of client and server applications.

Cloud computing, an extension of client-server architectures, introduced new challenges and opportunities for operating systems. Operating systems had to adapt to the dynamic nature of cloud environments, where resources are provisioned and de-provisioned on demand. Cloud operating systems, such as Linux-based distributions tailored for cloud deployments and Microsoft's Windows Server offerings with Azure integration, evolved to provide scalable and resilient solutions for client-server applications in the cloud.

Mobile computing marked another phase in the evolution of client-server architectures, and operating systems designed for mobile devices had to address the unique challenges of connectivity, resource constraints, and diverse device form factors. Mobile operating systems like iOS and Android facilitated seamless communication between mobile clients and remote servers, enabling users to access data and services on the go.

As the internet of things (IoT) gained prominence, operating systems adapted to support the unique characteristics of distributed computing in IoT ecosystems. IoT devices, acting as clients, communicate with central servers to exchange data and receive commands. Operating systems tailored for IoT environments prioritize low-power consumption, real-time processing, and secure communication to ensure the reliability and efficiency of client-server interactions.

In conclusion, the evolution of operating systems to support client-server architectures has been a dynamic and ongoing process, driven by the demands of scalable, collaborative, and distributed computing. Operating systems have played a central role in enabling the development and deployment of applications that leverage the client-server model, from the early days of LANs to the current era of cloud computing and IoT. The adaptability of operating systems to diverse networking environments, coupled with advancements in networking protocols, security measures, and virtualization technologies, has shaped the interconnected world of computing we experience today. As technology continues to evolve, operating systems will likely continue to play a crucial role in facilitating the seamless integration and communication of client and server components in increasingly complex and interconnected computing environments.

Discuss the challenges and benefits of distributed operating systems.

Distributed operating systems (DOS) present a paradigm that has both significant challenges and notable benefits, reflecting the complexities inherent in coordinating computing resources across multiple interconnected machines. One of the foremost challenges lies in achieving transparency, wherein the distributed nature of the system is hidden from users and applications. Ensuring transparency across various aspects, such as location transparency (hiding the physical location of resources), access transparency (uniform access mechanisms), and failure transparency (masking faults and failures), demands sophisticated mechanisms within the operating system. Achieving transparency is crucial for providing a seamless experience to users and applications, allowing them to interact with the distributed environment as if it were a centralized system.

A key challenge in distributed operating systems is managing the heterogeneity of the underlying hardware and software. Distributed systems often comprise diverse machines with different architectures, operating systems, and software stacks. Ensuring interoperability and seamless communication across such heterogeneous environments necessitates the development of standardized protocols, middleware, and compatibility layers within the operating system. The management of various hardware and software configurations poses a constant challenge in maintaining a unified and coherent distributed computing environment.

Scalability is a critical concern in distributed operating systems, particularly as the system grows in terms of the number of nodes and the volume of data. Ensuring that the system can efficiently handle an increasing load without compromising performance requires careful design and optimization. Scalability challenges often arise in areas such as resource allocation, data distribution, and communication protocols. Additionally, achieving load balancing across distributed nodes becomes crucial to prevent bottlenecks and optimize the overall system performance.

Another significant challenge is fault tolerance, as distributed systems are prone to failures in individual nodes, network links, or components. Developing mechanisms to detect, isolate, and recover from faults without disrupting the entire system is a complex task. Distributed operating systems often implement redundancy, replication, and consensus algorithms to maintain system integrity in the face of failures. Ensuring that the system can gracefully handle faults, recover quickly, and maintain data consistency is a continuous challenge in the design and implementation of distributed operating systems.

Consistency in distributed systems is a balancing act that presents both challenges and benefits. Achieving a consistent view of the system's state across all nodes is challenging due to factors like network delays and failures. The trade-off between consistency and performance is a central concern, and distributed operating systems must carefully choose between strong consistency models that ensure a uniform view of the data at the cost of performance, and weaker consistency models that prioritize performance but may lead to variations in the perceived state of the system.

Security is a paramount concern in distributed operating systems. The distributed nature of these systems introduces new attack vectors, making them susceptible to various security threats such as unauthorized access, data breaches, and denial-of-service attacks. Ensuring the confidentiality, integrity, and availability of data in a distributed environment requires robust security mechanisms within the operating system. Implementing secure communication channels, access controls, and encryption protocols becomes imperative to safeguard the distributed system from malicious activities.

Despite these challenges, distributed operating systems offer several compelling benefits that have driven their widespread adoption. One of the primary advantages is enhanced reliability through redundancy and fault tolerance. By distributing tasks and data across multiple nodes, distributed systems can continue to operate even if individual components fail. Redundancy and fault tolerance mechanisms, such as data replication and backup nodes, contribute to increased system reliability and availability.

Scalability is a significant benefit of distributed operating systems. These systems can efficiently scale to accommodate growing workloads and user demands by adding new nodes to the network. The ability to distribute tasks and resources across multiple nodes ensures that the system can handle increased computational and storage requirements without experiencing performance bottlenecks. This scalability is particularly advantageous in modern computing environments with dynamic and evolving workloads.

Distributed operating systems facilitate resource sharing and utilization across the network. By distributing tasks and data, these systems optimize resource utilization, ensuring that computing resources are efficiently allocated based on demand. This resource sharing model enhances overall system efficiency and can lead to cost savings by minimizing idle resources and maximizing utilization rates.

Geographical distribution is a key benefit of distributed operating systems, enabling collaboration and access to resources across different locations. Users and applications can seamlessly interact with resources regardless of their physical location. This geographical flexibility supports remote collaboration, data access, and resource utilization, making distributed operating systems essential in the context of globalized and geographically dispersed organizations.

Distributed operating systems contribute to improved performance and responsiveness through parallelism and load balancing. Tasks can be distributed across multiple nodes, allowing concurrent processing and reducing the time required to complete computations. Load balancing mechanisms ensure that each node in the system carries a fair share of the workload, preventing bottlenecks and optimizing overall performance.

Flexibility and adaptability are inherent benefits of distributed operating systems. These systems can evolve and scale to meet changing requirements without significant architectural overhauls. The modular and distributed nature of the operating system allows for seamless integration of new nodes, services, or applications, making it well-suited for dynamic and evolving computing environments.

Distributed operating systems also provide support for collaborative computing and distributed applications. Applications designed for distributed environments can harness the power of multiple nodes to perform complex computations, process large datasets, and achieve parallelism. This collaborative computing model is instrumental in scientific research, data analysis, and other domains where significant computational resources are required.

In conclusion, the challenges and benefits of distributed operating systems highlight the intricate balance between complexity and advantages. Overcoming challenges such as transparency, heterogeneity, scalability, fault tolerance, consistency, and security demands meticulous design and implementation. However, the benefits of enhanced reliability, scalability, resource utilization, geographical distribution, performance, flexibility, and support for collaborative computing underscore the significance of distributed operating systems in modern computing landscapes. As technological advancements continue, distributed operating systems will likely play an increasingly pivotal role in addressing the evolving demands of complex and interconnected computing environments.

Explore the impact of virtualization on operating system architecture.

Virtualization has profoundly impacted operating system architecture, revolutionizing the way computing resources are managed, utilized, and abstracted. At its core, virtualization involves creating virtual instances of physical resources, such as servers, storage, or networks, to enable multiple operating systems or applications to run independently on the same physical hardware. This paradigm shift has led to a fundamental rethinking of operating system design and has ushered in a new era of flexibility, efficiency, and resource optimization.

One of the primary impacts of virtualization on operating system architecture is the introduction of the hypervisor, also known as the Virtual Machine Monitor (VMM). The hypervisor is a critical component that sits between the physical hardware and the operating systems or virtual machines (VMs). It is responsible for managing and allocating physical resources to the virtual instances, ensuring isolation, and facilitating communication between the VMs and the underlying hardware. The hypervisor can be classified into two types: Type 1, which runs directly on the hardware, and Type 2, which runs on top of an existing operating system. The presence of the hypervisor alters the traditional relationship between the operating system and the hardware, introducing a layer of abstraction that enhances resource sharing and allocation.

Virtualization has also influenced how operating systems interact with hardware. In a virtualized environment, each VM operates as if it has its dedicated set of resources, including CPU, memory, and storage. The hypervisor abstracts the underlying physical hardware, presenting a virtualized view to each VM. This abstraction allows multiple operating systems, potentially different types or versions, to coexist on the same physical server without interference. Operating systems within VMs remain unaware of each other, believing they have exclusive access to the hardware, contributing to improved isolation and security.

The concept of virtual machines is central to the impact of virtualization on operating system architecture. Each virtual machine represents a complete and independent instance of an operating system, encapsulated with its applications and configurations. VMs enable the consolidation of multiple workloads on a single physical server, optimizing resource utilization and facilitating the efficient management of computing infrastructure. Operating systems within VMs can be different from the host operating system, allowing for greater flexibility and compatibility across diverse software environments.

Resource allocation and management have been redefined by virtualization, prompting changes in the way operating systems handle tasks such as memory management, CPU scheduling, and storage access. Traditional operating systems were designed to manage physical hardware directly, assuming exclusive access to resources. In a virtualized environment, the hypervisor controls resource allocation, and operating systems within VMs interact with the virtualized resources. This shift requires enhancements in memory management, such as dynamic allocation and resizing of virtual memory, to cater to the varying demands of VMs. Similarly, CPU scheduling algorithms are adapted to accommodate the multi-tenancy of virtualized environments, where multiple VMs contend for CPU cycles.

The impact of virtualization extends to storage architectures within operating systems. Virtualized storage introduces the concept of virtual disks or virtual storage volumes that exist independently of the underlying physical storage devices. Operating systems within VMs interact with these virtual storage entities, abstracted from the complexities of physical storage. This abstraction allows for more efficient storage management, including features like snapshotting, cloning, and dynamic resizing of virtual disks, without requiring direct intervention at the physical storage layer.

Another transformative impact of virtualization on operating system architecture is the rise of containerization. Containers represent lightweight, portable, and self-sufficient execution environments for applications, encapsulating the necessary libraries, dependencies, and configurations. Unlike traditional virtual machines, containers share the host operating system's kernel, which eliminates the need for a full operating system stack for each container. Technologies like Docker and Kubernetes have become integral to modern computing ecosystems, allowing developers to package, deploy, and manage applications consistently across diverse environments. The shift towards containerization has influenced how operating systems are designed, emphasizing modularity, efficiency, and compatibility with container runtimes.

The advent of virtualization has also led to advancements in the field of live migration, enabling the seamless movement of virtual machines between physical servers without disrupting ongoing operations. Live migration allows for load balancing, hardware maintenance, and resource optimization in virtualized environments. Operating systems have adapted to support live migration by incorporating features like checkpointing, which allows the state of a running VM to be captured and restored on another host. The ability to migrate VMs transparently across physical servers has become a crucial aspect of virtualized infrastructure, enhancing system reliability and flexibility.

Security considerations in operating system architecture have been reevaluated in the context of virtualization. Virtualized environments introduce new attack vectors, such as vulnerabilities in the hypervisor or the risk of unauthorized access to other VMs on the same host. Operating systems within VMs must address these challenges by implementing security features that account for the shared nature of the underlying hardware. Technologies like Virtual Trusted Platform Module (vTPM) and Secure Boot have been integrated into operating systems to enhance the security posture of virtualized environments. Additionally, the isolation provided by the hypervisor is leveraged to enhance the overall security of VMs and their hosted operating systems.

The impact of virtualization on operating system architecture extends beyond traditional server environments to desktop computing. Virtual Desktop Infrastructure (VDI) leverages virtualization to deliver desktop environments as services, allowing users to access their desktops remotely. Operating systems designed for VDI environments must address challenges related to user experience, resource allocation, and remote display protocols. Technologies like Microsoft

Remote Desktop Services and VMware Horizon have become integral to the virtualization of desktop computing, influencing the architectural considerations of operating systems in this context.

In conclusion, the impact of virtualization on operating system architecture has been transformative, ushering in a new era of efficiency, flexibility, and resource optimization. The introduction of hypervisors, virtual machines, and containerization has redefined the relationship between operating systems and hardware. Operating systems have adapted to the challenges posed by virtualization, including the need for enhanced resource management, support for diverse software environments, and the security considerations inherent in shared virtualized infrastructure. As virtualization continues to evolve, operating systems are likely to undergo further refinements to meet the demands of dynamic, scalable, and heterogeneous computing environments. The shift towards containerization and the integration of virtualization technologies into diverse computing scenarios will continue to shape the landscape of operating system architecture in the years to come.

Discuss the evolution of operating systems for mobile devices.

The evolution of operating systems for mobile devices represents a captivating journey driven by the convergence of technological advancements, user demands, and the quest for enhanced mobility. The early 2000s witnessed the emergence of mobile operating systems that laid the foundation for the smartphones we are familiar with today. One of the pioneering platforms was Symbian, developed by a consortium of mobile phone manufacturers. Symbian operated on a range of devices and played a crucial role in popularizing mobile computing. However, its dominance waned as more sophisticated alternatives emerged.

The introduction of Apple's iPhone in 2007 marked a pivotal moment in the evolution of mobile operating systems. The iPhone ran on iOS, a streamlined and intuitive platform that redefined user interactions with mobile devices. Characterized by its touch-based interface, the App Store for third-party applications, and a cohesive user experience, iOS set new standards for mobile operating systems. The success of the iPhone spurred a wave of innovation in the industry, prompting competitors to reimagine their approaches to mobile computing.

Android, developed by Google and released in 2008, emerged as a formidable competitor to iOS. One of Android's defining features was its open-source nature, fostering a diverse ecosystem of devices and manufacturers. Android's adoption by prominent smartphone manufacturers, coupled with its extensive customization options, contributed to its rapid rise in the market. The Android Market, later rebranded as Google Play, facilitated the distribution of applications, enhancing the platform's appeal to users and developers alike. The rivalry between iOS and Android became a defining characteristic of the mobile operating system landscape.

As smartphones gained popularity, mobile operating systems underwent significant advancements in terms of features, functionality, and user interfaces. iOS and Android, in particular, engaged in a continuous cycle of updates and improvements. iOS introduced features like the App Store, multitasking capabilities, and the iCloud ecosystem. Android responded with innovations such as the Google Assistant, improved notification systems, and enhanced customization options. The competition between these platforms fueled a rapid pace of innovation, benefitting users with an ever-expanding array of capabilities.

Microsoft entered the mobile operating system arena with Windows Mobile and later Windows Phone. While Windows Mobile gained traction in the early 2000s, Windows Phone, introduced in 2010, aimed to provide a fresh and distinctive user interface. The tile-based design of the Metro UI, later known as Modern UI, sought to differentiate Windows Phone from its competitors. However, despite its innovative design, Windows Phone struggled to gain significant market share against the formidable duopoly of iOS and Android.

The concept of app ecosystems became a defining element in the evolution of mobile operating systems. The App Store and Google Play transformed how users accessed, downloaded, and interacted with applications. The sheer volume and diversity of available apps became a crucial factor influencing users' preferences for a particular operating system. Both iOS and Android cultivated vibrant developer communities, leading to the creation of millions of apps catering to various needs, from productivity and entertainment to health and education.

The proliferation of mobile devices beyond smartphones, including tablets and wearables, further shaped the evolution of mobile operating systems. Apple's iOS expanded its reach to the iPad, offering a tablet-centric user experience. Android, being an open-source platform, was adopted by numerous manufacturers for a wide range of devices, from budget smartphones to high-end tablets. The diversification of form factors and use cases necessitated adaptations in the design and functionality of mobile operating systems to deliver optimal user experiences.

The integration of cloud services played a crucial role in enhancing the capabilities of mobile operating systems. Apple's iCloud and Google's suite of cloud services, including Google Drive and Google Photos, enabled seamless synchronization of data across devices. This shift towards cloud-centric models facilitated features such as automatic backup, device synchronization, and easy access to content from any connected device. The cloud became an integral component of the mobile computing experience, contributing to the evolution of mobile operating systems.

Security became a paramount consideration as mobile devices became repositories of sensitive personal and corporate information. Mobile operating systems responded by incorporating advanced security features such as biometric authentication (fingerprint recognition and facial recognition), secure enclave technologies, and app permission controls. The emphasis on security aimed to protect users from data breaches, unauthorized access, and malicious applications, fostering trust in the use of mobile devices for sensitive tasks.

The advent of 4G and later 5G networks played a pivotal role in reshaping the capabilities of mobile operating systems. Faster and more reliable network connections facilitated real-time communication, high-definition streaming, and enhanced online experiences. Mobile operating systems optimized their architectures to leverage the increased bandwidth and reduced latency offered by these networks. The evolution towards faster and more efficient connectivity paved the way for innovations such as augmented reality (AR) and virtual reality (VR) applications, expanding the possibilities of mobile computing.

The concept of mobile operating systems for feature phones, which were prevalent before the smartphone era, also evolved. KaiOS, a lightweight operating system based on the Linux kernel, gained prominence as a successor to traditional feature phone platforms. Designed to run on devices with modest hardware specifications, KaiOS brought smartphone-like features, including app support and internet connectivity, to affordable devices. This evolution bridged the gap between feature phones and smartphones, providing a cost-effective solution for users seeking enhanced functionality without the high price tag.

The convergence of mobile and desktop experiences became a focal point in the evolution of mobile operating systems. Apple introduced macOS features such as Handoff, Continuity, and Universal Clipboard, allowing seamless transitions between Macs and iOS devices. Microsoft explored a similar vision with Windows 10, offering features like Continuum that aimed to create a unified experience across desktops, tablets, and smartphones. The goal was to enhance user productivity by providing a consistent environment regardless of the device being used.

The introduction of foldable devices added a new dimension to the evolution of mobile operating systems. Operating systems had to adapt to the unique challenges posed by devices with flexible displays, enabling seamless transitions between folded and unfolded states. Both Android and iOS incorporated optimizations for foldable devices, encouraging manufacturers to experiment with innovative form factors. The evolution of mobile operating systems reflected the industry's commitment to pushing the boundaries of device design and user interaction.

In recent years, privacy

concerns have come to the forefront of the mobile operating system landscape. Both Apple and Google have taken steps to empower users with greater control over their personal data. Features like App Tracking Transparency on iOS and enhanced privacy settings on Android devices give users more transparency and control over how their data is collected and used by applications. This focus on privacy aligns with growing awareness and concerns about digital privacy and data security.

The ongoing evolution of mobile operating systems is characterized by a continuous quest for innovation, user-centric design, and adaptability to emerging technologies. As artificial intelligence (AI) and machine learning (ML) become integral to computing, mobile operating systems are integrating these technologies to provide smarter, more personalized user experiences. The future may witness further convergence between mobile and desktop computing, the maturation of 5G networks, and the exploration of new frontiers such as wearable computing and augmented reality. The journey of mobile operating systems reflects the dynamic nature of the technology landscape, where adaptation and innovation are key drivers of progress.

Discuss the role of operating systems in the internet age.

In the internet age, the role of operating systems has evolved into a central and indispensable aspect of computing, shaping the way individuals, businesses, and societies interact with and leverage the vast resources of the digital realm. Operating systems serve as the foundation for a diverse range of devices, from traditional computers and servers to smartphones, tablets, and embedded systems. Their significance lies not only in managing hardware resources but also in facilitating seamless connectivity, security, and the efficient execution of applications in an interconnected world.

One of the primary roles of operating systems in the internet age is to provide a robust and user-friendly interface for individuals accessing a variety of digital devices. Graphical user interfaces (GUIs) have become standard, offering intuitive interactions that hide the complexities of underlying hardware and software. Operating systems like Microsoft Windows, macOS, and various Linux distributions have played a pivotal role in shaping these interfaces, ensuring accessibility for users with varying technical backgrounds. The interface acts as a gateway, enabling users to harness the power of the internet for communication, information retrieval, entertainment, and productivity.

Connectivity is a defining characteristic of the internet age, and operating systems play a crucial role in managing network resources and interactions. Networking protocols, such as Transmission Control Protocol/Internet Protocol (TCP/IP), have become integral components of modern operating systems. These protocols enable devices to communicate across local and global networks, forming the backbone of the internet. Operating systems ensure that devices can seamlessly connect to the internet, access remote resources, and communicate with other devices, fostering a globally interconnected ecosystem.

The internet age has witnessed a profound shift towards mobile computing, with smartphones and tablets becoming ubiquitous. Mobile operating systems, such as iOS and Android, have emerged to address the unique challenges and opportunities presented by portable, connected devices. These operating systems optimize resource management, power consumption, and connectivity to provide users with a fluid and responsive mobile experience. The role of mobile operating systems extends beyond traditional computing to encompass communication, navigation, entertainment, and an ever-expanding array of applications and services accessible through app stores.

In the realm of servers and data centers, operating systems continue to play a critical role in managing resources efficiently and supporting the delivery of internet services. Server operating systems, such as Linux distributions and Windows Server, are designed to handle high-performance computing, networking, and storage tasks. They provide the foundation for web servers, database servers, cloud computing platforms, and other internet-facing services that underpin the digital infrastructure of the internet age.

Security is a paramount concern in the internet age, given the constant threat of cyberattacks, data breaches, and unauthorized access. Operating systems incorporate a range of security features to protect users and their data. These include user authentication mechanisms, access controls, encryption protocols, and secure boot processes. Regular security updates and patches are essential components of operating systems, addressing vulnerabilities and ensuring the resilience of devices and networks against evolving threats in the interconnected landscape of the internet.

The internet age has witnessed the proliferation of cloud computing, transforming the way computing resources are provisioned, managed, and accessed. Cloud operating systems, such as Linux-based distributions tailored for cloud environments and Microsoft's Windows Server offerings with cloud integration, have become instrumental in delivering scalable and flexible computing services. Operating systems in the cloud provide the foundation for virtualization, containerization, and orchestration technologies, enabling the efficient deployment and management of applications in distributed and dynamic computing environments.

Virtualization technologies have become integral to the role of operating systems in the internet age. Hypervisors, such as VMware, Microsoft Hyper-V, and open-source solutions like KVM, enable the creation of virtual machines, allowing multiple operating systems to run on a single physical server. Virtualization enhances resource utilization, scalability, and flexibility in data centers and cloud environments. Operating systems within virtual machines operate independently, enabling diverse workloads to coexist on shared infrastructure while maintaining isolation and security.

The internet age has witnessed the rise of containerization as a paradigm for deploying and managing applications. Container orchestration platforms, such as Kubernetes, rely on operating systems to provide the underlying infrastructure for containerized applications. Operating systems tailored for containerized environments, like CoreOS and Container Linux, prioritize minimalism, security, and rapid boot times to optimize the deployment and scaling of containerized workloads. The orchestration of containers has become a key driver of agility and efficiency in the development and deployment of internet-scale applications.

The evolution of internet browsers as ubiquitous tools for accessing online content has influenced the role of operating systems. While browsers are standalone applications, they rely on the underlying operating system for resource management, security, and integration with other system components. Operating systems play a crucial role in supporting features like sandboxing, secure socket layer (SSL) protocols, and efficient memory management, contributing to the overall security and performance of web browsing experiences.

The role of operating systems in the internet age extends to the management of vast amounts of data generated, shared, and processed online. File systems, a core component of operating systems, are responsible for organizing and storing data on storage devices. Distributed file systems, such as the Hadoop Distributed File System (HDFS) and Google File System (GFS), have emerged to handle the scale and distribution requirements of big data processing in the internet age. Operating systems facilitate the efficient access, retrieval, and storage of data across local and distributed storage environments.

Artificial intelligence (AI) and machine learning (ML) have become transformative technologies in the internet age, influencing the role of operating systems. Operating systems integrate AI and ML capabilities to enhance user experiences, automate tasks, and improve system performance. Features like voice recognition, predictive text input, and recommendation algorithms leverage AI and ML within operating systems to deliver personalized and context-aware interactions.

The internet age has witnessed the growing importance of edge computing, where computing resources are distributed closer to the location where data is generated. Edge operating systems play a crucial role in managing these distributed resources and supporting applications that require low-latency and real-time processing. Operating systems in edge computing environments must address the challenges of resource constraints, varied connectivity, and the need for seamless coordination among distributed components.

Interoperability has become a key consideration in the internet age, as users expect seamless integration between diverse devices and services. Operating systems facilitate interoperability through standardized communication protocols, application programming interfaces (APIs), and support for open standards. Interconnected devices, often part of the Internet of Things (IoT), rely on operating systems to enable communication and collaboration across a heterogeneous landscape of devices and platforms.

The role of operating systems in the internet age extends to user privacy and data protection. Operating systems implement privacy features such as user consent controls, data encryption, and transparent data handling practices. As regulations and user expectations evolve, operating systems are adapting to provide users with more granular control over their data and a heightened awareness of how applications handle personal information.

In conclusion, the role of operating systems in the internet age is multifaceted and central to the functioning of modern computing ecosystems. From traditional computers to smartphones, servers, cloud environments, and emerging technologies like edge computing and IoT, operating systems provide the foundation for connectivity, security, resource management, and user experiences. As the internet age continues to evolve, operating systems will remain at the forefront of innovation, adapting to new technologies, security challenges, and user expectations in the dynamic and interconnected landscape of the digital era.

Chapter 3: Key Components and Functions of Modern Operating Systems

Define the key components that constitute a modern operating system.

A modern operating system is a complex and sophisticated software entity that serves as the intermediary between the hardware of a computer system and the software applications that run on it. Its design encompasses a range of key components, each playing a crucial role in facilitating efficient and secure computing experiences. At the core of an operating system lies the kernel, the central component responsible for managing hardware resources, such as the CPU, memory, and peripheral devices. The kernel serves as the bridge between the hardware and higher-level software, executing essential tasks like process scheduling, memory allocation, and device management.

Memory management is a fundamental component of a modern operating system, ensuring the efficient utilization of a computer's memory resources. Memory management involves tasks such as allocating memory space to running processes, managing memory hierarchies (including RAM and virtual memory), and implementing techniques like paging and segmentation to optimize memory usage. The memory manager must coordinate the retrieval and storage of data in a way that minimizes conflicts between different processes and maximizes the overall system performance.

Process management is another critical aspect of modern operating systems, focusing on the execution and coordination of processes or tasks. A process can be thought of as an independent program in execution, and the operating system's process manager oversees their creation, scheduling, and termination. The scheduler, a key subcomponent of process management, determines the order in which processes receive access to the CPU, striving for fairness, efficiency, and responsiveness. Process synchronization and communication mechanisms are implemented to ensure proper coordination between concurrent processes, preventing data corruption and race conditions.

File systems constitute a vital component of modern operating systems, providing a hierarchical structure for the storage and retrieval of data on storage devices such as hard drives, solid-state drives, and network-attached storage. File systems manage file organization, storage allocation, and access permissions. They abstract the underlying complexity of storage devices, presenting a unified interface for users and applications to interact with stored data. File systems also contribute to data integrity and reliability through mechanisms like journaling and redundancy.

Device drivers and the Input/Output (I/O) subsystem are instrumental in enabling communication between the operating system and hardware peripherals. Device drivers serve as intermediaries, translating generic operating system commands into instructions specific to each hardware device. The I/O subsystem manages the flow of data between the CPU, memory, and peripherals, ensuring efficient and coordinated data transfer. Modern operating systems support a wide array of devices, from basic input devices like keyboards and mice to complex network interfaces, graphics cards, and storage devices.

The user interface (UI) is a visible and interactive component of the operating system, serving as the bridge between users and the underlying system functionality. The UI can take various forms, including command-line interfaces (CLI), graphical user interfaces (GUI), and touch-based interfaces in the case of mobile operating systems. The UI provides users with a means to interact with the system, launch applications, and configure settings. Accessibility features and customization options enhance the inclusivity and user-friendliness of the interface, accommodating diverse user needs and preferences.

Security features and mechanisms are paramount in modern operating systems, considering the increasing threats to data and privacy. Authentication mechanisms, such as passwords, biometrics, and multi-factor authentication, safeguard access to the system. Authorization controls define the permissions and privileges granted to users or processes, ensuring that sensitive resources remain protected. Encryption technologies play a crucial role in securing data both at rest and during transmission. Security patches and updates are regularly issued to address vulnerabilities and enhance the resilience of the operating system against evolving threats.

Networking capabilities are integral to the modern operating system, enabling communication and connectivity in a networked world. Networking components facilitate the implementation of communication protocols, such as TCP/IP, allowing devices to exchange data over local area networks (LANs) or the internet. Network stacks manage the flow of data between applications and network interfaces, handling tasks like packet routing, error detection, and protocol translation. The integration of networking capabilities into the operating system supports functionalities like remote file access, internet browsing, and cloud services.

Modern operating systems also incorporate power management features to optimize energy consumption and prolong battery life in portable devices. Power management mechanisms dynamically adjust the operating frequency of the CPU, control peripheral device power states, and implement strategies like sleep modes to conserve energy during periods of inactivity. These features are crucial for devices like laptops, smartphones, and tablets, where efficient power utilization is essential for user mobility and overall device sustainability.

Graphical subsystems and windowing systems contribute to the visual presentation of information on computer displays. Graphical subsystems handle the rendering of graphical elements, such as images and fonts, while windowing systems manage the organization and interaction of multiple application windows on the screen. These components enhance the user experience by providing a visually intuitive environment for multitasking, navigation, and content consumption.

Interprocess communication (IPC) mechanisms facilitate communication and data exchange between different processes within the operating system. IPC is crucial for enabling collaboration and coordination among concurrently running applications, allowing them to share data, synchronize actions, and communicate effectively. Various IPC mechanisms, such as message passing, shared memory, and inter-process signaling, cater to diverse communication needs while maintaining the security and integrity of the operating system.

System libraries and APIs (Application Programming Interfaces) provide a set of pre-built functions and interfaces that application developers can leverage to interact with the underlying operating system functionality. System libraries abstract low-level operations, offering a standardized and consistent programming interface for developers. APIs enable applications to access operating system services, including file operations, network communication, and hardware interaction. This abstraction layer fosters portability and allows developers to create applications that can run on different operating systems without extensive modification.

Error handling and fault tolerance mechanisms are integrated into modern operating systems to address and recover from unexpected events, errors, and system failures. These mechanisms include error detection and correction codes, system logs, and recovery procedures. The operating system's ability to gracefully handle faults contributes to system reliability, data integrity, and the prevention of catastrophic failures.

Resource allocation and management form a critical component of modern operating systems, ensuring that hardware resources are efficiently distributed among competing processes and applications. The resource manager oversees CPU scheduling algorithms, memory allocation policies, and prioritization mechanisms to optimize overall system performance. These components aim to balance the demands of concurrent processes, preventing resource contention and bottlenecks.

The evolution of modern operating systems has also seen the integration of virtualization technologies. Virtualization allows the creation of virtual machines or containers, each running its instance of an operating system on a shared physical host. Hypervisors and container runtimes manage the virtualization process, providing isolation, resource allocation, and efficient utilization of hardware resources. Virtualization is instrumental in scenarios like server consolidation, cloud computing, and development and testing environments.

In conclusion, a modern operating system is a complex and multifaceted software entity that orchestrates the interaction between hardware and software components in a computing system. The key components discussed, including the kernel, memory management, process management, file systems, device drivers, user interface, security features, networking capabilities, power management, graphical subsystems, interprocess communication, system libraries, error handling, and resource allocation, collectively contribute to the functionality, efficiency, and user experience of modern operating systems. The intricate interplay of these components reflects the ongoing evolution and adaptation of operating systems to meet the demands of contemporary computing environments.

Explore the evolution of GUIs in modern operating systems.

The evolution of Graphical User Interfaces (GUIs) in modern operating systems represents a captivating journey from the early days of computing to the sophisticated interfaces we interact with today. The roots of GUIs can be traced back to the Xerox Palo Alto Research Center (PARC) in the 1970s, where researchers developed the first graphical computing environment. Xerox's Alto, released in 1973, featured a graphical display, mouse, and a desktop metaphor, laying the foundation for the GUI revolution. However, it was Apple that brought the GUI to mainstream attention with the introduction of the Macintosh in 1984. The Macintosh showcased a revolutionary interface with icons, windows, and a mouse, making computing more accessible and intuitive for a broader audience. This watershed moment marked the beginning of the GUI era.

Microsoft, recognizing the potential of GUIs, embarked on its GUI journey with Windows 1.0 in 1985. Initially, Windows served as a graphical shell for MS-DOS, providing a multitasking environment with overlapping windows. Windows 3.0, released in 1990, marked a significant leap forward, introducing improved graphics, virtual memory, and enhanced support for third-party applications. This version of Windows played a crucial role in popularizing GUIs among PC users. The competition between Apple's Macintosh and Microsoft's Windows fueled innovation, leading to the refinement of GUI elements such as icons, menus, and drag-and-drop interactions.

The 1990s witnessed a proliferation of GUI-based operating systems, each vying for user attention and market share. Apple continued to enhance its Macintosh interface, introducing the colorful Mac OS 8 in 1997. Meanwhile, Microsoft Windows evolved through versions like Windows 95, Windows 98, and Windows Me, each bringing improvements in performance, visual design, and user experience. The era was characterized by the transition from 16-bit to 32-bit architectures, enabling more robust multitasking and support for larger memory spaces.

The introduction of Microsoft Windows 95 in particular was a defining moment in GUI evolution. Windows 95 featured the Start Menu, Taskbar, and a revamped desktop, setting the standard for subsequent Windows versions. The Start Menu, with its cascading menus, became an iconic element of the Windows interface. Additionally, the desktop paradigm with icons representing files and applications became more ingrained in user expectations.

The late 1990s also saw the emergence of alternative operating systems with compelling GUIs. Linux, which had predominantly been a command-line environment, embraced GUIs with desktop environments like KDE and GNOME. These environments brought graphical richness and user-friendly features to the Linux ecosystem, contributing to its growing popularity on both desktops and servers. The graphical Linux desktop experience offered users a choice beyond the dominant Windows and Macintosh platforms.

Apple, facing financial challenges in the late 1990s, underwent a significant transformation with the return of Steve Jobs. The acquisition of NeXTSTEP, a Unix-based operating system, formed the basis for Mac OS X, released in 2001. Mac OS X featured the Aqua interface, characterized by translucency, vibrant colors, and a brushed metal appearance. This version marked the convergence of the Macintosh's user-friendly interface with the robustness of Unix underpinnings, appealing to both creative professionals and general consumers.

The early 2000s witnessed the continuation of GUI refinement and innovation. Microsoft introduced Windows XP in 2001, with a redesigned taskbar, visual styles, and enhanced multimedia capabilities. The Start Menu underwent further enhancements, and the overall visual appeal of the interface improved. Windows XP became one of Microsoft's most enduring operating systems, maintaining its presence for well over a decade.

In 2007, Apple once again redefined the GUI landscape with the introduction of the iPhone. The iPhone featured a touch-based interface, introducing gestures like pinch-to-zoom and swipe navigation. The success of the iPhone propelled the adoption of touchscreen interfaces in smartphones and later in tablets. The iOS interface, with its app icons arranged on a grid, became a standard for mobile operating systems.

Microsoft responded to the changing landscape with the release of Windows 8 in 2012. Windows 8 introduced the Metro interface, characterized by a tile-based Start Screen with live tiles displaying real-time information. This departure from the traditional Start Menu stirred mixed reactions, as users navigated a paradigm shift. The interface was designed with touch screens in mind, reflecting the growing prevalence of touch-based devices.

With the release of Windows 10 in 2015, Microsoft sought to reconcile the desktop and touch experiences. Windows 10 brought back the Start Menu in a hybrid form, incorporating live tiles alongside a familiar menu. The operating system introduced the concept of universal apps that could run across various Windows devices, promoting a seamless experience across desktops, laptops, tablets, and even the Xbox.

On the macOS front, Apple transitioned from Mac OS X to macOS with the release of macOS Sierra in 2016. macOS maintained its sleek design language and introduced features like Siri integration, continuity across Apple devices, and a refined system font. Apple continued to iterate on the macOS interface, introducing visual enhancements, dark mode, and further integration with iOS devices.

Linux desktop environments also experienced evolution and diversification. GNOME 3, introduced in 2011, brought a new interface paradigm with its Activities overview, dynamic workspaces, and a streamlined design. KDE Plasma, another popular Linux desktop environment, underwent significant improvements, offering users a customizable and feature-rich experience.

In the mobile space, Android, Google's operating system, gained prominence as a robust and customizable platform. Android's GUI evolved through various versions, with each iteration introducing refinements and new features. The introduction of Material Design in Android 5.0 Lollipop in 2014 brought a cohesive design language with a focus on simplicity, depth, and intuitive interactions.

The convergence of computing experiences across devices became a notable trend in GUI evolution. Microsoft's Fluent Design System, introduced with Windows 10, aimed to provide a consistent design language across a spectrum of devices, including PCs, tablets, and mixed reality headsets. Apple's macOS and iOS ecosystems showcased a similar approach, allowing users to seamlessly transition between Macs, iPhones, iPads, and Apple Watches.

Dark mode became a notable GUI trend in the late 2010s, offering users an alternative color scheme for interfaces that reduced eye strain in low-light conditions. Major operating systems, including macOS, Windows, and Android, introduced dark mode options, reflecting a focus on user comfort and customization.

The advent of augmented reality (AR) and virtual reality (VR) introduced new possibilities for GUIs. Operating systems and interfaces tailored for AR and VR environments aimed to provide immersive and spatial computing experiences. Microsoft's HoloLens, for instance, featured a holographic interface, merging the physical and digital worlds.

As of the last knowledge update in January 2022, the GUI evolution continues with ongoing refinements and innovations. Operating systems are increasingly integrating AI-driven features, such as predictive actions and contextual suggestions, to enhance user experiences. The GUI journey, from the pioneering days of Xerox PARC to the present, underscores the continual pursuit of interfaces that balance functionality, aesthetics, and adaptability to the evolving needs of users in an increasingly interconnected and diverse computing landscape.

Discuss various process scheduling algorithms used in modern operating systems.

In modern operating systems, process scheduling algorithms play a pivotal role in managing the execution of multiple processes concurrently, ensuring efficient utilization of CPU resources. Various scheduling algorithms have been developed, each with its characteristics and trade-offs. One of the earliest and simplest algorithms is the First-Come, First-Served (FCFS) scheduling algorithm. In FCFS, processes are executed in the order they arrive in the ready queue. While easy to understand and implement, FCFS suffers from the "convoy effect," where short processes get delayed by longer ones that arrive earlier. To address this, Shortest Job Next (SJN) or Shortest Job First (SJF) scheduling prioritizes processes based on their burst time. The idea is to minimize waiting time by executing the shortest job first. However, predicting the exact burst time is often challenging, leading to variations like Shortest Remaining Time First (SRTF), which preempts the currently running process if a shorter one arrives.

Another class of scheduling algorithms is priority-based, where each process is assigned a priority, and the scheduler executes the process with the highest priority. Priority scheduling can be either preemptive or non-preemptive. In preemptive priority scheduling, a higher-priority process can interrupt the execution of a lower-priority one. Conversely, in non-preemptive priority scheduling, a process holds the CPU until it completes its execution. While priority-based scheduling provides flexibility, it may lead to starvation if lower-priority processes are continually pushed to the background. To address this, techniques like aging, where the priority of waiting processes increases over time, are employed.

Round Robin (RR) scheduling is another widely used algorithm that allocates fixed time slices, or time quanta, to each process in a cyclic manner. If a process's execution doesn't complete within its time quantum, it is moved to the back of the queue to wait for the next turn. RR ensures fairness and prevents starvation, but it may lead to higher turnaround times and waiting times, especially for CPU-bound tasks. To balance fairness and efficiency, variations like Weighted Round Robin (WRR) introduce priorities or weights for processes, influencing their share of CPU time.

Multilevel Queue Scheduling is an extension of the priority scheduling approach. Processes are divided into multiple queues, each with its priority level. The scheduler selects processes from the highest-priority non-empty queue, and aging mechanisms ensure that lower-priority processes eventually get a chance. This approach is suitable for systems with a mix of short and long tasks, preventing the latter from monopolizing the CPU. Additionally, Multilevel Feedback Queue Scheduling incorporates the idea of dynamically adjusting process priorities based on their behavior. Processes that use less CPU time are moved to higher-priority queues, while those requiring more CPU time are shifted to lower-priority queues.

The Lottery Scheduling algorithm introduces a probabilistic element into the scheduling process. Each process is assigned a number of lottery tickets, and the scheduler randomly selects a ticket to determine the next process to execute. This approach provides a level of fairness, as each process has a chance to be selected, but it requires a random number generator and may result in inefficient allocations if not properly managed.

Real-time operating systems demand scheduling algorithms that meet specific timing constraints. Earliest Deadline First (EDF) scheduling ensures that the process with the earliest deadline is selected for execution. If a task's deadline is missed, it can lead to serious consequences in real-time systems. Rate Monotonic Scheduling

(RMS) assigns priorities based on the inverse of the task's period, assuming shorter periods are associated with higher priorities. RMS is optimal for periodic tasks with known execution times but may not be suitable for aperiodic tasks.

In recent years, computing environments have become increasingly diverse, with multiprocessor and multicore systems becoming prevalent. This evolution has led to the development of parallel and distributed scheduling algorithms. The Symmetric Multiprocessing (SMP) scheduling algorithm focuses on distributing processes evenly across multiple processors, preventing load imbalances. In contrast, the Asymmetric Multiprocessing (AMP) scheduling algorithm allows each processor to have its own scheduler, providing flexibility but requiring careful coordination to avoid inefficiencies.

Thread scheduling introduces an additional layer of complexity, as each process may consist of multiple threads sharing the same resources. The Many-to-Many model maps multiple user threads to an equal or smaller number of kernel threads, allowing for concurrency but potentially leading to contention. In the One-to-One model, each user thread corresponds to a kernel thread, providing better concurrency at the cost of increased kernel overhead. The Many-to-One model involves mapping multiple user threads to a single kernel thread, simplifying thread management but potentially leading to poor parallelism.

In conclusion, process scheduling algorithms are a fundamental component of modern operating systems, determining the allocation of CPU resources among competing processes. The choice of a scheduling algorithm depends on the system's requirements, characteristics of the processes, and the desired balance between fairness, throughput, and responsiveness. From early FCFS and SJF algorithms to more complex schemes like Round Robin, Multilevel Queue, Lottery, and real-time scheduling, the evolution of scheduling algorithms reflects the dynamic nature of computing environments and the ongoing quest for optimizing system performance in diverse scenarios.

Explore advanced memory management techniques in modern operating systems.

In modern operating systems, advanced memory management techniques play a crucial role in optimizing the utilization of memory resources, ensuring efficient and secure operation. One key approach is demand paging, a technique that allows an operating system to bring data into memory only when it is required, rather than loading entire programs or processes at once. Demand paging minimizes the initial load time of programs and allows the operating system to handle larger programs than the physical memory can accommodate. By dividing memory into fixed-size blocks, known as pages, demand paging enables the operating system to selectively load pages into physical memory as needed, swapping them in and out of secondary storage, such as a hard disk or SSD.

Virtual memory is another advanced memory management technique that extends the available address space beyond the physical memory capacity. In a virtual memory system, each process is allocated a contiguous block of virtual address space, which is divided into pages. The operating system uses a page table to map virtual addresses to physical addresses, allowing processes to operate as if they have more memory than is physically available. Virtual memory enables efficient multitasking and supports the execution of larger programs, as not all of a program's code and data need to be loaded into physical memory simultaneously.

Memory protection mechanisms are essential for ensuring the security and stability of a system. Modern operating systems implement various memory protection techniques to prevent unauthorized access and ensure the isolation of processes. Access control bits in the page table allow the operating system to specify whether a particular page is readable, writable, or executable. This prevents one process from accessing or modifying the memory of another process, enhancing security and stability. Additionally, the use of hardware-based features, such as memory segmentation and privilege levels, further contributes to the enforcement of memory protection.

The concept of shared memory facilitates efficient communication and collaboration between processes. Shared memory allows multiple processes to access the same region of physical memory, enabling data exchange without the need for inter-process communication mechanisms. Modern operating systems provide APIs and mechanisms for processes to establish shared memory regions, enabling faster communication and data sharing between collaborating processes. This is particularly valuable in scenarios such as inter-process communication in parallel computing or communication between different components of a complex software system.

Memory-mapped files represent a technique where a file is associated with a region of virtual memory. This enables direct reading and writing to the file as if it were an array in memory. Memory-mapped files simplify file I/O operations by allowing processes to access files using memory operations, offering performance benefits over traditional file I/O mechanisms. This technique is commonly used in scenarios where large datasets or files need to be efficiently processed.

To optimize memory utilization and minimize fragmentation, modern operating systems employ advanced memory allocation algorithms. The buddy system algorithm is one such technique that divides memory into fixed-size blocks and allocates memory in powers of two. When a request for a block is made, the system allocates the smallest available block that can satisfy the request. When a block is freed, the system checks if its buddy (an adjacent block of the same size) is also free; if so, they are combined into a larger block. This approach minimizes external fragmentation and efficiently manages memory allocation.

The Slab Allocation algorithm is another memory management technique designed to efficiently allocate and deallocate small memory objects. It divides memory into slabs, each dedicated to a specific object size. Objects of the same size are allocated from the corresponding slab, reducing fragmentation and improving cache locality. The Slab Allocation algorithm is commonly used in the Linux kernel for managing memory for data structures like file descriptors and inodes.

Garbage collection is a memory management technique employed in languages with automatic memory management, such as Java and C#. The garbage collector identifies and reclaims memory occupied by objects that are no longer accessible or in use. Different garbage collection algorithms, such as mark-and-sweep, generational, and concurrent garbage collection, aim to balance the trade-offs between performance and memory reclamation efficiency. These algorithms use various strategies to identify unreachable objects and reclaim memory in a way that minimizes impact on program execution.

Memory compression is an innovative technique used in modern operating systems to address memory pressure and avoid swapping to slower storage devices. When physical memory becomes scarce, the operating system can compress inactive pages in memory, reducing their size and freeing up space for more critical processes. This allows the system to postpone or minimize the need for swapping pages to disk, which can significantly impact performance. Memory compression is particularly beneficial in scenarios where swapping to disk is undesirable due to latency concerns.

Huge Pages represent a memory management technique aimed at improving system performance for memory-intensive applications. In systems that support huge pages, the operating system allows the allocation of larger page sizes than the standard small page size. Huge pages reduce the overhead associated with managing a large number of small pages, leading to improved translation looka-side buffer (TLB) efficiency and reduced page table overhead. This is particularly advantageous for applications that work with large datasets, such as databases and scientific simulations.

Modern operating systems also employ memory prefetching techniques to optimize memory access patterns and enhance overall system performance. Prefetching involves predicting which memory locations a process will access in the future and proactively loading them into cache before they are requested. This helps reduce memory latency and ensures that the CPU has timely access to the data it needs. Prefetching algorithms use various strategies, including hardware-based prefetching and software-based techniques, to anticipate and streamline memory access patterns.

In the context of security, Address Space Layout Randomization (ASLR) is a technique used to mitigate the risk of memory-related security vulnerabilities. ASLR randomizes the memory addresses of system components and processes, making it more challenging for attackers to predict the location of specific functions or data structures. By introducing randomness into the memory layout, ASLR adds an additional layer of defense against certain types of exploits, such as buffer overflow attacks.

In conclusion, advanced memory management techniques in modern operating systems are critical for ensuring efficient, secure, and responsive computing environments. From demand paging and virtual memory to memory protection, shared memory, memory-mapped files, and advanced memory allocation algorithms, these techniques collectively contribute to optimal memory utilization, performance, and system reliability. As computing environments evolve and hardware capabilities advance, the ongoing development and refinement of memory management strategies will remain integral to meeting the demands of diverse applications and workloads.

Discuss modern file system design principles.

Modern file system design principles reflect the evolving landscape of computing, storage technologies, and user requirements, aiming to provide efficient, reliable, and scalable solutions for managing data. One key principle is the adoption of hierarchical structures to organize files and directories. The hierarchical file system structure allows users to create a logical and intuitive organization of data, facilitating easy navigation and retrieval. This hierarchical organization is typically represented as a tree-like structure, with directories serving as branches and files as leaves. This design principle has proven to be robust and user-friendly, with each level of the hierarchy representing a level of abstraction, making it easier for users to manage and locate their data.

Concurrency and multi-threading support are essential considerations in modern file system design. With contemporary computing systems featuring multiple processors or cores, file systems must efficiently handle concurrent access from multiple applications or users. Concurrent access poses challenges related to data consistency, integrity, and performance. File systems implement locking mechanisms, such as fine-grained or coarse-grained locks, to manage concurrent access and prevent data corruption. Additionally, support for multi-threading ensures that file operations can be parallelized, enhancing overall system responsiveness and throughput.

Security is a paramount concern in modern file system design, given the increasing frequency and sophistication of cyber threats. File systems incorporate access control mechanisms to govern user permissions on files and directories. These mechanisms often leverage user accounts, groups, and permission flags to regulate read, write, and execute privileges. Encryption is another crucial aspect of file system security, protecting data both at rest and in transit. Modern file systems may implement encryption algorithms to safeguard sensitive information, offering features like full-disk encryption or per-file encryption to enhance data privacy.

Data integrity and reliability are core principles guiding modern file system design. Redundancy and error-checking mechanisms, such as checksums and error-correcting codes, are integrated to detect and correct data corruption caused by hardware failures or other anomalies. File systems may also employ journaling or transactional approaches to ensure atomicity and consistency during write operations. These techniques enhance the robustness of file systems, minimizing the risk of data loss or corruption due to unforeseen events.

Scalability is a critical consideration as storage demands continue to grow exponentially. Modern file systems are designed to handle vast amounts of data efficiently, both in terms of storage capacity and performance. Distributed file systems, such as the Google File System (GFS) or Hadoop Distributed File System (HDFS), exemplify scalability principles by distributing data across multiple nodes and facilitating parallel access. Techniques like sharding, partitioning, and replication contribute to the scalability of file systems, allowing them to accommodate diverse workloads and support the storage requirements of large-scale applications.

Adaptability to various storage media is a key design principle in the face of the evolving storage landscape. File systems must seamlessly support traditional hard disk drives (HDDs), solid-state drives (SSDs), and emerging storage technologies. Techniques like wear leveling, which ensures even distribution of write and erase cycles in SSDs, are essential for prolonging the lifespan of flash-based storage. Modern file systems are designed to optimize performance based on the characteristics of different storage media, employing strategies like prefetching, caching, and tiered storage to enhance overall efficiency.

Metadata management is a foundational aspect of file system design, involving the efficient storage and retrieval of file-related information. Metadata encompasses details such as file names, sizes, creation dates, and permissions. Modern file systems employ various indexing and caching mechanisms to expedite metadata access and retrieval. Techniques like hierarchical storage management (HSM) enable the seamless transition of less frequently accessed data to slower or archival storage tiers, optimizing the use of high-performance storage for more active data.

Snapshot and versioning capabilities are increasingly integrated into modern file systems, allowing users to capture and restore previous states of their data. Snapshots provide point-in-time copies of file systems, enabling users to recover from accidental deletions or modifications. Versioning allows users to track changes to files over time, offering a safety net against data loss or unintentional alterations. These features enhance data protection, supporting recovery scenarios and providing users with greater control over their data.

Modern file systems often incorporate advanced search and indexing mechanisms to facilitate rapid and efficient data retrieval. Full-text search, metadata indexing, and content-based searching are examples of techniques employed to enhance the discoverability of files. These capabilities are particularly crucial as data volumes increase, enabling users to quickly locate relevant information within large file repositories.

Compression and deduplication are employed to optimize storage efficiency in modern file systems. Compression reduces the size of stored data, conserving storage space and facilitating faster data transfers. Deduplication identifies and eliminates duplicate copies of data, further reducing storage requirements. These techniques are especially valuable in environments with large-scale data storage demands, where minimizing the physical footprint of data contributes to cost-effectiveness and resource utilization.

As cloud computing becomes increasingly prevalent, file systems are designed to seamlessly integrate with cloud storage services. Cloud-native file systems provide features such as scalability, accessibility from diverse locations, and seamless collaboration among users. Integration with cloud storage also enables features like automatic synchronization, ensuring that files are consistently updated across multiple devices and locations.

The principle of backward compatibility is integral to modern file system design, acknowledging the need for systems to support legacy applications and data formats. Compatibility ensures that users can seamlessly transition to newer file system versions or platforms without sacrificing access to their existing data. Robust migration tools and well-defined file system APIs contribute to the longevity and interoperability of file systems, supporting a diverse ecosystem of applications and services.

In conclusion, modern file system design principles reflect a holistic approach to addressing the challenges and opportunities presented by evolving computing environments, storage technologies, and user expectations. From hierarchical organization and concurrency support to security, scalability, adaptability, and advanced features like snapshots and search capabilities, these principles collectively contribute to the efficiency, reliability, and usability of file systems in the contemporary computing landscape. As technology continues to advance, the ongoing evolution of file system design will play a crucial role in shaping the future of data management and storage.

Discuss how modern operating systems handle device management.

In the intricate architecture of modern operating systems, device management is a critical component responsible for the efficient coordination and utilization of hardware peripherals. The handling of devices involves a comprehensive set of processes and mechanisms, each designed to ensure seamless interaction between software applications and the diverse array of hardware components. A fundamental aspect of device management is the abstraction layer that shields software applications from the complexities of specific hardware implementations. This abstraction allows applications to communicate with devices through standardized interfaces and drivers, promoting portability and ease of development across various hardware platforms.

Device drivers are essential software components that facilitate communication between the operating system and specific hardware devices. These drivers serve as intermediaries, translating generic operating system commands into instructions that are understandable and executable by individual devices. Modern operating systems maintain extensive repositories of device drivers, ensuring compatibility with a wide range of peripherals. The process of identifying and loading the appropriate driver for a connected device is known as Plug and Play, a feature that automates much of the device configuration process and enhances user experience by eliminating the need for manual driver installations in many cases.

The concept of Plug and Play extends beyond driver loading to encompass dynamic device recognition and configuration. When a new device is connected to the system, the operating system is designed to detect it automatically and initiate the necessary processes for device configuration and driver loading. This capability simplifies the user experience, allowing for the seamless integration of new hardware components without requiring extensive user intervention. Additionally, hot-swappable devices, such as USB drives, can be connected or disconnected while the system is running, with the operating system dynamically responding to these changes.

To manage the multitude of connected devices efficiently, modern operating systems employ device management frameworks and architectures. These frameworks provide a structured approach to handling devices, encompassing layers of abstraction, modularization, and standardization. The Universal Serial Bus (USB) architecture, for example, is a prevalent framework that allows multiple devices to connect through a single standardized interface. USB supports a variety of devices, ranging from input peripherals like keyboards and mice to storage devices, cameras, and smartphones. The operating system's USB stack manages the communication protocols, power distribution, and device enumeration within the USB framework.

Device enumeration is a crucial step in the device management process, involving the identification and assignment of unique identifiers to connected devices. Enumeration ensures that each device is recognized and distinguished from others, enabling the operating system to establish communication channels and allocate resources appropriately. Enumeration is often facilitated through standardized protocols such as the Plug and Play Extensions (PnP-X), which allows devices to announce their presence and capabilities to the operating system.

Interrupt handling is a fundamental mechanism in device management, enabling devices to asynchronously signal the CPU when they require attention. When a device generates an interrupt, the operating system interrupts the current execution flow to handle the device's request promptly. Interrupt service routines (ISRs) are specific functions within the operating system that manage the processing of interrupts, ensuring timely and efficient responses to device events. Modern operating systems implement interrupt prioritization and handling mechanisms to manage concurrent interrupt requests and maintain responsiveness.

I/O scheduling is a critical aspect of device management, particularly in scenarios where multiple processes or applications are competing for access to a shared device. The operating system's I/O scheduler determines the order in which pending I/O requests are serviced, optimizing for factors such as throughput, response time, and fairness. Various scheduling algorithms, such as the Completely Fair Queuing (CFQ) algorithm in Linux or the Deadline scheduler, are employed to manage I/O operations effectively. These algorithms aim to balance the needs of different processes and applications, preventing resource contention and ensuring equitable access to devices.

Power management is an integral facet of device management, particularly in mobile and battery-powered devices. Modern operating systems implement sophisticated power management features to optimize energy consumption and extend battery life. Techniques such as dynamic frequency scaling adjust the operating frequency of the CPU based on workload, allowing the system to conserve power during periods of low activity. Furthermore, devices and components can enter low-power states or sleep modes when not in use, reducing overall energy consumption without compromising functionality. Advanced power management features contribute to the sustainability and efficiency of computing devices, aligning with broader environmental and energy conservation goals.

Modern operating systems often integrate support for advanced input devices, including touchscreens, gyroscopes, accelerometers, and biometric sensors. These devices enhance user interactions and provide novel input modalities, contributing to the versatility and user-friendliness of computing platforms. The operating system's input subsystem manages the communication and interpretation of data from these devices, translating gestures, touches, or sensor readings into meaningful inputs for applications. Accessibility features, such as screen readers and voice recognition, further expand the range of supported input methods, ensuring inclusivity for users with diverse needs.

Networking components are an integral part of device management in modern operating systems, enabling communication and connectivity in networked environments. The operating system's network stack implements communication protocols, such as the Transmission Control Protocol (TCP) and Internet Protocol (IP), facilitating data exchange over local area networks (LANs) or the internet. Device drivers for network interfaces handle the transmission and reception of data packets, while the operating system's networking subsystem manages tasks like packet routing, error detection, and protocol translation. Networking features extend to support for wireless communication standards, such as Wi-Fi and Bluetooth, enabling seamless connectivity with a wide range of devices and services.

The concept of virtualization has introduced new dimensions to device management, particularly in server environments and cloud computing platforms. Virtualization allows multiple virtual machines (VMs) to share the same physical hardware, each with its operating system and set of virtualized devices. Hypervisors, or virtual machine monitors, manage the allocation of physical resources to virtual machines and coordinate interactions with virtualized devices. This abstraction layer introduces flexibility in resource allocation, allowing for dynamic scaling and efficient utilization of hardware in virtualized environments.

Security considerations permeate every aspect of device management in modern operating systems. Secure boot mechanisms ensure the integrity of the operating system by verifying the authenticity of bootloader and kernel components during the system startup process. Device drivers undergo rigorous validation to prevent malicious software from exploiting vulnerabilities. Additionally, sandboxing and access control mechanisms restrict the privileges of applications and processes, minimizing the potential impact of security breaches. The secure management of cryptographic keys, biometric data, and other sensitive information further enhances the security posture of device management in modern operating systems.

Fault tolerance and error recovery mechanisms are critical for maintaining system stability and availability. Redundancy and error-checking techniques are implemented at various levels of device management to mitigate the impact of hardware failures or unexpected errors. RAID (Redundant Array of Independent Disks) configurations, for instance, provide fault tolerance for storage devices by distributing data across multiple disks. Error correction codes (ECC) in memory modules detect and correct errors in memory operations, preventing data corruption. These fault-tolerant features contribute to the overall reliability and resilience of modern operating systems.

In conclusion, modern operating systems employ a sophisticated and multifaceted approach to device management, encompassing abstraction layers, driver frameworks, plug-and-play mechanisms, interrupt handling, I/O scheduling, power management, support for diverse input devices, networking components, virtualization, security measures, and fault tolerance mechanisms. These elements collectively contribute to the seamless interaction between software applications and a diverse array of hardware peripherals, ensuring a user-friendly, efficient, and reliable computing experience. As technology continues to advance, the evolution of device management principles will remain integral to meeting the demands of ever-changing hardware landscapes and user expectations.

Explore the networking capabilities of modern operating systems.

The networking capabilities of modern operating systems play a pivotal role in enabling communication and connectivity in today's interconnected world. These capabilities are designed to facilitate the exchange of data between devices, support diverse network architectures, and ensure seamless access to resources across local and global networks. At the heart of these capabilities is the network stack, a layered architecture that manages the complexities of communication protocols, data transmission, and network interactions.

The Transmission Control Protocol/Internet Protocol (TCP/IP) is the foundational protocol suite that underpins modern networking capabilities. The TCP/IP stack is composed of multiple layers, each serving a specific function in the communication process.

The Link layer is responsible for the physical and data link aspects of communication, while the Internet layer handles the routing of data packets across networks. The Transport layer, with protocols like TCP and User Datagram Protocol (UDP), ensures reliable and connection-oriented or connectionless data transfer, respectively. Finally, the Application layer supports networked applications, providing a framework for processes to communicate over the network.

Ethernet, a widely used networking technology, forms the backbone of local area networks (LANs). Operating systems incorporate Ethernet drivers to manage communication over Ethernet networks, handling tasks such as packet framing, addressing, and collision detection. The Ethernet protocol is foundational for local network connectivity, enabling devices to communicate within the same network segment.

Wireless networking has become ubiquitous, and modern operating systems integrate robust support for various wireless communication standards. Wi-Fi, based on the IEEE 802.11 standard, allows devices to connect to wireless networks. Operating systems manage Wi-Fi connections, handling tasks such as authentication, encryption, and signal strength monitoring. The integration of wireless networking capabilities extends the reach of connectivity, providing users with the flexibility to access networks without physical constraints.

Mobile data connectivity is a vital aspect of modern operating systems, particularly in the era of smartphones and mobile devices. Operating systems support cellular data communication standards such as 3G, 4G LTE, and 5G, enabling devices to connect to mobile networks. Mobile data capabilities are fundamental for accessing the internet, sending and receiving data, and supporting a wide range of mobile applications. Operating systems seamlessly switch between Wi-Fi and cellular data based on availability and user preferences, ensuring continuous connectivity.

Virtual Private Network (VPN) support is a crucial feature in modern operating systems, addressing the need for secure and private communication over public networks. VPNs create encrypted tunnels between devices and remote servers, safeguarding data from interception or unauthorized access. Operating systems manage VPN connections, allowing users to establish secure connections for remote access to corporate networks, safeguarding sensitive information transmitted over the internet.

Firewall capabilities are integrated into modern operating systems to enhance network security. Firewalls monitor and control incoming and outgoing network traffic based on predefined security rules. By inspecting packets and applying access control policies, firewalls help protect devices from unauthorized access, malware, and other security threats. Operating systems provide users with tools to configure firewall settings and define rules tailored to their security requirements.

Dynamic Host Configuration Protocol (DHCP) and Domain Name System (DNS) services are integral components of modern networking capabilities. DHCP enables automatic assignment of IP addresses to devices on a network, simplifying network configuration. DNS translates human-readable domain names into IP addresses, facilitating the resolution of network addresses. Operating systems manage DHCP interactions for automatic address assignment and DNS resolution to streamline the network configuration process for users.

Network Address Translation (NAT) is a key feature employed by operating systems to manage the scarcity of IPv4 addresses. NAT allows multiple devices within a private network to share a single public IP address when accessing the internet. Operating systems implement NAT functionality, enabling devices within a local network to communicate externally while appearing to have the same public IP address. This approach extends the usability of IPv4 addresses, mitigating the impact of address exhaustion.

Quality of Service (QoS) mechanisms are integrated into modern operating systems to prioritize network traffic and optimize performance. QoS ensures that critical applications receive preferential treatment over the network, enhancing user experience for real-time applications such as voice and video communication. Operating systems implement QoS policies that prioritize certain types of traffic, allocate bandwidth appropriately, and manage network congestion to maintain optimal performance.

Multicast and broadcast support are fundamental networking capabilities that enable efficient communication in specific scenarios. Multicast allows a device to send data to a select group of recipients, conserving network bandwidth compared to unicast communication to individual devices. Broadcast facilitates communication to all devices within a network segment. Operating systems manage multicast and broadcast traffic, ensuring efficient and targeted communication in situations where these modes are beneficial.

Network File System (NFS) and Server Message Block (SMB) protocols are essential for file sharing and collaborative work in networked environments. NFS, commonly used in Unix-like systems, allows users to access files on remote servers as if they were local. SMB, prevalent in Windows environments, enables file and printer sharing between devices on a network. Operating systems provide built-in support for these protocols, simplifying file sharing and collaboration across diverse networked environments.

Remote Desktop Protocol (RDP) and Virtual Network Computing (VNC) are protocols supported by modern operating systems for remote desktop access. These protocols enable users to control and view the desktop of a remote device over a network. Operating systems implement RDP (common in Windows environments) and VNC (used in Unix-like systems), offering users the ability to remotely manage computers, troubleshoot issues, and collaborate across geographical distances.

IPv6 adoption is a crucial aspect of modern networking capabilities, addressing the limitations of IPv4 address space. Operating systems support IPv6 to ensure continued connectivity as the world transitions to a larger address space. IPv6 facilitates the identification and location of devices on the internet, supporting the growing number of connected devices and addressing the exhaustion of available IPv4 addresses.

Software-defined networking (SDN) principles are increasingly influencing modern networking capabilities. SDN separates the control plane from the data plane, allowing for centralized network management and dynamic configuration. Operating systems incorporate SDN-compatible features to enhance network flexibility, programmability, and scalability, particularly in large-scale data center and cloud environments.

Container networking is a contemporary development in modern operating systems, aligning with the rise of containerization technologies like Docker and Kubernetes. Containers encapsulate applications and their dependencies, and container orchestration platforms manage their deployment. Operating systems support container networking, enabling efficient communication between containers, load balancing, and the establishment of microservices architectures.

Network monitoring and diagnostic tools are integral components of modern operating systems, providing users with insights into network performance, troubleshooting capabilities, and security monitoring. Operating systems include tools like ping, traceroute, netstat, and Wireshark, empowering users to analyze network activity, identify connectivity issues, and diagnose network-related problems.

In conclusion, the networking capabilities of modern operating systems are foundational to the seamless communication, connectivity, and collaboration that define contemporary computing environments. From supporting diverse network technologies and protocols to ensuring security, privacy, and efficient resource utilization, these capabilities play a central role in shaping the user experience and facilitating the complex interactions within today's interconnected world. As technology continues to evolve, the ongoing development and refinement of networking features in operating systems will remain essential to meeting the demands of a dynamic and interconnected digital landscape.

Discuss security measures implemented in modern operating systems.

Security measures in modern operating systems constitute a multifaceted and comprehensive framework designed to protect systems, data, and users from a myriad of potential threats and vulnerabilities. One fundamental aspect of security is the secure boot process, which ensures the integrity of the operating system during startup. Secure boot mechanisms, often based on technologies like Unified Extensible Firmware Interface (UEFI) and Trusted Platform Module (TPM), verify the authenticity and integrity of bootloader and kernel components, preventing the execution of malicious code during the boot sequence. This safeguard enhances the overall security posture by establishing a trustworthy foundation for the operating system.

Access control mechanisms form a cornerstone of modern operating system security, governing user permissions and system resource access. Operating systems implement user account management, assigning specific privileges and permissions to each user. Role-based access control (RBAC) and discretionary access control (DAC) are common models employed to regulate user access rights. RBAC defines access based on user roles, while DAC allows individual users to set access permissions on their files and directories. Access control lists (ACLs) offer a more granular approach, enabling users to specify detailed access policies for resources. These mechanisms collectively contribute to the principle of least privilege, limiting user access to only the resources essential for their tasks and minimizing the potential impact of security breaches.

File system encryption is a critical security measure in modern operating systems, addressing the need to protect sensitive data at rest. Full-disk encryption and file-level encryption mechanisms safeguard data from unauthorized access, even in the event of physical theft or unauthorized access to storage media. Technologies like BitLocker in Windows and FileVault in macOS implement encryption at the disk or file system level, ensuring that data remains confidential and secure. Encryption keys are securely managed to prevent unauthorized decryption and enhance the overall confidentiality of stored information.

Security updates and patch management are essential components of modern operating system security, addressing vulnerabilities and weaknesses discovered after the initial release. Operating system vendors regularly release security updates and patches to address known vulnerabilities and improve system resilience. Automatic update mechanisms streamline the process of applying patches, ensuring that systems remain protected against emerging threats. Timely and consistent application of updates is crucial to maintaining a secure operating environment and minimizing the risk of exploitation.

Firewalls are integrated into modern operating systems to monitor and control network traffic, forming a critical defense against unauthorized access and malicious activities. Firewalls operate at the network layer, inspecting incoming and outgoing packets and applying access control policies based on predefined rules. Ingress filtering and egress filtering mechanisms allow administrators to specify rules governing which traffic is allowed or denied. Firewalls contribute to the overall security posture by preventing unauthorized access, mitigating the impact of network-based attacks, and safeguarding sensitive information.

Intrusion detection and prevention systems (IDPS) are employed in modern operating systems to detect and respond to suspicious or malicious activities. IDPS mechanisms analyze system logs, network traffic, and behavior patterns to identify potential security incidents. Anomalies and known attack signatures trigger alerts or automated responses to thwart unauthorized access or exploitation attempts. IDPS technologies enhance the situational awareness of system administrators, providing insights into potential security threats and enabling proactive measures to protect the system.

Security auditing and logging mechanisms contribute to accountability and forensic analysis by recording system activities and events. Modern operating systems generate audit logs that capture details such as login attempts, privilege escalations, file access, and system configuration changes. Security information and event management (SIEM) tools can aggregate and analyze these logs, providing a comprehensive view of system activities. Auditing mechanisms support post-incident analysis, compliance reporting, and the identification of potential security incidents by tracking changes and activities across the operating system.

User authentication is a foundational security measure, ensuring that only authorized individuals can access a system. Modern operating systems implement a variety of authentication methods, including password-based authentication, biometric authentication (such as fingerprint or facial recognition), and multi-factor authentication (MFA). MFA combines multiple authentication factors, such as a password and a one-time code, to enhance security. Operating systems support robust password policies, including requirements for complexity, length, and periodic changes, to fortify the authentication process and mitigate the risk of unauthorized access.

Security sandboxing is a technique employed in modern operating systems to contain and isolate potentially malicious applications or processes. Sandboxing restricts the capabilities and access rights of applications, preventing them from interfering with other system components or accessing sensitive resources. Containerization technologies, such as Docker, extend the concept of sandboxing by encapsulating applications and their dependencies in isolated environments. Sandboxing mechanisms contribute to the overall security and stability of the operating system by confining potentially harmful activities to controlled environments.

Secure communication is a critical consideration in modern operating systems, particularly in networked environments. The implementation of secure communication protocols, such as Transport Layer Security (TLS) and Secure Sockets Layer (SSL), ensures the confidentiality and integrity of data transmitted over networks. Secure communication is essential for protecting sensitive information during activities like online banking, e-commerce transactions, and remote access to corporate networks. Operating systems provide libraries and frameworks to support secure communication, enabling developers to implement cryptographic protocols and secure their applications.

Virtualization technologies have introduced new dimensions to operating system security, particularly in scenarios involving hypervisors and virtual machines (VMs). Hypervisors manage the allocation of physical resources to multiple VMs, and security measures are implemented to prevent unauthorized access or escape from virtualized environments. Secure boot processes for VMs, secure isolation between VMs, and the implementation of trusted execution environments contribute to the security of virtualized environments. Operating systems that serve as hosts for VMs implement security features to safeguard the integrity and isolation of virtualized workloads.

Application whitelisting and blacklisting are security measures employed in modern operating systems to control which applications can run on a system. Whitelisting allows only approved applications to execute, while blacklisting prohibits the execution of known malicious or unauthorized applications. These measures help prevent the installation and execution of unauthorized software, reducing the attack surface and minimizing the risk of malware infections. Operating systems provide administrators with tools to define and enforce application control policies, enhancing overall system security.

Endpoint protection solutions are integral components of modern operating system security, providing defense against malware, ransomware, and other malicious software. Antivirus and anti-malware programs scan files, processes, and network traffic to identify and mitigate threats. Endpoint protection solutions often include features such as real-time scanning, behavior analysis, and threat intelligence integration to detect and respond to evolving security threats. Regular updates to virus definitions and heuristic analysis techniques contribute to the effectiveness of endpoint protection mechanisms.

Security information sharing and collaboration are essential aspects of modern operating system security. Threat intelligence feeds, security forums, and collaboration platforms enable information sharing about emerging threats and vulnerabilities. Operating system vendors collaborate with security researchers, industry partners, and the wider security community to identify and address security issues proactively. This collaborative approach enhances the collective ability to respond to security incidents and strengthens the overall security posture of modern operating systems.

Secure development practices and code integrity measures are critical for building secure operating systems. Operating system vendors adhere to secure coding standards, conduct code reviews, and employ static and dynamic analysis tools to identify and remediate security vulnerabilities during the development process. Code signing mechanisms ensure the integrity of executables and system components by validating their authenticity and preventing the execution of tampered or malicious code. Secure development practices contribute to the robustness and reliability of modern operating systems from the ground up.

Security education and awareness are integral components of modern operating system security. Users and administrators play a crucial role in maintaining a secure computing environment by understanding security best practices, recognizing potential threats, and adhering to

security policies. Operating systems provide educational resources, user guides, and security prompts to inform users about safe computing practices, phishing awareness, and the importance of regular updates. Security awareness programs contribute to a culture of security, empowering users to actively participate in safeguarding the integrity and confidentiality of system resources.

In conclusion, the security measures implemented in modern operating systems form a comprehensive and adaptive framework designed to protect against a diverse range of threats and vulnerabilities. From secure boot processes and access controls to encryption, intrusion detection, and collaborative threat intelligence, these measures collectively contribute to the resilience and integrity of operating systems. As the digital landscape evolves and cyber threats continue to advance, the ongoing development and enhancement of security measures will remain paramount to ensuring the trustworthiness and security of modern computing environments.

Discuss how modern operating systems optimize power consumption.

Optimizing power consumption has become a crucial consideration in modern operating systems as the proliferation of portable devices, laptops, and energy-efficient computing environments continues. One fundamental approach to power optimization is dynamic frequency scaling, a technique that adjusts the operating frequency of the CPU based on the current workload. Modern operating systems employ dynamic frequency scaling to dynamically scale the CPU clock frequency up or down, aligning with the processing demands of the system. When the system is under low load, the operating system reduces the CPU frequency to conserve power, minimizing energy consumption and heat generation. Conversely, during periods of high demand, the operating system increases the CPU frequency to ensure optimal performance, striking a balance between power efficiency and computational needs.

Operating systems leverage advanced power management features to regulate the energy consumption of various hardware components, such as the CPU, GPU, and peripheral devices. Advanced Configuration and Power Interface (ACPI) is a standard employed by modern operating systems to facilitate power management at the system level. ACPI enables the operating system to control the power states of individual devices, allowing them to enter low-power states or sleep modes when not in use. These power states help conserve energy and extend battery life in portable devices. Operating systems implement ACPI features to orchestrate the transitions between different power states based on user activity and system requirements.

In the context of mobile devices, modern operating systems optimize power consumption through a combination of strategies tailored for the specific challenges of these environments. Mobile operating systems, such as Android and iOS, incorporate aggressive power management policies to enhance battery life. Techniques like app standby, background process limitations, and network optimization are employed to minimize the energy impact of applications running in the background. Additionally, mobile operating systems implement Doze mode, a feature that suspends background activities during periods of device inactivity, further reducing power consumption and extending battery life.

Modern operating systems implement adaptive display brightness control to optimize power consumption in devices equipped with screens. Ambient light sensors detect the surrounding lighting conditions, allowing the operating system to dynamically adjust the display brightness. During well-lit environments, the operating system increases the display brightness for better visibility, while in darker conditions, it reduces the brightness to conserve power. This adaptive brightness control not only improves user experience but also contributes to energy efficiency by aligning the display's power consumption with the ambient lighting conditions.

Peripheral device management is a key aspect of power optimization in modern operating systems. USB selective suspend, for example, is a feature that allows the operating system to selectively suspend power to USB devices when they are not in active use. This helps reduce overall power consumption by preventing connected USB peripherals from drawing unnecessary power. Additionally, operating systems implement intelligent management of wireless connectivity, such as Wi-Fi and Bluetooth, by adjusting power states and optimizing the frequency of background scans. These measures contribute to power efficiency without compromising the user's ability to access wireless services.

Modern operating systems implement advanced sleep and hibernation modes to optimize power consumption during periods of inactivity. Sleep mode (or standby mode) involves placing the system into a low-power state while keeping the system's state in memory. This allows for quick resumption of operations when the user returns, minimizing the time and energy required to transition between active and idle states. Hibernation mode, on the other hand, involves saving the system's state to disk and then shutting down, consuming minimal power. Hibernation is particularly effective for devices with limited battery capacity, ensuring that power is conserved even when the device is completely powered off.

In server environments and desktop systems, modern operating systems implement power management features to optimize energy consumption without sacrificing performance. Advanced Configuration and Power Interface (ACPI) plays a crucial role in regulating power states, allowing the operating system to control the sleep states of the CPU and other hardware components. Operating systems dynamically adjust the system's power state based on the workload, transitioning to lower-power states during periods of low activity and returning to higher-power states when processing demands increase. Power management policies are often customizable to accommodate user preferences and organizational energy efficiency goals.

Modern operating systems incorporate support for heterogeneous architectures, such as systems with both high-performance cores and energy-efficient cores. This architecture, known as big.LITTLE in ARM-based systems, allows the operating system to intelligently distribute processing tasks to the appropriate core based on the computational demands. During periods of light workload, the operating system can assign tasks to energy-efficient cores, minimizing power consumption. When high-performance capabilities are required, the operating system can utilize the more powerful cores, balancing performance and energy efficiency dynamically.

The adoption of solid-state drives (SSDs) in modern storage solutions has influenced power optimization strategies in operating systems. Unlike traditional hard disk drives (HDDs), SSDs have no moving parts, resulting in lower power consumption and faster access times. Modern operating systems take advantage of the characteristics of SSDs by implementing power-aware storage management. Techniques like selective data prefetching, efficient wear leveling, and TRIM support enhance the energy efficiency of SSDs, contributing to overall power optimization in computing systems.

Cloud computing environments introduce new dimensions to power optimization, especially in data centers where energy efficiency is a critical concern. Modern operating systems implement power capping and dynamic voltage and frequency scaling (DVFS) mechanisms in collaboration with hypervisors to regulate the power consumption of virtualized server environments. These measures enable data center operators to align power consumption with workload demands, optimizing energy efficiency without compromising the performance and responsiveness of virtualized workloads.

Containerization technologies, such as Docker and Kubernetes, have gained prominence in modern computing architectures. Operating systems support power-efficient container orchestration by allowing dynamic scaling of container instances based on demand. Container platforms implement features like auto-scaling, which adjusts the number of running containers based on resource utilization, contributing to power optimization in cloud-native environments. Operating systems play a vital role in providing the underlying support for containerization and ensuring that resource utilization aligns with energy efficiency goals.

Machine learning algorithms are increasingly being integrated into modern operating systems to predict and optimize power consumption patterns. These algorithms analyze historical usage data, system configurations, and workload patterns to make predictions about future power requirements. Operating systems leverage these predictions to dynamically adjust power management policies, optimizing energy consumption based on anticipated user behavior and application workloads. This proactive approach to power optimization enhances the responsiveness of the operating system to changing conditions and contributes to more effective energy conservation.

The development of energy-efficient hardware architectures, such as ARM's big.LITTLE architecture and Intel's Lakefield processors, has influenced power optimization strategies in modern operating systems. These architectures feature a combination of high-performance and energy-efficient cores, allowing the operating system to intelligently distribute tasks based on workload demands. The operating system can direct less demanding tasks to energy-efficient cores, reducing power consumption during periods of low activity. This approach aligns with the growing emphasis on energy efficiency in mobile devices, laptops, and other computing platforms.

In conclusion, power optimization in modern operating systems is a multifaceted and dynamic endeavor that spans a range of strategies and technologies. From dynamic frequency scaling and advanced power management features to adaptive display brightness control, sleep modes, and support for heterogeneous architectures, operating systems employ a diverse set of tools to balance performance and energy efficiency. Whether in mobile devices, desktops, servers, or cloud environments, the ongoing evolution of power optimization techniques in operating systems remains integral to meeting the demands of users, organizations, and the broader goals of sustainability in computing.

Discuss user account control mechanisms in modern operating systems.

User Account Control (UAC) mechanisms play a pivotal role in modern operating systems, serving as a fundamental layer of defense against unauthorized access, malware, and potential security threats. Introduced with Windows Vista and present in subsequent Windows operating systems, UAC is designed to elevate the security posture by enforcing the principle of least privilege and minimizing the risk associated with elevated privileges. One key aspect of UAC is the separation of standard user accounts and administrative accounts. Standard user accounts operate with limited privileges, preventing inadvertent or unauthorized modifications to critical system files and settings. When administrative tasks are required, UAC prompts the user to provide explicit consent or credentials, ensuring that elevated privileges are only granted when necessary.

The core principle of UAC is to limit the default permissions of user accounts and prompt for explicit authorization when higher privileges are required. This approach reduces the attack surface by minimizing the time that user accounts operate with elevated privileges, mitigating the impact of potential security vulnerabilities. UAC achieves this by assigning two distinct integrity levels to processes: a standard level for regular user tasks and a high level for administrative tasks. When a standard user attempts to perform an action that requires elevated privileges, UAC prompts the user to enter the credentials of an administrator, thereby preventing unauthorized access and modifications.

One of the key components of UAC is the Consent Prompt, a dialog box that appears when an action requires administrative privileges. This prompt seeks user confirmation or administrator credentials before allowing the action to proceed. The Consent Prompt serves as a crucial point of control, ensuring that users are aware of potentially sensitive operations and preventing unauthorized changes to system settings or files. This explicit user confirmation mechanism enhances security by reducing the likelihood of unintended administrative actions and discouraging malicious activities that may attempt to exploit elevated privileges.

Beyond the Consent Prompt, UAC incorporates various levels of control to balance security and user experience. The UAC slider, introduced in Windows 7, allows users to customize the prompt behavior based on their preferences. The slider includes different levels ranging from "Always notify" to "Never notify," enabling users to define the frequency and granularity of UAC prompts. While "Always notify" ensures maximum security by prompting for consent before any administrative action, "Never notify" minimizes interruptions but exposes the system to potential security risks. The slider provides a flexible approach, allowing users to tailor UAC behavior according to their comfort level and security requirements.

User Account Control is not limited to traditional desktop environments; it extends its principles to modern computing scenarios, including remote access and virtual environments. In Remote Desktop scenarios, UAC prompts are transmitted to the connecting client, ensuring that administrative actions initiated remotely undergo the same scrutiny as local tasks. This consistency in UAC behavior across different access methods contributes to a unified security model, reinforcing the importance of explicit user consent in all administrative interactions regardless of the access point.

In virtualized environments, UAC mechanisms adapt to the unique challenges posed by virtual machines and hypervisors. UAC recognizes the distinction between local and remote sessions, tailoring the prompt behavior to maintain a consistent and secure user experience. Virtualized environments often involve complex interactions between host and guest operating systems, and UAC ensures that administrative actions within virtual machines adhere to the same principles of least privilege and explicit user authorization.

Another crucial aspect of UAC is its integration with application compatibility. Recognizing that many legacy applications were designed without considering the principles of least privilege, UAC includes virtualization mechanisms to address compatibility challenges. Virtualization allows legacy applications running with standard user privileges to function seamlessly by redirecting write operations to user-specific locations rather than system-wide directories. This ensures that older applications can run on modern operating systems without requiring modifications while still benefiting from the security enhancements introduced by UAC.

UAC extends its reach to script execution, acknowledging the prevalence of scripting languages in system administration and automation tasks. While scripts can be powerful tools, they can also pose security risks if executed with elevated privileges without proper scrutiny. UAC mitigates this risk by introducing script virtualization. When a script requires administrative privileges, UAC prompts the user for consent or administrator credentials, preventing potentially malicious scripts from executing unauthorized actions. This capability aligns with the broader goal of UAC to provide a layered defense against various vectors of unauthorized access and system manipulation.

Modern operating systems have evolved UAC in response to user feedback, security considerations, and advancements in technology. In Windows 10, for instance, UAC includes additional features such as the Secure Desktop environment for consent prompts. The Secure Desktop provides an isolated and visually distinct space for UAC prompts, minimizing the risk of spoofing or unauthorized interception by malware. This enhancement strengthens the integrity of UAC prompts, ensuring that users can trust the authenticity of the requests for administrative authorization.

Despite the security benefits, UAC prompts can be perceived as disruptive to the user experience. Recognizing this, modern operating systems implement technologies to reduce the frequency of prompts while maintaining security. For example, UAC introduces the concept of auto-elevation for certain trusted applications. Auto-elevation allows specific applications to request and receive elevated privileges without triggering a UAC prompt. However, this feature is carefully controlled to prevent misuse, and only applications with proper signatures and meeting specific criteria are eligible for auto-elevation.

In enterprise environments, UAC plays a crucial role in enforcing security policies and protecting against unauthorized system modifications. Group Policy settings allow administrators to configure UAC behavior across a network, defining the level of prompting, default privileges, and other UAC-related settings. This centralized control ensures a consistent and secure user experience across an organization, aligning with the principle of centralized management in enterprise IT environments.

The integration of UAC into the broader security ecosystem of modern operating systems contributes to a defense-in-depth strategy. UAC complements other security features such as firewall controls, antivirus protection, and encryption mechanisms, creating a layered approach to safeguarding systems and user data. By preventing unauthorized access to critical system components and enforcing the principle of least privilege, UAC enhances the overall security posture of modern operating systems.

In conclusion, User Account Control mechanisms in modern operating systems represent a crucial layer of defense against unauthorized access and potential security threats. From the separation of standard and administrative accounts to the Consent Prompt, UAC embodies the principles of least privilege and explicit user authorization. As operating systems continue to evolve, UAC adapts to new challenges, incorporates user feedback, and integrates with emerging technologies to provide a secure and user-friendly computing experience. The ongoing refinement of UAC reflects the commitment to balancing security and usability in the complex and dynamic landscape of modern computing.

Chapter 4: Operating System Architectures: Unveiling the Framework

Define the concept of operating system architectures.

Operating system architectures represent the fundamental structural frameworks that govern the design, functionality, and interaction of operating systems with hardware, software, and user applications. These architectures serve as the underlying blueprints dictating how the operating system manages resources, facilitates communication between components, and provides a cohesive environment for diverse applications. One prominent paradigm in operating system architecture is the monolithic architecture, where the entire operating system functions as a single, indivisible unit. In monolithic architectures, all components, including the kernel, device drivers, file systems, and system services, reside in a unified address space. This approach simplifies system management but can result in challenges related to complexity, maintainability, and extensibility as the system grows.

Contrasting the monolithic architecture is the microkernel architecture, which advocates for minimalism by delegating only essential functions, typically the kernel's core, into privileged mode. Additional system services and components operate in user mode, outside the privileged kernel space. This separation aims to enhance system reliability, security, and maintainability, as faults or errors in non-essential components do not directly impact the kernel's integrity. Microkernel architectures facilitate a modular design, allowing for easier updates and additions without necessitating modifications to the kernel. However, the overhead of inter-process communication between user-mode components and the microkernel may introduce performance considerations.

The client-server architecture extends the principles of modularity by distributing operating system functionality between clients and servers. In this model, client machines request services from dedicated server machines that fulfill these requests. This decentralized approach enhances scalability, as multiple clients can concurrently access shared resources provided by servers. Common implementations of the client-server model in operating systems include file servers, print servers, and network servers. While this architecture promotes resource sharing and efficient utilization, it introduces dependencies on network communication and server availability, making the system susceptible to issues related to latency and reliability.

A variation of the client-server architecture is the peer-to-peer architecture, where individual machines, or peers, share resources and services without a dedicated central server. This model promotes decentralization, fostering collaboration and resource sharing among peers. Operating systems with peer-to-peer architectures often facilitate file sharing, distributed processing, and collaborative applications. While this approach can enhance resilience and reduce dependencies on a central server, it may introduce challenges related to coordination, security, and consistency across peer systems.

Distributed operating system architectures extend the principles of client-server and peer-to-peer models to large-scale, networked environments. In distributed architectures, multiple machines collaborate to provide a unified and transparent computing environment. This involves the distribution of processes, data, and resources across interconnected nodes. Distributed operating systems often incorporate features such as transparency, fault tolerance, and scalability. Transparency aims to provide a seamless user experience regardless of the physical location of resources or processes. Fault tolerance mechanisms enhance system reliability in the face of failures, while scalability allows the system to accommodate an increasing number of nodes and users.

As the demand for virtualization and cloud computing has surged, virtual machine-based architectures have gained prominence. Hypervisors, or virtual machine monitors, facilitate the creation and management of virtual machines (VMs) that run independent operating systems. This architecture allows multiple operating systems to coexist on a single physical machine, enabling efficient resource utilization, isolation, and flexibility. Hypervisors can adopt either a Type 1 (bare-metal) or Type 2 (hosted) configuration. Type 1 hypervisors run directly on the hardware, while Type 2 hypervisors operate atop an existing operating system. Virtualization architectures are foundational to cloud computing platforms, where they empower the creation and deployment of virtualized instances across distributed infrastructure.

In the realm of real-time operating systems (RTOS), architectures are tailored to meet stringent timing constraints and predictability requirements. Real-time operating system architectures prioritize deterministic response times and reliability, crucial for applications where timing accuracy is paramount. The kernel of an RTOS is designed to manage tasks with precise timing characteristics, ensuring that critical tasks receive timely attention. In addition to the traditional monolithic and microkernel architectures, RTOS may employ specialized architectures such as the client-server model for real-time systems, where dedicated servers handle time-sensitive tasks, and clients submit requests for immediate execution.

The emergence of mobile computing has led to the development of mobile operating system architectures, catering to the unique demands of smartphones, tablets, and other portable devices. Mobile operating systems, such as Android and iOS, often feature a layered architecture where the kernel interacts with hardware, and higher-level layers handle user interfaces, applications, and services. The use of sandboxing mechanisms enhances security by isolating applications from each other and restricting their access to system resources.

Mobile operating systems also incorporate power management features to optimize energy consumption, reflecting the importance of resource efficiency in battery-powered devices.

In the context of embedded systems, operating system architectures are designed for resource-constrained environments, where memory and processing power are limited. Real-time embedded operating systems prioritize determinism and responsiveness, ensuring that tasks are executed within predefined time constraints. These architectures often adopt a modular and configurable design, allowing developers to tailor the operating system to the specific requirements of the embedded system. Lightweight kernels, such as those based on the microkernel model, are common in embedded systems to minimize overhead and maximize efficiency.

The concept of hybrid operating system architectures has gained traction, combining elements of different models to leverage their respective advantages. Hybrid architectures aim to strike a balance between simplicity, modularity, and performance. For example, a hybrid kernel may integrate features of both monolithic and microkernel designs, allowing for flexibility and extensibility while maintaining a streamlined core for efficiency. Hybrid architectures exemplify the adaptability of operating systems to diverse computing scenarios, where a one-size-fits-all approach may not be optimal.

The evolution of operating system architectures reflects the ever-changing landscape of computing paradigms, user expectations, and technological advancements. The diverse models discussed here demonstrate the versatility of operating systems in addressing the specific needs of different computing environments, from traditional desktops to cloud-based infrastructures, real-time systems, and embedded devices. As computing continues to evolve, operating system architectures will likely continue adapting, embracing new paradigms, and incorporating innovative features to meet the demands of emerging technologies.

Explore the monolithic kernel architecture and its characteristics.

The monolithic kernel architecture stands as one of the foundational designs in operating system development, characterized by its holistic approach where the entire operating system, including the kernel and various system services, resides within a single address space. In this architectural model, the kernel assumes a central and indispensable role, managing system resources, providing core functionalities, and mediating interactions between hardware and software components. At the heart of the monolithic kernel is the kernel space, a privileged region of memory that contains essential operating system components like process management, memory management, file systems, and device drivers. This architectural choice emphasizes simplicity, efficiency, and direct communication between kernel modules, as they share a common memory space, streamlining interactions and minimizing the overhead associated with interprocess communication.

One of the defining characteristics of the monolithic kernel is its unified view of the operating system as a monolithic entity. This unity facilitates seamless access to system resources and services without the need for elaborate communication mechanisms between disparate components. Processes, system calls, and device drivers coexist within the same address space, allowing for direct invocation of kernel functions and efficient communication between user-level applications and kernel-level services. While this integration enhances performance and simplifies design, it also introduces challenges related to modularity, as changes or updates to one component may impact the stability of the entire system.

The simplicity and cohesiveness of the monolithic kernel architecture result in a straightforward development process, where the kernel and associated services can be developed, compiled, and linked together as a single unit. This ease of development is advantageous for small to medium-sized operating systems where the entire codebase can be managed as a cohesive unit. However, as the size and complexity of the operating system increase, the monolithic architecture may face challenges related to maintainability and extensibility. Modifications or additions to the system may require recompilation and reloading of the entire kernel, disrupting system operation and potentially introducing errors.

Monolithic kernels are often associated with improved performance due to the absence of communication overhead between kernel modules. Direct access to shared memory allows for rapid data exchange and function invocation, contributing to efficient system operation. Additionally, the absence of inter-process communication overhead benefits real-time and resource-constrained environments, making monolithic kernels suitable for applications with stringent performance requirements, such as embedded systems, where low latency and predictable behavior are crucial.

Device drivers play a critical role in interfacing with hardware components, and in monolithic kernels, these drivers operate within the same address space as the kernel. This integration allows for direct communication between device drivers and kernel modules, simplifying the handling of hardware-related tasks. However, it also means that a malfunctioning or poorly designed device driver can potentially destabilize the entire system. Despite this vulnerability, the monolithic architecture provides a straightforward and efficient mechanism for device driver development and interaction with the core operating system.

The monolithic kernel architecture has evolved over time to address some of its inherent limitations, leading to variations such as the modular monolithic kernel. In a modular monolithic design, the kernel is organized into discrete modules or components that can be dynamically loaded or unloaded at runtime. This approach aims to enhance the modularity and flexibility of the monolithic architecture, allowing for the addition or removal of specific functionalities without the need to recompile and reload the entire kernel. While this mitigates some of the challenges related to maintainability, it introduces a degree of complexity associated with module management and inter-module dependencies.

The deployment of monolithic kernels has been widespread, notably in early Unix systems, Linux distributions, and certain versions of Microsoft Windows, such as Windows 95 and Windows 98. The success of these operating systems demonstrates the viability and efficiency of the monolithic architecture in various computing environments. However, as computing landscapes continue to evolve, alternative architectures, such as microkernels and hybrid designs, have gained prominence, each offering a different balance of trade-offs between simplicity, performance, and modularity.

In conclusion, the monolithic kernel architecture embodies a straightforward and efficient approach to operating system design, where the entire operating system, including the kernel and associated services, resides within a unified address space. Its characteristics of direct communication between kernel modules, simplicity of development, and strong performance make it suitable for a range of applications, especially in resource-constrained and real-time environments. However, the monolithic architecture faces challenges related to modularity, maintainability, and extensibility as system complexity increases. While alternative architectures have emerged to address some of these challenges, the monolithic kernel remains a foundational and influential design in the history of operating systems.

Discuss the microkernel architecture and its approach to system design.

The microkernel architecture represents a departure from the monolithic design philosophy by advocating a modular and minimalist approach to system design. In a microkernel system, the kernel's functionality is reduced to the bare essentials, typically encompassing process scheduling, inter-process communication (IPC), and basic memory management. Unlike the monolithic kernel where most operating system services reside in the kernel space, a microkernel delegates non-essential services, such as file systems, device drivers, and networking protocols, to user space as separate, isolated processes. This separation aims to enhance system modularity, scalability, and fault tolerance by isolating critical kernel functions from less critical components, mitigating the impact of errors or failures in non-essential services on the overall system stability.

One of the central tenets of the microkernel architecture is the emphasis on simplicity and minimalism within the kernel. By restricting the kernel's responsibilities to essential tasks, developers can create a lean and easily understandable core. This simplicity facilitates faster development, easier debugging, and a reduced likelihood of kernel-related errors. In addition, the small size of the microkernel often results in a smaller attack surface, making the system less vulnerable to security exploits and providing a foundation for secure and reliable computing environments.

The core concept driving microkernel design is the reliance on inter-process communication (IPC) to facilitate communication and collaboration between user-level processes handling various operating system services. IPC mechanisms, such as message passing or remote procedure calls (RPC), allow user-level processes to interact with each other while remaining isolated from the kernel's critical components. This isolation is a key characteristic of microkernel architectures, as it prevents errors or faults in user-level services from affecting the integrity of the kernel itself. However, the reliance on IPC introduces potential overhead, which must be carefully managed to maintain system performance.

The modularity introduced by the microkernel architecture enables a high degree of flexibility and extensibility in the system. New services can be added, modified, or removed without requiring changes to the core kernel. This adaptability facilitates the development of specialized operating systems tailored to specific requirements or environments. For example, an embedded system might include only the necessary components for its intended functionality, while a general-purpose system could incorporate a broader set of services. This flexibility contrasts with monolithic kernels, where modifications or additions often necessitate recompilation and reloading of the entire kernel.

Microkernel architectures often incorporate a notion of protection domains or address spaces, ensuring that each user-level service operates in a separate space with limited access to other services and the kernel. This isolation enhances system security by preventing unauthorized access or interference between services. While the microkernel itself is responsible for managing these protection domains, the actual enforcement of access control policies is delegated to user-level components. This separation of concerns contributes to the overall security and robustness of microkernel-based systems.

In microkernel systems, device drivers and file systems, traditionally part of the monolithic kernel, operate as user-level processes. This separation enhances system stability, as errors or failures in device drivers do not compromise the integrity of the kernel. Moreover, if a device driver encounters an issue, it can be restarted or replaced without affecting the overall system operation. This design choice aligns with the microkernel philosophy of isolating non-critical components from the core kernel, contributing to fault tolerance and ease of maintenance.

The microkernel architecture excels in scenarios where reliability and fault tolerance are critical requirements. By isolating critical kernel functions from user-level services, the impact of failures or errors in non-essential components is limited, reducing the likelihood of system crashes or disruptions. This characteristic is particularly advantageous in safety-critical systems, such as those used in aerospace, automotive, or medical applications, where system stability is paramount and failure could have severe consequences. The modular nature of microkernels also facilitates the development of redundant or hot-swappable components, further enhancing fault tolerance.

While the microkernel architecture offers numerous advantages, it introduces challenges related to performance, as communication between user-level processes incurs additional overhead compared to direct function calls in monolithic kernels. Efficient management of IPC is crucial for maintaining acceptable system performance, and optimizations, such as shared memory mechanisms or carefully designed communication protocols, are often implemented to mitigate this overhead. Additionally, the choice of IPC mechanisms can impact the overall responsiveness and efficiency of a microkernel-based system.

Historically, notable microkernel-based operating systems include Mach, developed at Carnegie Mellon University, and the L4 microkernel family. Mach, in particular, influenced the development of the macOS kernel and served as the foundation for various research projects. The L4 microkernel family has been widely used in research and commercial applications due to its focus on minimalism, security, and high performance.

The hybrid microkernel architecture represents a compromise between the microkernel and monolithic designs. In a hybrid approach, certain non-essential components, traditionally considered part of user space, may reside within the kernel space for performance reasons. This hybrid model seeks to retain the benefits of microkernel modularity while mitigating some of the IPC-related performance concerns. While it may not strictly adhere to the purist principles of the microkernel architecture, the hybrid model reflects a pragmatic approach that acknowledges the trade-offs between performance and modularity.

In conclusion, the microkernel architecture presents a paradigm shift in operating system design by advocating simplicity, modularity, and isolation of critical kernel functions. Its emphasis on IPC, protection domains, and user-level services contributes to enhanced reliability, security, and fault tolerance. While challenges related to performance must be carefully addressed, the microkernel architecture has demonstrated its efficacy in specialized environments where system stability and extensibility are paramount. The ongoing development of microkernel-based operating systems and the exploration of hybrid models highlight the enduring influence and adaptability of the microkernel design philosophy in the ever-evolving landscape of operating system architectures.

Explore the hybrid kernel architecture, combining elements of monolithic and microkernel designs.

The hybrid kernel architecture represents a nuanced and pragmatic approach to operating system design, seamlessly blending elements from both monolithic and microkernel models. In this hybrid model, certain components traditionally residing in the user space of monolithic kernels may find themselves incorporated into the kernel space for reasons of performance, while critical functions and services maintain a modular, microkernel-like structure. This synthesis aims to strike a balance between the efficiency of monolithic kernels, which benefit from direct communication between components within the kernel space, and the modularity and fault isolation principles championed by microkernels. By combining the best of both worlds, hybrid kernels seek to leverage the advantages of each architectural approach, offering improved performance, flexibility, and maintainability.

One of the key features of the hybrid kernel architecture is the strategic placement of specific components within the kernel space. Certain device drivers, file systems, and networking protocols, traditionally residing outside the monolithic kernel in user space, are brought inside the kernel space for optimized performance. This decision acknowledges that direct communication between these components and the kernel can result in lower overhead, contributing to more efficient operation. The kernel space in a hybrid design accommodates these components without necessarily incorporating the entire monolithic stack, thus retaining a degree of modularity and separation of concerns.

The hybrid model addresses some of the performance concerns associated with microkernels, which often rely on inter-process communication (IPC) mechanisms for interaction between user-level components. In microkernels, IPC can introduce overhead that impacts system responsiveness. By strategically placing certain components within the kernel space, the hybrid kernel minimizes the need for IPC in these critical areas, potentially enhancing overall system performance. This approach acknowledges that not all components have the same impact on system performance and stability, allowing for a more nuanced integration of monolithic and microkernel principles.

A crucial aspect of the hybrid kernel architecture is the modular design of critical kernel functions. These functions are organized into separate modules, each responsible for a specific aspect of system management, such as process scheduling, memory management, and basic IPC. This modular structure aligns with the microkernel philosophy of isolating essential kernel functions from non-essential services. The modularity enhances system maintainability and extensibility, enabling developers to update or replace specific modules without affecting the entire kernel. This adaptability is particularly beneficial for evolving system requirements and for incorporating new features or optimizations.

Hybrid kernels often introduce a layer called the "kernel server" or "executive," which serves as an intermediary between the kernel and user-level components. This layer encapsulates critical kernel services and provides an interface for user-level services to interact with the kernel. The kernel server essentially acts as a bridge, facilitating communication between user-level components and the modular kernel functions. This design choice contributes to the separation of concerns, as the kernel server handles critical operations, while user-level services remain isolated and focused on their specific functionalities.

An exemplary implementation of the hybrid kernel architecture is the Windows NT kernel, used in various Microsoft operating systems, including Windows NT, Windows 2000, Windows XP, and their successors. The Windows NT kernel encapsulates certain components, such as the memory manager and I/O manager, within the kernel space for optimized performance. However, the kernel maintains a modular structure with components like the Executive, which includes the Process Manager, Object Manager, and Security Reference Monitor, organized as separate modules. This modular design aligns with microkernel principles, offering benefits in terms of system stability and maintainability.

The hybrid kernel model finds practical application in diverse computing environments, including desktop operating systems, servers, and embedded systems. Its adaptability allows it to cater to a range of system requirements, from general-purpose computing to specialized applications. In desktop operating systems like Windows, the hybrid approach facilitates efficient communication between user-level applications and critical kernel functions, resulting in a responsive and versatile computing environment. In server environments, the modular design supports scalability and ease of management, enabling administrators to customize the system to meet specific demands. In embedded systems, the hybrid architecture accommodates the diverse requirements of resource-constrained devices while providing the necessary performance for real-time applications.

The integration of certain user-space components into the kernel space in the hybrid model poses challenges related to system security. The inclusion of device drivers and file systems within the kernel space increases the potential attack surface, as vulnerabilities in these components could directly impact the kernel's integrity. Security measures, such as thorough code reviews, robust privilege separation, and isolation mechanisms, are crucial for mitigating these risks. Additionally, the modular design introduces complexities related to inter-module dependencies and version compatibility, requiring careful management to ensure a cohesive and reliable system.

The hybrid kernel architecture reflects the evolving nature of operating system design, where a pragmatic approach embraces elements from different paradigms to address diverse requirements. This adaptability is evident in the ongoing development and refinement of hybrid kernels to meet the challenges posed by modern computing environments. As technology continues to advance, the hybrid model provides a flexible and resilient foundation for operating systems, demonstrating the viability of integrating monolithic and microkernel principles to achieve a well-balanced and efficient system design.

Discuss the exokernel architecture and its focus on flexibility and resource management.

The exokernel architecture represents a groundbreaking approach to operating system design that prioritizes flexibility, resource management, and fine-grained control over hardware resources. In contrast to traditional monolithic and microkernel designs, exokernels push the boundaries of abstraction by exposing low-level hardware resources directly to applications. At its core, the exokernel concept revolves around the idea of minimalism, granting applications unprecedented control and responsibility over hardware resources while the exokernel itself focuses on resource multiplexing, protection, and isolation.

One of the fundamental principles of the exokernel architecture is the concept of application-level resource management. Exokernels intentionally refrain from providing high-level abstractions, such as file systems or network stacks, that are traditionally offered by monolithic and microkernel designs. Instead, exokernels aim to expose raw hardware resources, such as CPU cycles, memory, and I/O operations, directly to applications. This raw exposure allows applications to make decisions about resource usage based on their specific requirements, tailoring resource management to the unique demands of each application. By avoiding unnecessary abstractions, exokernels eliminate potential overhead and empower applications to optimize resource utilization according to their specific needs.

In the exokernel model, protection and isolation mechanisms are crucial for maintaining system integrity while providing applications with direct access to hardware resources. Exokernels employ fine-grained protection mechanisms to ensure that applications cannot interfere with each other or compromise the stability of the system. Protection domains are established to isolate applications, and the exokernel enforces access controls at the granularity of individual hardware resources. This fine granularity allows for more precise control over resource access and sharing, facilitating efficient use of system resources while minimizing the risk of unintended interference.

An essential feature of exokernels is the careful multiplexing of hardware resources among competing applications. Unlike traditional kernels that may impose global policies on resource allocation, exokernels enable applications to negotiate and manage resources dynamically. This negotiation is achieved through explicit resource allocation interfaces exposed by the exokernel. Applications can request resources based on their specific needs, and the exokernel, acting as a resource arbiter, makes allocation decisions according to policies specified by the application or system administrator. This approach introduces a level of flexibility that is unparalleled in more conventional kernel architectures.

To facilitate resource multiplexing, exokernels implement a mechanism known as a library operating system or a library OS. The library OS runs in user space and provides a set of abstractions and services tailored to the needs of a specific application or set of applications. Unlike the monolithic or microkernel designs, where the entire operating system provides a uniform set of abstractions to all applications, the library OS in exokernels is specialized for the particular requirements of each application. This specialization allows applications to have a lightweight and customized operating system environment, minimizing unnecessary overhead and maximizing performance.

The exokernel architecture challenges the traditional notion of a fixed and rigid operating system interface. Instead of imposing a predefined set of abstractions, exokernels encourage the creation of application-specific operating system environments. This adaptability is particularly advantageous in scenarios where the standard abstractions provided by traditional operating systems may be suboptimal or inefficient. For example, specialized applications in domains like high-performance computing, networking, or real-time systems can benefit from tailoring their operating system environment to meet the precise demands of their workloads.

Exokernels excel in scenarios where fine-tuned control over hardware resources is paramount. High-performance computing applications, such as scientific simulations or data analytics, often have unique resource requirements that may not be adequately addressed by generic abstractions provided by traditional operating systems. Exokernels empower such applications to directly manage and optimize their interaction with the underlying hardware, potentially leading to significant performance improvements. Similarly, networking applications, where low-level control over network interfaces is crucial, can benefit from the flexibility offered by exokernel architectures.

The principle of resource specialization in exokernels extends to the realm of security. Exokernels allow applications to define their own security policies, specifying how resources should be accessed and shared. This flexibility enables the implementation of application-specific security models, tailoring the security posture of each application to its unique characteristics. While this decentralization of security policies introduces challenges related to system-wide security enforcement, it provides a level of granularity and customization that can be advantageous in certain contexts, especially where traditional security models may not align with specific application requirements.

Despite the innovative concepts and potential advantages offered by exokernels, their adoption has been limited in practice. The complexity and effort required to develop and manage application-specific operating system environments pose challenges for application developers and system administrators. Additionally, the absence of standardized abstractions can make exokernel-based systems less accessible to a broad range of developers accustomed to the convenience of higher-level abstractions provided by traditional operating systems. As a result, exokernels have primarily remained a subject of academic research and experimentation rather than widespread adoption in mainstream computing environments.

In conclusion, the exokernel architecture represents a paradigm shift in operating system design, prioritizing flexibility, resource management, and fine-grained control over hardware resources. By exposing raw hardware resources directly to applications and embracing a library operating system model, exokernels empower applications to tailor their operating system environment according to their specific requirements. While the potential benefits of exokernels in terms of performance, resource optimization, and security are evident, their adoption has been limited by practical challenges and the comfort of developers with established abstractions provided by traditional operating systems. Nevertheless, the exokernel concept continues to influence discussions on operating system design, sparking innovative ideas and approaches that explore the boundaries of what is possible in the quest for efficient and adaptable computing environments.

Discuss operating system architectures that support virtualization.

Operating system architectures that support virtualization play a pivotal role in modern computing environments, enabling the creation and management of virtual machines (VMs) that operate as independent instances of an operating system on a shared physical host. This paradigm shift has transformed the landscape of computing by offering increased flexibility, resource utilization, and isolation. One of the prominent architectures facilitating virtualization is the hypervisor-based model, also known as the Type 1 or bare-metal hypervisor architecture. In this design, the hypervisor, a thin layer of software, runs directly on the hardware without the need for a host operating system. It assumes the responsibility of managing multiple VMs, allocating resources, and facilitating communication between VMs and the underlying hardware. Hypervisors like VMware ESXi, Microsoft Hyper-V, and Xen exemplify this architecture, showcasing its effectiveness in enterprise environments, data centers, and cloud infrastructures.

A key advantage of the hypervisor-based architecture is its ability to achieve high levels of isolation between VMs. Each VM operates independently, oblivious to the existence of other VMs on the same host. This isolation ensures that the failure or compromise of one VM does not impact others, enhancing system security and reliability. Furthermore, hypervisors provide a platform for running various operating systems concurrently, allowing for the consolidation of diverse workloads on a single physical machine. The hypervisor-based architecture is particularly well-suited for scenarios where strict isolation, resource partitioning, and efficient utilization of hardware resources are essential.

In contrast, the hosted or Type 2 hypervisor architecture involves running the hypervisor as an application on top of a host operating system. This model is prevalent in desktop and development environments, where the hypervisor, such as Oracle VirtualBox or VMware Workstation, coexists with the host operating system. While the hosted architecture may introduce an additional layer between VMs and the hardware, it offers greater flexibility for developers and enthusiasts to experiment with virtualization on their personal machines. Hosted hypervisors allow users to create and manage VMs without necessitating changes to the host operating system, making them an accessible choice for testing, development, and educational purposes.

The paravirtualization architecture represents another approach to virtualization, focusing on optimizing the performance of VMs by modifying the guest operating systems to be aware of their virtualized environment. Unlike traditional virtualization, which emulates complete hardware, paravirtualization leverages cooperation between the hypervisor and guest operating systems to achieve improved efficiency. This collaboration enables the guest operating systems to make direct calls to the hypervisor for certain operations, reducing the overhead associated with full hardware emulation. Xen, a hypervisor known for its paravirtualization support, demonstrates the benefits of this architecture in terms of enhanced performance and scalability, making it suitable for high-performance computing and cloud environments.

The container-based architecture, popularized by technologies like Docker and Kubernetes, represents a lightweight and efficient form of virtualization. Unlike traditional VMs, containers share the host operating system's kernel, leading to reduced overhead and faster instantiation. Containers encapsulate applications and their dependencies, providing a portable and consistent environment across different systems. This architecture is particularly well-suited for microservices-based applications, where each component can run in its own container, enabling easy deployment, scaling, and management. While containers lack the level of isolation provided by VMs, they offer a compelling solution for certain use cases, emphasizing agility, rapid deployment, and resource efficiency.

Unikernels represent a specialized form of virtualization architecture designed for lightweight and specialized workloads. In the unikernel model, the operating system is tailored to a specific application, incorporating only the necessary components and libraries required for that application to run. This minimalist approach aims to reduce the attack surface, enhance performance, and streamline resource utilization. Unikernels are typically designed to be deployed as single-purpose VMs, optimized for specific tasks such as network functions, microservices, or edge computing. While unikernels may not provide the general-purpose flexibility of traditional operating systems, their focus on efficiency and security makes them well-suited for certain specialized use cases.

The hardware-assisted virtualization architecture leverages specific features provided by modern processors to enhance the performance and efficiency of virtualization. Processors with virtualization extensions, such as Intel VT-x and AMD-V, introduce hardware-level support for virtualization, allowing the hypervisor to offload certain virtualization-related tasks to the CPU. This offloading improves the overall efficiency of virtualization, reducing the reliance on software-based techniques and enhancing the performance of VMs. Hardware-assisted virtualization is a key enabler for the success of hypervisor-based architectures, providing a foundation for efficient resource management and virtual machine execution.

In the context of cloud computing, virtualization architectures are integral to the delivery of Infrastructure as a Service (IaaS). Cloud service providers utilize hypervisor-based virtualization to offer virtual machines as scalable and on-demand resources. Users can provision VMs with varying configurations, deploy applications, and scale resources based on demand. This virtualized infrastructure provides flexibility, cost-effectiveness, and agility, enabling organizations to adapt to changing workloads and business requirements. Cloud platforms such as Amazon EC2, Microsoft Azure, and Google Cloud Platform rely on virtualization architectures to deliver the foundational services that underpin modern cloud computing.

As virtualization technologies continue to evolve, emerging architectures such as nested virtualization and hardware-based containerization further expand the possibilities and applications of virtualization. Nested virtualization allows running hypervisors within VMs, enabling scenarios like running a hypervisor on a VM hosted by another hypervisor. This capability is valuable for testing and development environments, as well as for certain cloud-based scenarios. Hardware-based containerization, exemplified by technologies like Intel Clear Containers and gVisor, aims to provide a balance between the lightweight nature of containers and the isolation of virtual machines. These innovations contribute to the ongoing evolution of virtualization architectures, addressing diverse use cases and requirements across different computing environments.

In conclusion, virtualization architectures have become fundamental to modern computing, transforming the way resources are provisioned, utilized, and managed. Whether through hypervisor-based models, containerization, paravirtualization, or specialized approaches like unikernels, virtualization technologies offer unprecedented flexibility, efficiency, and scalability. These architectures have become instrumental in the evolution of cloud computing, enabling the creation of dynamic, on-demand infrastructure. As virtualization continues to shape the future of computing, ongoing innovations and advancements will likely further refine and expand the capabilities of virtualization architectures to meet the evolving needs of diverse applications and industries.

Discuss the client-server model as an architectural choice in operating systems.

The client-server model stands as a foundational architectural choice in operating systems, shaping the way applications and services interact within distributed computing environments. At its core, this model divides the responsibilities between two distinct entities: the client, which requests services or resources, and the server, which provides those services or resources. This architectural paradigm has become pervasive in the design of networked systems, offering a scalable and modular approach to organizing computing tasks and facilitating communication across a network.

One of the defining characteristics of the client-server model is its clear separation of concerns between the client and server components. Clients are responsible for initiating requests, typically in the form of service or resource demands, while servers are dedicated to fulfilling these requests. This separation allows for the specialization of functionalities, with clients focusing on user interfaces and interaction, and servers handling the underlying processing, data storage, or computation. Such a division of labor enhances modularity, simplifies development, and enables the scaling of systems by deploying multiple servers to handle increasing workloads.

The client-server model manifests in various configurations, each serving distinct purposes within the broader landscape of computing. A common instantiation is the two-tier architecture, where a client communicates directly with a server to request and receive services. This architecture is often employed in traditional client-server applications, such as database management systems, where a client application interacts with a database server to retrieve or update data. While effective for certain scenarios, the two-tier model may face limitations in scalability and flexibility, especially as applications grow in complexity.

In response to the challenges posed by the two-tier model, the three-tier architecture emerged, introducing an additional layer known as the application server. In this model, clients interact with an application server, which, in turn, communicates with a database server. This separation allows for a more modular and flexible design, as the application server can handle business logic independently of the client and database server. The three-tier architecture enhances scalability, as changes to the application logic can be implemented on the application server without impacting the client or database components.

The client-server model is not limited to a fixed number of tiers, and the n-tier architecture represents a generalized extension of the concept. In an n-tier architecture, the system is divided into multiple layers or tiers, each serving a specific function. This flexibility accommodates a wide range of applications, from simple two-tier setups to more complex configurations with multiple layers, such as presentation, application, business logic, and data storage tiers. The n-tier approach provides a scalable and adaptable framework, allowing for the efficient distribution of tasks across various components based on their roles and responsibilities.

The advent of distributed computing and the proliferation of networked systems have further propelled the client-server model into various forms, such as the client-server computing model and the more contemporary client-server computing model. The client-server computing model leverages the power of distributed processing by distributing tasks among multiple servers, each specializing in a particular aspect of computation or service provision. This model facilitates parallel processing, allowing for improved performance and resource utilization. On the other hand, the client-server computing model extends the traditional client-server architecture by incorporating elements of peer-to-peer computing. In this model, nodes in the network can act as both clients and servers, sharing resources and responsibilities dynamically.

Client-server architectures have proven instrumental in the evolution of the internet, forming the backbone of numerous applications and services. The World Wide Web itself operates on a client-server model, where web browsers act as clients, requesting and rendering web pages served by web servers. This architecture enables the scalable and efficient delivery of content to a vast number of users worldwide. Moreover, web applications often employ the client-server model, with the client running in the user's browser and communicating with a server to fetch data or perform computations. The ubiquity of web-based services underscores the enduring relevance and adaptability of the client-server model in contemporary computing.

An essential aspect of client-server architectures is the communication protocol that facilitates interaction between clients and servers. The most prevalent protocol in this context is the Hypertext Transfer Protocol (HTTP), which governs communication on the World Wide Web. HTTP defines the rules for clients to request resources and servers to respond, enabling the seamless exchange of information. Additionally, other protocols, such as the Simple Object Access Protocol (SOAP) and Representational State Transfer (REST), have emerged to support specific types of interactions between clients and servers, particularly in the context of web services.

The client-server model is not confined to traditional desktop or web-based applications; it extends to various domains, including file servers, print servers, and database servers. File servers, for instance, store and manage files that clients can access or modify. Print servers manage printing tasks on a network, allowing multiple clients to send print jobs to a centralized printer. Database servers store and manage data, responding to queries and updates from client applications. These specialized implementations showcase the adaptability of the client-server model across diverse computing scenarios.

The benefits of the client-server model extend beyond its modular and scalable design. The separation of concerns between clients and servers facilitates a clear and organized development process. Developers can focus on designing user interfaces and client-side interactions independently of the underlying server logic. This modularization enhances code maintainability and supports collaboration among development teams working on different components of a system. Moreover, the client-server model facilitates the reuse of server-side components, allowing multiple clients to interact with the same server services, fostering efficiency and consistency in application development.

While the client-server model offers numerous advantages, it is not without challenges. The reliance on central servers introduces potential points of failure and bottlenecks, impacting system reliability and scalability. High server loads can lead to degraded performance or service interruptions. Additionally, the need for network communication between clients and servers introduces latency, influencing the responsiveness of applications, particularly in scenarios where real-time interactions are critical. To address these challenges, various strategies, such as load balancing, caching, and content delivery networks (CDNs), are employed to optimize server performance and enhance the overall user experience.

Security considerations also play a crucial role in client-server architectures. Protecting the confidentiality and integrity of data exchanged between clients and servers is paramount. Encryption protocols, such as Transport Layer Security (TLS), are commonly employed to secure communications over networks. Access controls and authentication mechanisms ensure that only authorized clients can access specific services or resources on the server. Server-side security measures, such as firewalls and intrusion detection systems, further safeguard against unauthorized access or malicious activities.

The advent of cloud computing has introduced new dimensions to the client-server model, with the emergence of cloud-based services and the shift toward serverless computing. Cloud services leverage the client-server model to provide scalable, on-demand resources, enabling organizations to deploy applications without the need for extensive infrastructure management. Serverless computing takes the decentralization of server responsibilities a step further by abstracting away the management of servers entirely. In serverless architectures, clients execute functions in response to events, and cloud providers handle the underlying infrastructure automatically. This model simplifies deployment, scales dynamically, and charges users based on actual resource consumption.

In conclusion, the client-server model stands as a cornerstone in the architecture of operating systems, defining the structure of distributed computing environments. From traditional two-tier setups to modern n-tier and distributed computing models, the client-server paradigm continues to shape how applications and services interact over networks. Its modularity, scalability, and clear separation of concerns have contributed to the development of diverse and sophisticated systems, from web applications to cloud services. As technology evolves, the client-server model adapts to new challenges and opportunities, remaining a foundational framework for designing and implementing distributed computing solutions across various domains.

Discuss architectural considerations in distributed operating systems.

Architectural considerations in distributed operating systems are paramount as these systems orchestrate the collaboration and coordination of multiple interconnected nodes to achieve collective computing goals. The architectural decisions influence the system's performance, scalability, fault tolerance, and overall efficiency. A foundational aspect of distributed operating systems architecture is the choice between a monolithic and a microservices-based approach. In a monolithic architecture, all components are tightly integrated into a single, cohesive unit, simplifying development and deployment but potentially limiting scalability and modularity. In contrast, a microservices architecture decomposes the system into smaller, independently deployable services, enabling better scalability, fault isolation, and ease of maintenance. This architectural decision reflects a trade-off between simplicity and flexibility, with implications for system complexity and adaptability.

Another critical architectural consideration is communication mechanisms within the distributed system. Communication between nodes is essential for sharing information and coordinating actions. The choice between synchronous and asynchronous communication introduces trade-offs in terms of responsiveness and reliability. Synchronous communication, such as Remote Procedure Call (RPC), enables real-time interactions but may lead to increased latency and dependencies between nodes. Asynchronous communication, exemplified by message queues or publish-subscribe patterns, enhances decoupling and fault tolerance at the cost of potential delays. Selecting the appropriate communication paradigm depends on the system's requirements, latency tolerance, and the need for fault tolerance.

Consistency and availability, often characterized by the CAP theorem, represent pivotal considerations in distributed systems architecture. The CAP theorem posits that a distributed system can achieve at most two out of three guarantees: consistency, availability, and partition tolerance. Consistency ensures that all nodes in the system have a consistent view of the data, availability guarantees that every request receives a response without guaranteeing its content, and partition tolerance ensures the system's resilience to network partitions. Architectural choices must carefully balance these trade-offs based on the system's requirements. Systems adopting an eventual consistency model, like many NoSQL databases, prioritize availability and partition tolerance, accepting that consistency may be achieved over time.

Fault tolerance is a fundamental consideration in distributed operating systems architecture to ensure system robustness in the face of node failures or network issues. Replication, redundancy, and error detection mechanisms are integral components of fault-tolerant architectures. Replication involves duplicating data or services across multiple nodes to provide backup in case of failures. Redundancy ensures that critical components exist in multiple places, minimizing the impact of node outages. Error detection mechanisms, such as heartbeat protocols or timeouts, enable nodes to identify and respond to failures promptly. These fault tolerance strategies contribute to system reliability, resilience, and continuous operation in dynamic and unpredictable environments.

Load balancing is another architectural consideration to optimize resource utilization and improve system performance. In distributed systems, load balancing involves distributing incoming requests or tasks evenly across nodes to prevent resource bottlenecks and ensure efficient use of computational resources. Load balancing algorithms, such as round-robin, least connections, or weighted distribution, guide the allocation of tasks among nodes based on factors like node capacity, current load, or response time. Effective load balancing enhances scalability and responsiveness in distributed systems, enabling them to handle increased workloads and dynamic changes in resource demand.

Security considerations play a crucial role in designing distributed operating systems architectures. As data and communication traverse multiple nodes over interconnected networks, ensuring the confidentiality, integrity, and availability of information becomes imperative. Encryption mechanisms, secure communication protocols, and access controls are essential components of a secure distributed system. Authentication and authorization mechanisms validate the identity of nodes and regulate access to resources, safeguarding the system against unauthorized access or malicious activities. Additionally, distributed systems must be resilient to various security threats, such as denial-of-service attacks, data breaches, and man-in-the-middle attacks, necessitating a comprehensive and layered security architecture.

Scalability is a key architectural concern, especially in systems that need to accommodate growing workloads or dynamic user demands. Scalability can be achieved through horizontal scaling, involving the addition of more nodes to the system, or vertical scaling, where individual nodes are upgraded with increased resources. The choice between these scaling approaches depends on factors like the nature of the workload, system architecture, and resource constraints. Well-designed distributed systems should exhibit the ability to scale seamlessly, ensuring that performance remains optimal as the system evolves and faces varying levels of demand.

Consolidating and managing distributed system configurations is a non-trivial task, demanding thoughtful architectural decisions. Configuration management involves defining and maintaining the settings, parameters, and behavior of distributed system components. Centralized configuration management systems, such as Apache ZooKeeper or Consul, provide a unified platform for configuring and synchronizing settings across distributed nodes. Alternatively, decentralized approaches, like configuration files distributed with each node, offer simplicity but may lack centralized control and consistency. Efficient configuration management is crucial for maintaining system coherence, reducing potential misconfigurations, and enabling easier updates or changes across the distributed environment.

Distributed file systems represent a critical architectural consideration, providing a means for storing and retrieving data across multiple nodes. Distributed file systems aim to deliver reliable and scalable storage solutions while addressing challenges like data consistency and fault tolerance. Traditional file systems, such as Network File System (NFS) or Common Internet File System (CIFS), may be extended or adapted to operate in distributed environments. Alternatively, distributed file systems like Google File System (GFS) or Hadoop Distributed File System (HDFS) are specifically designed to meet the demands of large-scale distributed computing, emphasizing fault tolerance, scalability, and efficient data processing.

Containerization and orchestration technologies have emerged as influential architectural considerations in modern distributed systems. Containers encapsulate applications and their dependencies, offering consistency and portability across different environments. Orchestration frameworks, like Kubernetes or Docker Swarm, streamline the deployment, scaling, and management of containerized applications in distributed environments. Containerization enhances resource utilization, accelerates deployment, and fosters a microservices architecture, allowing components to scale independently. The architectural choice between containerization and traditional virtualization depends on factors like resource efficiency, operational overhead, and the need for isolation.

Deciding on the appropriate data storage model is a nuanced architectural consideration in distributed systems. The choice between relational databases, NoSQL databases, or NewSQL databases depends on the system's requirements, data structure, and query patterns. Relational databases offer structured and ACID-compliant data management, suitable for applications with well-defined schemas and complex queries. NoSQL databases, including key-value stores, document stores, column-family stores, and graph databases, provide flexibility and scalability for unstructured or rapidly evolving data. NewSQL databases seek to combine the benefits of traditional and NoSQL databases, offering scalability and consistency without compromising on ACID properties.

Event-driven architectures represent a contemporary architectural consideration in distributed systems, focusing on asynchronous communication and responsiveness to events. In event-driven systems, components emit or subscribe to events, triggering actions or processes in response. This approach enables loose coupling between components, allowing for better scalability, fault isolation, and adaptability to changing conditions. Event-driven architectures are well-suited for scenarios where real-time processing, responsiveness, and modularity are crucial, such as in financial systems, IoT applications, or distributed streaming platforms.

As the complexity and scale of distributed systems continue to evolve, architectural considerations must adapt to meet the challenges posed by dynamic environments, diverse workloads, and emerging technologies. Future architectures may explore advancements in edge computing, federated learning, and serverless computing to address evolving requirements in areas like IoT, AI, and data analytics. Embracing decentralized and autonomous architectures may become more prevalent to enhance resilience and reduce single points of failure. Architectural decisions in distributed operating systems will remain pivotal in shaping the landscape of computing, guiding the development of systems that deliver efficiency, reliability, and innovation across a distributed and interconnected world.

Explore architectures designed for fault tolerance and reliability.

Architectures designed for fault tolerance and reliability represent a critical facet of systems engineering, especially in the context of distributed and mission-critical applications. Fault tolerance aims to ensure system stability and continued operation in the face of component failures, unexpected events, or adverse conditions. A fundamental principle guiding the design of fault-tolerant architectures is redundancy, which involves replicating critical components to mitigate the impact of failures. Various architectural strategies and mechanisms contribute to achieving fault tolerance and reliability, encompassing hardware, software, and communication aspects.

At the hardware level, redundant components and systems are a foundational element of fault-tolerant architectures. Redundant hardware involves duplicating critical components such as processors, memory modules, or storage devices. In the event of a hardware failure, the redundant components seamlessly take over, preserving system functionality. This redundancy can be implemented at different levels, ranging from individual components within a server to entire servers within a data center. Hardware redundancy strategies, such as RAID (Redundant Array of Independent Disks) for storage or dual power supplies for servers, exemplify how redundant hardware components enhance system reliability by providing failover mechanisms.

Beyond redundant hardware, architectural decisions in fault-tolerant systems often involve the integration of fault-tolerant middleware or software layers. These layers operate at the system or application level, orchestrating redundant components, managing failover processes, and ensuring continuity of service. Clustering is a prevalent architectural strategy that involves grouping multiple servers or nodes into a cluster, allowing them to work in concert to achieve fault tolerance. In a clustered environment, if one node fails, others within the cluster can assume the workload, ensuring uninterrupted service. Clustering can be implemented at different layers, from database clusters that distribute data across multiple servers to application clusters that distribute processing tasks.

One notable approach to fault tolerance is the use of replication. Replication involves creating duplicate copies of data, processes, or services across multiple nodes. This redundancy ensures that if one node or instance fails, another can seamlessly take over, minimizing downtime. Database replication is a common application of this principle, where data is replicated across multiple database servers. In the event of a server failure, the system can switch to a replica, ensuring data availability. Replication can also be applied to critical processes or services, ensuring that if one instance becomes unavailable, another can continue to provide the required functionality.

The concept of active-passive redundancy is foundational in fault-tolerant architectures. In an active-passive setup, one component (the active component) handles the primary workload, while a redundant component (the passive component) remains on standby, ready to take over in the event of a failure. This approach is prevalent in scenarios where maintaining continuous operation is crucial but the backup component does not need to be fully utilized unless a failure occurs. Active-passive redundancy is often implemented in server configurations, where one server handles the traffic, and a standby server is ready to assume the load if the primary server fails.

Load balancing is an architectural consideration that contributes significantly to both fault tolerance and reliability. Load balancing distributes incoming requests or tasks across multiple nodes to prevent resource bottlenecks and ensure efficient resource utilization. By evenly distributing the workload, load balancers enhance system responsiveness and availability. Moreover, load balancers can detect the health of individual nodes and direct traffic away from faulty or overloaded nodes, preventing them from becoming single points of failure. Load balancing strategies, such as round-robin, least connections, or weighted distribution, play a crucial role in optimizing resource usage and maintaining system reliability.

Closely related to load balancing is the concept of horizontal scaling. Horizontal scaling involves adding more nodes or instances to a system to distribute the workload. This architectural strategy enhances fault tolerance by providing additional capacity and redundancy. Cloud computing platforms exemplify horizontal scaling, where additional virtual machines or containers can be provisioned dynamically to accommodate increased demand or compensate for failed instances. The ability to scale horizontally enables systems to adapt to changing workloads and maintain performance, making it a key consideration in fault-tolerant architectures.

Checkpointing is an architectural technique designed to ensure the recoverability of systems in the event of failures. Checkpointing involves periodically saving the state of a system, including its processes, data, and configuration, to persistent storage. In the event of a failure, the system can be restored to a previous checkpoint, minimizing data loss and downtime. Checkpointing is particularly useful in long-running or computation-intensive applications, where the cost of recomputing lost work is substantial. While checkpointing introduces some overhead, it is a valuable mechanism for maintaining system reliability and recovering from faults efficiently.

The concept of graceful degradation is an architectural consideration that acknowledges the inevitability of failures and seeks to ensure that a system can continue to operate with reduced functionality in the presence of faults. In a gracefully degrading system, components or services are designed to gracefully transition to a degraded state when faults occur. This approach allows the system to prioritize essential functionalities, ensuring that critical services remain available even in compromised conditions. Architectures that embrace graceful degradation often incorporate strategies such as feature toggles, circuit breakers, or fallback mechanisms to manage the impact of faults on system performance.

Distributed consensus algorithms play a vital role in ensuring fault tolerance and reliability, particularly in distributed systems where nodes must agree on a common state or decision. Consensus algorithms, such as the Paxos algorithm or the Raft consensus algorithm, facilitate agreement among nodes even in the presence of failures or network partitions. These algorithms ensure that the distributed system reaches a consistent state, preventing divergent behavior among nodes. Consensus is crucial for maintaining data consistency, coordinating distributed transactions, and ensuring the overall reliability of distributed systems.

Architectural considerations for fault tolerance also extend to communication patterns within distributed systems. The use of message queues, publish-subscribe patterns, or event-driven architectures contributes to fault tolerance by decoupling components and enabling asynchronous communication. Asynchronous communication patterns allow components to continue operating independently, even if some components experience delays or failures. This decoupling enhances fault isolation, resilience, and adaptability in distributed systems, making them more robust in the face of unpredictable conditions.

The implementation of health monitoring and self-healing mechanisms is an architectural consideration that enhances fault tolerance by proactively identifying and addressing issues. Health monitoring involves continuously assessing the status of system components, including hardware, software, and services. If a component is detected to be unhealthy or exhibiting anomalous behavior, self-healing mechanisms can automatically initiate corrective actions, such as restarting a service or redirecting traffic away from a faulty node. These proactive measures contribute to maintaining system reliability and minimizing the impact of failures on end-users.

In the context of distributed databases, the choice of consistency models is a critical architectural consideration that balances fault tolerance, reliability, and performance. Consistency models, such as eventual consistency, causal consistency, or strong consistency, define how distributed databases handle the visibility of data changes across multiple nodes. Architectures that prioritize eventual consistency allow for continued operation in the presence of network partitions but may exhibit temporary inconsistencies. On the other hand, architectures emphasizing strong consistency prioritize immediate consistency at the cost of potential increased latency or reduced availability during network partitions.

In conclusion, architectures designed for fault tolerance and reliability are essential for building resilient and robust systems, particularly in the context of distributed and mission-critical applications. Redundancy, replication, load balancing, and horizontal scaling are foundational principles that contribute to fault tolerance by mitigating the impact of failures and ensuring continuous operation. Checkpointing, graceful degradation, and distributed consensus algorithms address the challenges posed by faults and failures in distributed systems. The use of asynchronous communication patterns, health monitoring, and self-healing mechanisms further enhances fault tolerance by providing proactive measures and adaptability. The careful consideration of these architectural principles and mechanisms is crucial for designing systems that can withstand failures, deliver consistent performance, and provide a reliable foundation for diverse applications and services.

Discuss the challenges of scalability in operating system design.

Scalability in operating system design represents a complex challenge that arises from the need to accommodate growing workloads, varying user demands, and evolving hardware architectures. Operating systems must be able to efficiently scale to handle increased computational tasks, data processing, and user interactions without compromising performance or system responsiveness. Several interrelated challenges contribute to the complexity of achieving scalability in operating systems, spanning hardware limitations, resource management, communication overhead, and design trade-offs.

One fundamental challenge in achieving scalability is related to the underlying hardware architecture. As technology advances, the number of processing cores on a single chip increases, leading to a shift towards multi-core and many-core processors. While this provides the potential for parallelism and improved performance, operating systems must be designed to effectively utilize these resources. Scalability challenges arise from the need to develop parallel algorithms, manage concurrent execution, and synchronize processes across multiple cores. Ensuring that the operating system kernel can efficiently distribute and balance workloads among cores while avoiding contention for shared resources becomes a critical aspect of achieving scalability.

Resource management is a central aspect of scalability challenges in operating systems. Efficiently allocating and managing resources such as CPU time, memory, and storage becomes increasingly complex as the scale of the system grows. In scalable operating systems, resource management mechanisms must adapt dynamically to varying workloads and prioritize tasks based on their importance and impact on overall system performance. The challenge lies in devising scheduling algorithms, memory management strategies, and I/O optimizations that scale gracefully with increasing demands, avoiding bottlenecks or resource contention that could hinder system scalability.

Communication overhead introduces significant challenges to scalability, particularly in distributed and networked environments. As operating systems scale across multiple nodes or systems, communication between these entities becomes a crucial factor. Inter-process communication (IPC) mechanisms, network protocols, and data exchange patterns must be designed to minimize latency and overhead. Scalable operating systems need to handle communication efficiently, avoiding unnecessary serialization, deserialization, and synchronization costs. The challenge lies in developing communication models that balance the need for coordination with the imperative to minimize delays, especially in scenarios where real-time or near-real-time responsiveness is crucial.

The design trade-offs inherent in operating systems present challenges to achieving scalability. Operating systems must balance various conflicting requirements, such as responsiveness versus throughput, generality versus specialization, and consistency versus availability. Scalable designs often involve making choices that impact the system's behavior under different conditions. For instance, a trade-off may be required between the simplicity of centralized control and the complexity of distributed coordination in large-scale systems. Striking the right balance in design trade-offs is challenging, as the operating system must cater to a diverse range of applications and workloads while maintaining scalability across different scenarios.

Another significant challenge in achieving scalability is related to load balancing. Load balancing becomes increasingly critical as the system scales to handle a larger number of tasks or processes. Ensuring that workloads are distributed evenly across available resources, whether within a single machine or across a cluster of machines, is a non-trivial task. Operating systems must implement effective load balancing algorithms that consider factors such as resource utilization, task dependencies, and communication patterns. The challenge lies in dynamically adapting load balancing strategies to changing conditions, preventing resource imbalances that can lead to degraded performance or inefficient resource utilization.

Scalability challenges are amplified in the context of real-time operating systems (RTOS) where predictable and deterministic behavior is crucial. Real-time applications, such as those in embedded systems or critical control systems, demand precise and timely execution. Achieving scalability in real-time operating systems requires addressing challenges related to minimizing interrupt latencies, ensuring bounded response times, and efficiently managing priority-based scheduling. The challenge lies in accommodating the scalability needs of real-time applications while maintaining the predictability and determinism required for mission-critical tasks.

Security considerations pose additional challenges to scalability in operating system design. As systems scale, they become more susceptible to security threats and vulnerabilities. Scalable operating systems must implement robust security mechanisms to protect against various attacks, unauthorized access, and data breaches. The challenge lies in integrating security measures without introducing significant overhead that could impede scalability. Balancing the need for security with the imperative to maintain performance and responsiveness becomes a delicate task, especially in environments where the operating system interacts with diverse and potentially untrusted applications.

The emergence of virtualization and containerization technologies introduces unique challenges to scalability in operating system design. Virtualized environments, where multiple virtual machines or containers share a physical host, demand efficient resource isolation, allocation, and coordination. Scalable operating systems must adapt to the dynamic nature of virtualized workloads, ensuring that resources are allocated judiciously and that the overhead introduced by virtualization does not become a scalability bottleneck. Additionally, achieving scalability in container orchestration systems, such as Kubernetes, involves addressing challenges related to container scheduling, network orchestration, and service discovery at scale.

The complexity of achieving scalability in operating system design is further heightened by the rise of edge computing and IoT (Internet of Things). Edge computing environments involve distributed systems that span a multitude of edge devices with diverse capabilities. Operating systems must be designed to scale across these heterogeneous devices while addressing challenges such as intermittent connectivity, resource constraints, and varying processing capabilities. Scalability in the context of IoT introduces challenges related to data management, edge-to-cloud communication, and the need for localized decision-making. Operating systems must adapt to these constraints and efficiently scale to support the growing landscape of edge computing.

In conclusion, achieving scalability in operating system design is a multifaceted challenge that involves addressing issues related to hardware architectures, resource management, communication overhead, design trade-offs, load balancing, real-time requirements, security, virtualization, and the complexities of emerging computing paradigms such as edge computing and IoT. As technology continues to evolve, operating systems must adapt to support increasingly diverse workloads and user demands. Overcoming the scalability challenges requires innovative solutions, thoughtful design principles, and a holistic understanding of the intricate interplay between hardware, software, and the dynamic nature of computing environments. Operating system designers face the ongoing task of navigating these challenges to ensure that scalable, reliable, and responsive systems underpin the diverse range of applications in our interconnected and ever-expanding digital landscape.

Chapter 5: User Interfaces and Interaction in Operating Systems

Trace the historical development of user interfaces in operating systems.

The historical development of user interfaces in operating systems has undergone a remarkable journey, evolving from rudimentary command-line interfaces to sophisticated graphical user interfaces (GUIs) and, more recently, incorporating touch, voice, and gesture-based interactions. The earliest operating systems, including those for mainframes and early personal computers, predominantly relied on command-line interfaces (CLIs). Users interacted with these systems by entering text commands, often requiring a memorization of specific commands and syntax. This era, epitomized by systems like MS-DOS and Unix, laid the foundation for user interactions with computers.

The transformative moment in the history of user interfaces came with the advent of graphical user interfaces in the 1980s. Xerox PARC's Alto computer, developed in the 1970s, introduced the concept of a graphical desktop with icons, windows, and a pointing device called a mouse. However, it was Apple's Macintosh, released in 1984, that brought these innovations to the mainstream. The Macintosh featured a graphical desktop environment with icons representing files and folders, and users interacted with the system using a mouse. Concurrently, Microsoft Windows, starting with Windows 1.0 in 1985, adopted a similar GUI approach, allowing users to navigate through the system visually. These GUIs marked a paradigm shift by making computers more accessible to a broader audience and reducing the learning curve associated with command-line interfaces.

The 1990s witnessed the refinement and widespread adoption of graphical interfaces. Operating systems like Microsoft Windows 95 introduced the Start menu, taskbar, and a more intuitive user experience. Additionally, the rise of the World Wide Web prompted the development of web browsers, such as Netscape Navigator, which brought graphical interfaces to internet navigation. With the increasing popularity of the internet, graphical interfaces became synonymous with the computing experience, and users became accustomed to interacting with applications and content visually.

As technology progressed into the 21st century, a new era of user interfaces emerged with the proliferation of touch-based interactions. Apple's iPhone, introduced in 2007, revolutionized the concept of user interfaces by popularizing capacitive touchscreens and introducing gestures like pinch-to-zoom and swipe. This innovation influenced not only mobile operating systems like iOS and Android but also desktop environments. Microsoft, with Windows 8 in 2012, embraced a touch-centric interface featuring a Start screen with live tiles, reflecting the growing importance of touch interactions in computing.

The advent of smartphones and tablets spurred further exploration of natural user interfaces (NUIs), which encompass touch, voice, and gesture-based interactions. Voice-controlled virtual assistants, like Apple's Siri and Amazon's Alexa, became integral to operating systems, offering hands-free control and personalized assistance. Additionally, gesture-based interfaces, popularized by devices like Microsoft's Kinect, allowed users to interact with computers through body movements. These advancements expanded the accessibility of computing interfaces and catered to diverse user preferences and abilities.

In recent years, user interfaces have witnessed a convergence of technologies, including augmented reality (AR) and virtual reality (VR). Operating systems are incorporating AR interfaces that overlay digital information onto the physical world, enhancing user experiences in fields like gaming, education, and navigation. VR interfaces immerse users in virtual environments, offering new possibilities for simulations, training, and collaborative workspaces. Platforms like Microsoft's Windows Mixed Reality showcase the integration of AR and VR within traditional operating systems.

Accessibility has become a focal point in the evolution of user interfaces. Modern operating systems prioritize inclusive design, incorporating features like screen readers, magnification, and customizable color schemes to cater to users with diverse needs. The goal is to ensure that technology is accessible to individuals with disabilities, empowering them to engage with digital interfaces effectively.

The trajectory of user interface development in operating systems reflects not only technological advancements but also changing societal expectations and user behaviors. The shift from command-line interfaces to graphical interfaces to touch, voice, and gesture-based interactions exemplifies a continuous effort to enhance usability and make computing more intuitive. Additionally, the influence of mobile devices, the internet, and emerging technologies like AR and VR underscores the dynamic nature of user interfaces, as they adapt to meet the demands of evolving computing paradigms. The ongoing development of user interfaces remains an integral aspect of shaping the user experience, fostering innovation, and ensuring that operating systems remain accessible and relevant in the ever-changing landscape of technology.

Explore key design principles of modern GUIs.

Modern Graphical User Interfaces (GUIs) embody a multifaceted amalgamation of design principles that converge to provide users with intuitive, efficient, and aesthetically pleasing interactions. One of the pivotal tenets shaping contemporary GUIs is user-centered design, a philosophy that places end-users at the forefront of the design process. This principle underscores the significance of understanding user needs, behaviors, and preferences, thereby ensuring that the interface aligns seamlessly with the cognitive patterns of its intended audience. Furthermore, the concept of consistency is indispensable in modern GUI design. Consistency manifests in the uniformity of visual elements, interaction patterns, and terminology across the interface, fostering a sense of predictability and reducing cognitive load for users.

Accessibility emerges as another pivotal facet in the design paradigm, emphasizing the imperative to create interfaces that cater to users with diverse abilities and disabilities. Integrating principles of universal design ensures that GUIs are not only inclusive but also accommodate a spectrum of user requirements, fostering an environment where digital interactions are accessible to all. Responsive design is an extension of this ethos, acknowledging the ubiquity of devices with disparate screen sizes and resolutions. It mandates the creation of interfaces that dynamically adapt to various screen dimensions, ensuring a consistent and optimal user experience across a plethora of devices.

The aesthetic dimension is encapsulated by the principle of visual hierarchy, wherein designers employ various design elements such as color, size, and contrast to guide users through the interface, emphasizing key elements and facilitating intuitive navigation. The judicious use of whitespace, an integral aspect of modern GUIs, not only contributes to a visually pleasing design but also enhances legibility and comprehension by preventing visual clutter. Additionally, the incorporation of affordances and signifiers is paramount in steering users towards understanding the interactive elements within the interface, reinforcing the learnability aspect of GUI design.

Navigation within modern GUIs is underpinned by the principle of simplicity, advocating for streamlined pathways that enable users to accomplish tasks with minimal cognitive effort. This extends to the concept of information architecture, dictating the organization and structure of content to facilitate easy retrieval and comprehension. The principle of feedback complements this by providing users with real-time responses to their actions, fostering a sense of control and transparency in their interactions. Microinteractions, subtle animations or visual cues, further contribute to this feedback loop, enriching the overall user experience and imbuing interfaces with a sense of dynamism.

The dynamic nature of contemporary digital interactions necessitates a focus on adaptability, encapsulated by the principle of flexibility. GUIs should be designed to accommodate evolving user needs and technological advancements, ensuring a future-proof interface that remains relevant over time. Moreover, the emergence of touch interfaces and gesture-based interactions has introduced the principle of direct manipulation, wherein users interact directly with on-screen elements, fostering a tangible and engaging experience.

Security and privacy considerations form an integral part of modern GUI design, reflecting the growing concern for safeguarding user data and digital identities. Designers must incorporate features such as clear privacy settings, secure authentication processes, and unambiguous security indicators to instill confidence in users and mitigate potential risks. Furthermore, the rise of multi-platform experiences necessitates the integration of cross-platform consistency, ensuring a cohesive user experience across diverse operating systems and devices.

Collaboration and social integration underscore the communal aspect of contemporary digital experiences, prompting designers to incorporate features that facilitate seamless collaboration and social interactions within the interface. This includes the integration of social media sharing options, collaborative editing tools, and real-time communication features, aligning the GUI with the interconnected nature of modern digital ecosystems.

In conclusion, the design principles shaping modern GUIs coalesce into a nuanced framework that prioritizes user-centricity, accessibility, responsiveness, aesthetics, simplicity, adaptability, security, and collaboration. This holistic approach not only caters to the diverse needs of users but also anticipates the evolving landscape of technology, ensuring that GUIs remain effective, engaging, and relevant in an ever-changing digital milieu.

Discuss different user interaction models in operating systems.

User interaction models in operating systems encompass a diverse array of paradigms that dictate how users communicate with and manipulate the underlying computing environment. One prevalent model is the Command-Line Interface (CLI), which traces its roots to early computing systems. In a CLI, users interact with the system by typing text-based commands into a terminal. This model provides a direct and powerful means of controlling the computer, offering efficiency and flexibility to users with a proficiency in command syntax. However, it often demands a steep learning curve for novices and lacks the graphical richness that characterizes modern user interfaces.

Contrasting with the CLI, the Graphical User Interface (GUI) has become the predominant interaction model in contemporary operating systems. GUIs leverage graphical elements such as icons, windows, buttons, and menus to facilitate user interactions. This paradigm emphasizes visual representations and intuitive controls, fostering a more user-friendly experience. GUIs abstract complex command structures, making computing accessible to a broader audience. Iconic exemplars include the Windows, macOS, and Linux desktop environments, which enable users to manipulate files, run applications, and configure system settings through a visual and interactive interface.

Touch-based interaction models have gained prominence in the era of smartphones and tablets, representing a departure from traditional input devices like keyboards and mice. Operating systems like iOS and Android prioritize touch gestures, enabling users to interact with the system by tapping, swiping, and pinching on the screen. This tactile approach enhances the intuitiveness of the user experience and is particularly well-suited for mobile devices. Gestures mimic real-world actions, making the interaction more natural, though the transition from physical keyboards to virtual touch keyboards poses challenges for certain users.

Voice-based interaction models leverage natural language processing and voice recognition technologies to enable users to control and command the operating system verbally. Systems like Apple's Siri, Amazon's Alexa, and Google Assistant exemplify this paradigm, allowing users to perform tasks, retrieve information, and navigate interfaces using spoken commands. Voice interaction models aim to provide a hands-free and convenient alternative, catering to users with mobility issues or those seeking a more seamless integration of technology into daily life.

Gesture-based interaction models extend beyond touchscreens to encompass motion-sensing technologies like accelerometers and cameras. Microsoft's Kinect for Xbox and certain features in Apple's MacBook trackpad exemplify this model, enabling users to control applications and interfaces through hand movements, gestures, or even facial expressions. This approach enhances user engagement and is prevalent in gaming, virtual reality, and augmented reality environments.

Pen-based interaction models revolve around the use of stylus or digital pens for input. Operating systems like Microsoft Windows and certain tablet interfaces support this model, enabling users to draw, write, or navigate with precision. Pen-based interactions often find applications in creative fields, note-taking, and digital artistry, offering users a tactile and fine-grained control that complements touch-based input.

Natural User Interfaces (NUIs) constitute an emerging paradigm that integrates multiple interaction modalities seamlessly, fostering a more immersive and intuitive user experience. NUIs aim to mimic real-world interactions, incorporating elements like touch, voice, gesture, and even gaze tracking. Technologies like Microsoft's Surface Studio, which combines touch and pen input, exemplify the potential of NUIs in creating a cohesive and natural user interface.

Augmented Reality (AR) and Virtual Reality (VR) introduce interaction models that immerse users in computer-generated environments. Operating systems designed for AR and VR, such as Microsoft's Windows Mixed Reality, prioritize spatial awareness, hand tracking, and gesture recognition. Users navigate and interact with digital content as if it were part of the physical world, creating novel opportunities for gaming, simulations, and collaborative experiences.

In conclusion, user interaction models in operating systems have evolved significantly over time, driven by advancements in technology and the quest for more intuitive and immersive computing experiences. From the text-centric interfaces of early computing to the graphical richness of contemporary GUIs, and the emergent paradigms of touch, voice, gesture, pen, and natural user interfaces, each model brings its own strengths and challenges. The future promises further innovation as augmented and virtual reality reshape the landscape, offering new dimensions of user interaction and transforming how individuals engage with computing environments.

Discuss how operating systems incorporate accessibility features.

Operating systems, cognizant of the imperative to foster inclusivity and accommodate users with diverse abilities, have integrated a multitude of accessibility features that aim to enhance the usability of computing environments. One pivotal aspect of accessibility is the provision of alternative input methods. Operating systems often include features such as on-screen keyboards, voice recognition, and gesture controls to cater to users with motor impairments or those who may face challenges using traditional input devices. These alternatives empower individuals with varying physical abilities to interact with the system in a manner that suits their specific needs and capabilities.

Visual impairments pose a significant challenge to effective computing, and in response, operating systems have implemented a plethora of features to enhance accessibility for individuals with limited or no vision. Screen readers, an essential component of modern accessibility suites, convert on-screen text and graphical elements into synthesized speech or braille output, enabling users with visual impairments to navigate the interface, read documents, and engage with digital content. Additionally, high contrast and large font options, as well as customizable color schemes, contribute to a more legible and visually adaptable interface for users with low vision.

Operating systems also prioritize auditory accessibility, recognizing the significance of sound cues and feedback for individuals with visual impairments. Screen readers often include audio descriptions of on-screen events and interfaces. Additionally, operating systems provide options for users to customize system sounds, enabling them to assign distinct sounds to specific events or notifications. This auditory feedback aids users in understanding system status, alerts, and prompts, creating a more comprehensive and inclusive computing experience.

Cognitive accessibility features are designed to support users with cognitive impairments or conditions such as dyslexia, attention deficit disorders, or learning disabilities. Text-to-speech functionalities assist users in comprehending written content, while speech-to-text capabilities enable them to express themselves through spoken words rather than written text. Furthermore, operating systems may include features like simplified interfaces, consistent navigation structures, and the ability to adjust animation speeds, all aimed at reducing cognitive load and enhancing the overall usability for individuals with diverse cognitive needs.

Inclusivity extends to the realm of mobility, where operating systems strive to cater to users with limited dexterity or those who rely on assistive devices. Customizable keyboard layouts, dwell-clicking options, and gesture recognition technologies empower users to interact with the system using alternative input methods, accommodating a wide spectrum of motor abilities. Furthermore, voice commands and dictation functionalities provide users with hands-free alternatives, ensuring that mobility challenges do not impede effective interaction with the operating system.

Operating systems also prioritize the creation of inclusive interfaces for users with photosensitive conditions or epilepsy. To mitigate the risk of triggering seizures or discomfort, accessibility features may include options to adjust screen brightness, disable certain animations or flashing elements, and apply color filters to the display. These adjustments not only cater to individuals with specific sensitivities but also contribute to creating a more comfortable and inclusive computing environment for all users.

As part of their commitment to accessibility, operating systems often include features that facilitate content comprehension for users with language-related challenges. Multilingual support, integrated translation tools, and text simplification options aim to break down language barriers and make digital content more accessible to individuals with diverse linguistic backgrounds or those facing language-related difficulties.

In the context of hearing impairments, operating systems have integrated features to enhance accessibility for individuals who are deaf or hard of hearing. Real-time captioning and transcription services, often used in conjunction with video and audio content, provide a textual representation of spoken words. Additionally, visual alerts and notifications, such as flashing lights or on-screen indicators, serve as alternatives to auditory signals, ensuring that users with hearing impairments receive important information in a timely manner.

Accessibility in operating systems extends beyond individual features to encompass the concept of universal design, aiming to create interfaces that are inherently inclusive and adaptable. This approach emphasizes the importance of designing interfaces that can be used effectively by the widest possible range of users, without the need for specialized adaptations. Operating systems strive to incorporate universal design principles, ensuring that accessibility is woven into the fabric of the user experience and is not treated as an afterthought.

In conclusion, the integration of accessibility features within operating systems represents a concerted effort to make computing environments inclusive and empowering for users with diverse abilities. Through alternative input methods, visual enhancements, auditory cues, cognitive support, mobility accommodations, and a commitment to universal design, operating systems seek to break down barriers and create a digital landscape where everyone, regardless of their abilities or challenges, can engage with technology in a meaningful and equitable manner. This ongoing commitment to accessibility reflects a broader societal acknowledgment of the importance of ensuring that the benefits of technology are accessible to all.

Explore the integration of gesture and touch interfaces in modern operating systems.

The integration of gesture and touch interfaces in modern operating systems represents a paradigm shift in user interaction, transforming the way individuals engage with computing devices. Touch interfaces, pioneered by mobile devices such as smartphones and tablets, have become ubiquitous, reshaping the user experience across a spectrum of devices and operating systems. In these interfaces, users interact directly with the screen, manipulating digital content through gestures like tapping, swiping, and pinching. This tactile and intuitive approach has been a hallmark of operating systems such as Apple's iOS and Google's Android, revolutionizing how users navigate menus, interact with applications, and engage with digital content.

Gesture interfaces, which involve recognizing and interpreting specific movements or gestures made by users, have gained prominence as technology has advanced. Operating systems like Microsoft's Windows 10 incorporate gesture recognition technologies, allowing users to control various aspects of the interface through hand movements, swipes, or even facial expressions. This integration of gesture controls enhances the user experience by providing a more natural and immersive means of interaction. For example, users can swipe to scroll through documents, pinch to zoom in on images, or use hand gestures to control applications, bringing a sense of direct manipulation to the digital realm.

One of the primary drivers behind the integration of touch and gesture interfaces is the widespread adoption of smartphones and tablets. Operating systems for mobile devices have embraced touch interactions as a fundamental component of their design philosophy. Apple's iOS, with its emphasis on touch gestures like tapping and swiping, and Google's Android, which has similarly embraced touch-centric interactions, have set the standard for intuitive and fluid touch interfaces. The success of these mobile operating systems has influenced the design principles of other platforms, leading to touch-centric features being incorporated into desktop operating systems as well.

The evolution of touch interfaces has extended beyond mere touchpoints on flat screens to encompass innovations like pressure-sensitive screens and haptic feedback. Pressure-sensitive displays, as seen in devices like Apple's iPhone with 3D Touch, introduce an additional layer of interaction by recognizing varying levels of pressure applied to the screen. This capability opens new possibilities for context-sensitive actions, providing users with more nuanced control over their interactions. Haptic feedback, in the form of tactile vibrations or responses, further enhances the touch experience by providing sensory confirmation for actions like button presses or gestures, contributing to a more immersive and responsive user interface.

Gesture and touch interfaces have found a natural home in 2-in-1 devices that combine the form factors of laptops and tablets. Operating systems like Microsoft's Windows 10 have been designed with touch functionality in mind, allowing users to seamlessly transition between traditional keyboard and mouse inputs to touch-based interactions. The versatility of these devices, exemplified by the Microsoft Surface series, underscores the adaptability of modern operating systems to cater to a range of input methods, offering users a unified experience across different modes of interaction.

The integration of gesture controls in operating systems is not limited to consumer electronics; it has also permeated the realm of augmented reality (AR) and virtual reality (VR). Operating systems designed for AR and VR environments leverage gesture recognition to enable users to interact with digital content in a three-dimensional space. Technologies like Microsoft's HoloLens and Oculus Touch controllers exemplify this fusion of gesture controls with immersive computing, allowing users to reach out, grab, and manipulate virtual objects, further blurring the lines between the physical and digital worlds.

Accessibility considerations play a crucial role in the design and implementation of touch and gesture interfaces. Operating systems strive to ensure that these interfaces are inclusive, providing alternative means of interaction for users with mobility challenges or impairments. Features such as customizable gestures, voice commands, and dwell-clicking options empower users with diverse abilities to navigate and interact with the system effectively. The pursuit of accessibility aligns with the broader goal of making technology more inclusive and breaking down barriers to digital participation.

The integration of touch and gesture interfaces has also influenced the design of desktop operating systems. Microsoft's Windows 10, for instance, introduced touch-friendly features like the Start screen with live tiles and tablet mode, optimizing the interface for touch-based interactions. Similarly, Apple's macOS incorporates touchpad gestures, allowing users to navigate through applications, switch between desktops, and perform various functions with intuitive swipe gestures. These adaptations reflect an awareness of the changing landscape of computing devices and the diverse ways users expect to interact with them.

Collaboration and productivity have been enhanced by the integration of touch and gesture interfaces. Operating systems incorporate features that facilitate collaboration in real-time, leveraging touch and gesture controls for activities such as collaborative drawing, document editing, and brainstorming sessions. For instance, Microsoft's Surface Hub, running Windows 10, integrates touch and pen input to create a collaborative canvas for team interactions, exemplifying how touch interfaces can foster collaborative work environments.

The fusion of touch and gesture interfaces with artificial intelligence (AI) technologies has introduced new dimensions to user interactions. Voice-activated virtual assistants, such as Apple's Siri, Google Assistant, and Microsoft's Cortana, complement touch and gesture controls by allowing users to perform tasks, retrieve information, and execute commands through natural language. The synergy of these interaction modalities creates a more holistic and responsive computing experience, where users can seamlessly switch between touch, gestures, and voice inputs based on their preferences and the context of their activities.

In conclusion, the integration of gesture and touch interfaces in modern operating systems marks a transformative era in user interaction. From the touch-centric interfaces of mobile devices to the gesture-driven interactions in augmented and virtual reality environments, operating systems have adapted to accommodate a diverse array of input methods. The seamless integration of touch and gesture controls has not only redefined how users engage with computing devices but has also influenced the design philosophy of operating systems, fostering a more intuitive, immersive, and inclusive computing experience. As technology continues to evolve, the marriage of touch and gesture interfaces with emerging technologies is poised to shape the future landscape of human-computer interaction.

Discuss the role of voice recognition and natural language processing in user interfaces.

Voice recognition and natural language processing (NLP) have emerged as transformative technologies, revolutionizing user interfaces and reshaping the way individuals interact with digital systems. At the heart of this evolution is the ability of machines to comprehend and respond to human language, enabling a more natural and intuitive interaction between users and devices. Voice recognition, a subset of speech technology, involves converting spoken words into written text, allowing users to communicate with devices through verbal commands. This technology has found extensive application in user interfaces, ranging from virtual assistants to voice-controlled smart devices.

One of the primary domains where voice recognition and NLP have made significant inroads is in the realm of virtual assistants. Platforms like Apple's Siri, Amazon's Alexa, Google Assistant, and Microsoft's Cortana leverage voice recognition to understand and process user queries, enabling hands-free interactions. Users can ask questions, request information, set reminders, or perform various tasks simply by speaking to their devices. The integration of NLP enhances the capabilities of virtual assistants, enabling them to interpret the context, understand user intent, and generate contextually relevant responses, creating a more conversational and user-friendly experience.

Beyond virtual assistants, voice recognition and NLP have permeated various aspects of user interfaces, contributing to the development of voice-controlled applications and systems. Smartphones, smart speakers, and other connected devices have embraced voice as a prominent input modality, allowing users to dictate messages, initiate calls, or search the internet using natural language. This shift towards voice-driven interactions reflects a broader trend in making technology more accessible, especially in scenarios where hands-free operation is advantageous, such as while driving or multitasking.

In the context of accessibility, voice recognition plays a pivotal role in empowering individuals with disabilities. Users with mobility impairments or those who face challenges with traditional input methods can benefit from voice-controlled interfaces, enabling them to navigate devices, compose text, and execute commands using verbal interactions. The inclusivity offered by voice recognition aligns with the principles of universal design, striving to create interfaces that cater to users with diverse abilities.

Moreover, the integration of voice recognition in user interfaces extends to the field of smart homes and Internet of Things (IoT) devices. Voice-controlled smart speakers, thermostats, lighting systems, and other connected devices allow users to control their environment effortlessly. The marriage of voice recognition and NLP enables users to issue complex commands, set automation routines, and interact with a multitude of devices using natural language, fostering a seamless and intuitive smart home experience.

In the evolution of voice-controlled user interfaces, natural language processing serves as the linchpin that elevates the interaction from simple command-based transactions to more sophisticated and context-aware engagements. NLP enables systems to understand the nuances of human language, including context, sentiment, and intent. This contextual understanding enhances the accuracy of voice recognition, enabling systems to discern between homophones, understand colloquial language, and even recognize user emotions based on their tone and cadence.

Furthermore, NLP enables conversational interfaces, where users can engage in more dynamic and contextually rich interactions with systems. Chatbots and virtual agents leverage NLP to comprehend user queries, respond appropriately, and engage in dialogues that simulate natural conversation. The application of NLP in chatbots spans customer service, e-commerce, and various online platforms, providing users with instant and personalized interactions without the need for explicit command-driven inputs.

Voice recognition and NLP have also found a significant role in the healthcare sector, where natural language interfaces facilitate more efficient and accurate documentation. Healthcare professionals can use voice recognition to dictate patient notes, record observations, and navigate electronic health records, streamlining the documentation process and allowing practitioners to focus more on patient care. The integration of NLP ensures that the transcribed text retains context and coherence, contributing to more accurate and meaningful medical records.

As the capabilities of voice recognition and NLP continue to advance, their integration into education technology has become increasingly prominent. Language learning applications, virtual tutors, and educational platforms leverage these technologies to provide personalized and interactive learning experiences. Users can practice pronunciation, receive feedback, and engage in conversational exercises, fostering language acquisition in a more immersive and dynamic manner.

Despite the advancements, challenges persist in refining the accuracy and naturalness of voice recognition and NLP systems. Accents, dialects, and variations in speech patterns present hurdles in achieving universal comprehension. Ongoing research and development efforts focus on improving the adaptability of these systems to diverse linguistic contexts, ensuring that voice-controlled interfaces cater to a global user base with linguistic diversity.

In the era of ambient computing, where computing is seamlessly woven into the fabric of daily life, the role of voice recognition and NLP becomes even more pivotal. Wearable devices, smart appliances, and connected cars leverage these technologies to enable users to interact with their surroundings using natural language commands. The ubiquity of voice-controlled interfaces in various domains underscores their potential to redefine how we interact with the digital world, making technology more pervasive and integrated into our everyday activities.

Security and privacy considerations loom large in the landscape of voice-controlled interfaces. The collection and processing of voice data raise concerns about data security, potential misuse, and the need for robust privacy safeguards. Operating systems and technology providers must implement stringent security measures, transparent data handling practices, and user consent mechanisms to address these concerns and foster trust in voice-controlled systems.

In conclusion, the integration of voice recognition and natural language processing in user interfaces marks a paradigm shift in how individuals interact with technology. From virtual assistants and smart homes to healthcare and education applications, voice-controlled interfaces are becoming increasingly ubiquitous. The fusion of voice recognition and NLP not only enhances accessibility and inclusivity but also contributes to more intuitive, context-aware, and conversational user experiences. As these technologies continue to evolve, they hold the potential to redefine the nature of human-computer interaction, making technology more attuned to human needs and seamlessly integrated into the fabric of our daily lives.

Discuss features that allow users to customize their operating system experience.

Modern operating systems recognize the diverse preferences and needs of users, and as such, they incorporate a plethora of features that allow for extensive customization, empowering individuals to tailor their computing experience. One prominent avenue for customization lies in the personalization of the user interface. Operating systems like Microsoft Windows, Apple macOS, and various Linux distributions offer users the ability to customize desktop backgrounds, themes, and color schemes. This visual customization not only allows users to express their individuality but also contributes to creating a workspace that is aesthetically pleasing and conducive to productivity.

The customization of desktop icons is another facet that provides users with a means to personalize their operating system environment. Users can rearrange icons, change their sizes, or even choose custom icons for applications and shortcuts. This level of customization extends to the taskbar or dock, where users can decide which applications to pin for quick access and how these elements are displayed. Such flexibility in arranging the desktop and taskbar ensures that users can organize their workspace in a way that aligns with their workflow and preferences.

Operating systems also offer users the ability to personalize their file management experience. This includes options for customizing folder views, icon arrangements, and sorting preferences. Users can choose between detailed lists, icon grids, or thumbnail views, and customize the size and appearance of icons to suit their visual preferences. Additionally, the option to assign custom folder icons or background images to specific directories adds a layer of personalization to the file management interface.

Themes and visual styles represent another avenue for users to customize the overall look and feel of their operating system. Windows operating systems, for example, allow users to download and apply third-party visual styles that alter the appearance of window borders, buttons, and other graphical elements. This level of customization goes beyond the default themes provided by the operating system, enabling users to create a more personalized and unique visual identity for their computing environment.

The personalization of the desktop extends to widgets and gadgets, which provide at-a-glance information and quick access to specific functionalities. Widgets can range from weather updates and news feeds to system monitoring tools. Users can choose, rearrange, and customize these widgets based on their preferences, transforming the desktop into an information hub that aligns with their specific needs and interests.

The customization of system sounds is another feature that allows users to add a personal touch to their operating system experience. Users can assign custom sounds to various system events, such as startup, shutdown, or error notifications. This auditory personalization contributes to creating a more immersive and individualized computing environment, where users can tailor the sensory feedback to align with their preferences.

Fonts and text settings provide an additional layer of customization for users who seek a more personalized reading experience. Operating systems offer options to change default fonts, adjust text sizes, and even enable features like font smoothing or anti-aliasing. These customization options cater to users with specific preferences for text appearance, enhancing the readability and overall visual comfort of the operating system interface.

Accessibility features in modern operating systems also extend the customization paradigm to better serve users with diverse needs. Accessibility options may include features like screen readers, magnification tools, and color contrast adjustments. Users can customize these settings based on their specific requirements, ensuring that the operating system is accessible and accommodating to individuals with visual, auditory, or motor impairments.

Keyboard shortcuts and hotkeys constitute a powerful tool for users who wish to streamline their interactions with the operating system. Modern operating systems allow users to customize or create new keyboard shortcuts for various actions, applications, or system functions. This level of customization not only enhances efficiency but also caters to users who prefer specific key combinations for common tasks, aligning the system's operation with their workflow.

Taskbar and system tray customization options contribute to a more tailored user experience. Users can choose which icons appear on the taskbar, customize their order, and configure system tray settings to display or hide specific notifications. This level of control allows users to declutter their desktop, prioritize essential applications, and manage system notifications in a way that aligns with their preferences and workflow.

Operating systems with multiple desktops or workspaces offer users the ability to customize and organize these virtual environments. Users can assign specific desktop backgrounds to each workspace, arrange applications in a way that mirrors their workflow, and switch between desktops seamlessly. This feature enhances multitasking capabilities, allowing users to create distinct environments for different tasks and projects.

Browser integration and synchronization contribute to a cohesive and personalized computing experience. Operating systems often integrate with web browsers, allowing users to sync bookmarks, history, and settings across devices. This feature ensures a consistent browsing experience, enabling users to seamlessly transition between devices while maintaining a personalized and familiar online environment.

Customization also extends to security and privacy settings, allowing users to configure their operating system to align with their preferences for data protection. Users can customize privacy settings, control app permissions, and manage security features such as firewall settings and antivirus configurations. This level of control empowers users to strike a balance between security and convenience based on their individual preferences and priorities.

The customization of notification settings represents a key aspect of tailoring the user experience. Operating systems provide users with the ability to customize how notifications are displayed, including the choice of banner notifications, sounds, or pop-up alerts. Users can also prioritize or mute specific app notifications, ensuring that they receive relevant information without being overwhelmed by unnecessary distractions.

The integration of cloud services within operating systems enhances the customization and continuity of the user experience across devices. Features like cloud-based storage, synchronization of settings, and seamless access to documents and applications contribute to a unified computing environment. Users can personalize their experience on one device, and these customizations seamlessly propagate to other devices, creating a consistent and personalized computing experience.

Moreover, operating systems often provide users with the ability to customize energy and power settings. Users can configure power plans, set screen brightness preferences, and establish sleep or hibernation settings. This level of customization is particularly valuable for users on laptops or portable devices, allowing them to optimize power usage based on their preferences and usage patterns.

In conclusion, the extensive array of customization features embedded in modern operating systems empowers users to tailor their computing experience to an unprecedented degree. From visual elements and themes to file management preferences, accessibility settings, and security configurations, users have the flexibility to shape their operating system environment to suit their individual needs and preferences. This commitment to customization not only enhances user satisfaction but also reflects the recognition by operating system developers that computing is a deeply personal and individualized experience. As technology continues to advance, the customization paradigm will likely remain a central tenet in the ongoing evolution of operating systems.

Discuss how modern operating systems facilitate multitasking.

Modern operating systems have undergone significant evolution to adeptly accommodate the increasingly complex demands of multitasking – the concurrent execution of multiple tasks or processes. One of the foundational features contributing to effective multitasking is the concept of preemptive multitasking. Operating systems, such as Microsoft Windows, macOS, and various Linux distributions, employ preemptive multitasking to manage and switch between multiple processes seamlessly. This approach allows the operating system to allocate CPU time to different tasks based on priority, ensuring that each task receives a fair share of processing resources. Preemptive multitasking enhances system responsiveness, prevents any single task from monopolizing resources, and enables a smooth and efficient sharing of computational power among concurrently running applications.

Task management interfaces in modern operating systems play a pivotal role in facilitating multitasking. The taskbar in Windows, the dock in macOS, and similar elements in various Linux desktop environments provide users with a visual representation of running applications. Users can effortlessly switch between open applications, launch new ones, or close unnecessary processes through these interfaces. Additionally, task management features often include thumbnail previews, window stacking, and the ability to group related tasks, enhancing the overall organization and accessibility of concurrently running applications.

The integration of virtual desktops or workspaces is another key feature that modern operating systems leverage to enhance multitasking capabilities. Virtual desktops allow users to create distinct desktop environments, each with its set of open applications and tasks. This feature facilitates the organization of workspaces based on projects or activities, providing users with a dynamic and efficient way to switch between different contexts. Users can allocate specific applications to different virtual desktops, preventing clutter and streamlining the multitasking experience.

Window management features contribute significantly to multitasking efficiency. Modern operating systems incorporate features such as window snapping, resizing, and tiling to optimize screen real estate and streamline the arrangement of open applications. Users can quickly snap windows to specific regions of the screen or resize them proportionally, enabling a more granular control over the layout of concurrently running applications. These window management tools enhance multitasking by providing users with the flexibility to configure their workspace based on individual preferences and workflow requirements.

The task switcher, often accessible through keyboard shortcuts or dedicated hotspots, is a fundamental component of modern operating systems that streamlines the process of switching between open applications. Task switchers present users with a visual overview of running tasks, making it easy to navigate and select the desired application. Some operating systems, like Windows, also include features such as Alt-Tab previews, enabling users to preview the content of each open application before making a selection. This visual representation enhances the efficiency of multitasking, especially when managing numerous open windows.

Furthermore, the development of advanced graphical compositing engines in modern operating systems has introduced features like transparency, animations, and visual effects that enhance the user interface and contribute to a more engaging multitasking experience. These graphical enhancements not only add aesthetic appeal but also serve a functional purpose by providing users with visual cues and context when managing multiple tasks. Elements like taskbar previews, live window thumbnails, and fluid transitions between applications contribute to a more intuitive and visually coherent multitasking environment.

The advent of multiple-core processors has profoundly impacted multitasking capabilities in modern operating systems. Operating systems are designed to leverage the power of multi-core CPUs, allowing them to execute multiple tasks simultaneously. Task scheduling algorithms allocate threads and processes across available cores, maximizing computational efficiency and improving the overall responsiveness of the system. Multicore support enhances multitasking performance, enabling users to run resource-intensive applications concurrently without compromising system stability or responsiveness.

Memory management plays a critical role in multitasking, and modern operating systems employ sophisticated techniques to optimize the utilization of system memory. Virtual memory systems, which involve the use of both RAM and secondary storage (like a hard drive or SSD), enable operating systems to efficiently handle large amounts of data. This allows users to run numerous applications concurrently, even if the physical RAM is insufficient to accommodate all active processes. Swap space or paging mechanisms facilitate the seamless movement of data between RAM and storage, ensuring that multitasking remains fluid and responsive.

Modern operating systems also prioritize energy efficiency in multitasking scenarios, especially on portable devices like laptops and tablets. Power management features dynamically adjust CPU frequencies, screen brightness, and other hardware parameters based on the workload and user activity. This adaptive approach optimizes energy consumption, extending battery life while ensuring that the system remains responsive during multitasking. Operating systems often include power plans or profiles that users can customize to strike a balance between performance and energy efficiency based on their preferences and usage patterns.

The integration of notification systems in modern operating systems contributes to efficient multitasking by keeping users informed about important events and updates without interrupting their workflow. Notifications appear as unobtrusive alerts, providing users with timely information about emails, messages, calendar events, or system updates. Users can manage and respond to notifications without leaving their current task, promoting a seamless integration of information into the multitasking experience. Operating systems typically allow users to customize notification preferences, ensuring that they align with individual preferences and do not become a source of distraction.

Cloud integration has introduced a new dimension to multitasking, allowing users to seamlessly transition between devices while maintaining continuity in their work. Modern operating systems often integrate with cloud services, enabling users to sync files, settings, and even open applications across multiple devices. This feature enhances multitasking by providing users with a consistent computing environment regardless of the device they are using. The ability to access and edit documents, view browser history, and even resume tasks from one device to another streamlines the multitasking experience in an increasingly interconnected digital landscape.

Security features embedded in modern operating systems contribute to a secure multitasking environment. Features such as sandboxing and containerization isolate individual processes and applications, preventing potential security threats from spreading across the system. Operating systems implement robust user privilege models to restrict unauthorized access and ensure that each task operates within defined security boundaries. These security measures bolster the reliability and integrity of multitasking, allowing users to run diverse applications without compromising the overall system security.

Moreover, the integration of search functionalities within operating systems streamlines multitasking by providing users with quick and efficient access to files, applications, and information. Search features, often integrated into the Start menu or system bar, allow users to locate and launch applications, access documents, or initiate system actions with minimal effort. This accelerates task switching and reduces the time spent navigating through menus and directories, enhancing the overall efficiency of multitasking.

The incorporation of voice recognition and natural language processing further enriches multitasking capabilities in modern operating systems. Users can execute commands, open applications, or perform specific tasks using voice interactions, reducing the reliance on manual inputs and mouse clicks. Voice-controlled virtual assistants, such as Siri, Google Assistant, or Cortana, enable users to initiate multitasking actions through spoken commands, offering a hands-free and intuitive approach to managing tasks concurrently.

In conclusion, modern operating systems have evolved to facilitate multitasking in a myriad of ways, offering users a rich and dynamic computing experience. From preemptive multitasking and task management interfaces to virtual desktops, window management features, and advanced graphical compositing engines, operating systems provide users with the tools and flexibility to navigate seamlessly between multiple tasks. The synergy of hardware advancements, such as multicore processors, with sophisticated memory management and energy-efficient strategies, ensures that users can multitask efficiently without compromising system stability. As technology continues to advance, the focus on enhancing multitasking capabilities reflects the commitment of operating systems to meet the diverse and evolving needs of users in an interconnected and dynamic digital landscape.

Explore emerging interfaces in virtual and augmented reality environments.

The emergence of virtual and augmented reality (VR and AR) has ushered in a new era of human-computer interaction, introducing innovative interfaces that transcend traditional modes of engagement. In virtual reality environments, where users are fully immersed in computer-generated worlds, the primary interface revolves around immersive experiences facilitated by VR headsets and motion controllers. These devices enable users to interact with the virtual environment through gestures, movements, and spatial awareness. Hand tracking, an evolving technology, further enhances the VR interface by enabling users to manipulate virtual objects using their hands without the need for controllers. This intuitive interaction paradigm offers a sense of presence and engagement, creating an immersive experience that extends beyond the limitations of conventional interfaces.

Gesture recognition plays a central role in virtual reality interfaces, allowing users to communicate with the digital environment using natural hand movements. Advanced sensors in VR headsets and controllers capture the nuances of hand gestures, translating them into corresponding actions within the virtual space. This technology not only enhances user agency but also contributes to a more intuitive and immersive VR experience. Companies like Oculus and

Valve have integrated gesture recognition capabilities into their VR systems, enabling users to point, grab, and interact with virtual objects using hand movements, fostering a more natural and immersive form of interaction.

Augmented reality interfaces, on the other hand, blend digital content with the real world, creating a hybrid environment where virtual elements coexist with the user's physical surroundings. AR interfaces leverage devices such as smart glasses, smartphones, and tablets to overlay digital information onto the user's view of the real world. Smart glasses, equipped with transparent displays, depth-sensing cameras, and sensors, offer users a hands-free AR experience, allowing them to see and interact with digital content seamlessly integrated into their field of view. Companies like Microsoft with the HoloLens and Google with Google Glass have pioneered the development of AR smart glasses, opening up possibilities for applications in fields ranging from enterprise to education and healthcare.

Spatial computing, a fundamental concept in both VR and AR, plays a crucial role in shaping interfaces in these environments. Spatial computing refers to the ability of systems to understand and respond to the physical space around them. In VR, spatial computing enables the creation of immersive environments where users can move, explore, and interact within a three-dimensional space. In AR, spatial computing allows digital content to be anchored and responsive to the user's physical environment. This convergence of digital and physical spaces is redefining how users engage with information and interact with their surroundings, leading to the development of more contextual and adaptive interfaces in both VR and AR environments.

Hand tracking technology has gained prominence in both VR and AR interfaces, offering users a more natural and direct means of interaction. In VR, hand tracking allows users to engage with the virtual environment without the need for handheld controllers.

Companies like Oculus have integrated hand tracking features into their VR headsets, enabling users to use their hands directly to interact with objects and navigate menus within the virtual space. In AR, hand tracking facilitates interactions with digital content overlaid onto the real world. This technology is particularly valuable in scenarios where users need to manipulate virtual objects or interact with augmented information in a hands-free manner, contributing to a more seamless and immersive AR experience.

Voice recognition and natural language processing are integral components of emerging interfaces in both VR and AR environments. Voice commands offer users a hands-free and intuitive way to control and interact with virtual and augmented content. In VR, voice recognition allows users to navigate menus, initiate actions, and communicate with virtual characters using spoken commands. In AR, smart glasses equipped with microphones and voice recognition capabilities enable users to access information, receive directions, and perform tasks through verbal interactions. The integration of natural language processing further enhances the sophistication of these interfaces, enabling systems to understand and respond to contextual language input, creating a more immersive and user-friendly experience in both VR and AR.

Haptic feedback, or the sense of touch, is a critical aspect of emerging interfaces in virtual and augmented reality. Haptic feedback technologies provide users with tactile sensations, enhancing the sense of presence and realism in virtual environments. In VR, haptic feedback is commonly integrated into motion controllers, allowing users to feel the sensation of touching and interacting with virtual objects. Advancements in haptic gloves further refine this experience, enabling users to experience a more nuanced sense of touch and interaction in virtual spaces. In AR, haptic feedback can be applied through wearables or handheld devices, providing users with tactile feedback when interacting with augmented content overlaid onto the real world. These haptic interfaces add a new layer of immersion, making VR and AR experiences more sensory-rich and engaging.

The concept of eye tracking is gaining prominence in both VR and AR interfaces, offering new possibilities for interaction and user experience optimization. Eye tracking technology monitors the movement and focus of the user's eyes, allowing systems to respond dynamically to gaze direction. In VR, eye tracking enhances realism by simulating natural eye movements, enabling more realistic avatars and dynamic rendering where only the area within the user's gaze is rendered in high detail. In AR, eye tracking can optimize the presentation of information by adjusting the placement and visibility of digital content based on the user's gaze. This technology introduces a new dimension to interface design, where interactions can be initiated or influenced by the user's gaze, providing a more intuitive and personalized experience.

Biometric interfaces are emerging as a novel approach to authentication and personalization in both VR and AR environments. Biometric technologies, such as facial recognition and fingerprint scanning, offer secure and seamless user identification in virtual and augmented spaces. In VR, facial recognition can be used to create realistic avatars that mimic the user's facial expressions. In AR, smart glasses equipped with biometric sensors can provide secure access to augmented information based on the user's identity. These biometric interfaces contribute to a more personalized and secure user experience, aligning with the trend towards enhancing privacy and security in immersive computing environments.

Gesture-based interfaces, beyond hand tracking, are evolving to offer users more nuanced and expressive ways of interacting with virtual and augmented content. In VR, gesture recognition technologies enable users to convey emotions, commands, and complex interactions through predefined hand gestures or movements. This adds a layer of expressiveness to virtual interactions, allowing users to communicate with virtual characters or manipulate objects in a more intuitive manner. In AR, gesture-based interfaces can be employed through smart glasses or wearables, enabling users to control augmented content with simple hand movements or gestures. These interfaces leverage the natural language of gestures, making interactions more intuitive and engaging in both VR and AR environments.

The convergence of AI and machine learning with VR and AR interfaces is reshaping how these environments respond to user inputs and adapt to individual preferences. AI-driven interfaces can learn and anticipate user behavior, providing personalized and context-aware experiences in virtual and augmented spaces. In VR, AI algorithms can dynamically adjust the virtual environment based on user preferences, creating adaptive and immersive scenarios. In AR, machine learning can enhance the recognition and understanding of the user's surroundings, enabling more accurate and contextually relevant augmentation of the real world. This integration of AI and machine learning amplifies the intelligence of VR and AR interfaces, making them more responsive and attuned to individual users.

The concept of mixed reality (MR), which seamlessly blends elements of both VR and AR, introduces interfaces that dynamically transition between fully immersive virtual environments and augmented realities integrated into the real world. MR interfaces leverage technologies like depth-sensing cameras and spatial mapping to anchor virtual objects within the physical environment. Users can interact with these objects as if they coexist with real-world elements. Microsoft's HoloLens exemplifies the potential of mixed reality interfaces, offering a spectrum of experiences ranging from fully virtual simulations to holographic augmentations in the user's surroundings. The fluidity of MR interfaces provides users with a versatile and dynamic spectrum of interaction possibilities, combining the best of both virtual and augmented realities.

In conclusion, the evolution of interfaces in virtual and augmented reality environments represents a paradigm shift in human-computer interaction. From immersive VR experiences facilitated by hand tracking and gesture recognition to AR interfaces that overlay digital content onto the real world using smart glasses and wearables, the landscape of interfaces is diversifying and becoming more intuitive. The integration of technologies like voice recognition, haptic feedback, eye tracking, and biometrics adds layers of richness and personalization to these interfaces. As AI and machine learning continue to advance, VR and AR interfaces are poised to become even more adaptive, context-aware, and seamlessly integrated into the fabric of our daily lives, shaping the future of immersive computing experiences.

Discuss current trends in user experience design for operating systems.

User experience design for operating systems is undergoing continuous evolution, driven by technological advancements, changing user expectations, and the growing complexity of digital ecosystems. One prevailing trend is the emphasis on minimalism and simplicity. Operating systems across various platforms, including Windows, macOS, and Linux distributions, are adopting clean and uncluttered interfaces. This design philosophy aims to streamline user interactions, reduce cognitive load, and enhance overall usability. Flat design, characterized by simple icons, straightforward layouts, and a focus on essential functionalities, has become pervasive. The shift towards minimalism not only provides a visually appealing aesthetic but also prioritizes user efficiency and accessibility, aligning with the principle that less visual noise leads to a more intuitive and user-friendly experience.

Dark mode has emerged as a prominent trend in user experience design for operating systems. Dark mode, characterized by a darker color scheme for the interface elements, offers benefits such as reduced eye strain in low-light environments and improved visual hierarchy. Major operating systems, including Windows, macOS, and various Linux desktop environments, have integrated dark mode options. This trend is not merely an aesthetic choice but also a response to user preferences and a recognition of the importance of providing adaptable interfaces that cater to diverse user needs and environmental conditions.

Personalization features are gaining prominence in the design of modern operating systems, reflecting a shift towards user-centric design. Operating systems now offer extensive customization options, allowing users to personalize their desktop backgrounds, themes, and color schemes. Customizable taskbars, widgets, and desktop icons enable users to tailor the interface to their preferences, fostering a sense of ownership and a more individualized computing experience. This trend acknowledges the diverse needs and preferences of users, emphasizing the importance of providing a flexible and personalized environment within the operating system.

Accessibility has become a central focus in user experience design, reflecting a commitment to inclusivity and usability for individuals with diverse abilities. Operating systems are integrating a range of accessibility features, including screen readers, magnification tools, and voice control. These features empower users with visual, auditory, or motor impairments, ensuring that the operating system is accessible to a broader user base. Inclusive design principles are driving the development of interfaces that prioritize usability for everyone, aligning with the goal of creating technology that accommodates diverse needs and abilities.

The integration of AI-driven features is transforming user experience design in operating systems. AI algorithms are being leveraged to enhance predictive capabilities, personalization, and context-aware interactions. Features like intelligent suggestions, contextually relevant notifications, and adaptive interfaces that learn from user behavior contribute to a more dynamic and responsive user experience. Operating systems are becoming increasingly adept at understanding user preferences, predicting actions, and adapting the interface based on individual usage patterns, creating a more seamless and personalized computing environment.

Gesture-based interfaces are gaining traction in user experience design for operating systems, especially in touch-enabled devices. Operating systems for smartphones, tablets, and 2-in-1 devices are incorporating gesture controls to enable users to navigate, switch between applications, and perform various actions through intuitive hand movements. Gesture-based interfaces offer a more natural and interactive way of interacting with devices, bridging the gap between physical and digital interactions. This trend aligns with the prevalence of touchscreens and the desire to create interfaces that leverage human gestures for a more immersive and engaging user experience.

Cross-platform consistency is becoming a key consideration in user experience design as users increasingly engage with multiple devices and platforms. Operating systems are striving to provide a consistent user experience across different devices, ensuring that users encounter familiar interfaces and workflows regardless of whether they are using a desktop, laptop, tablet, or smartphone. Cross-platform design principles prioritize coherence in visual elements, interaction patterns, and feature parity, creating a seamless transition for users moving between different devices within the same ecosystem.

Integration of virtual assistants and voice interactions is shaping the future of user experience in operating systems. Virtual assistants like Siri, Google Assistant, and Cortana are becoming integral parts of operating systems, allowing users to perform tasks, get information, and control devices using voice commands. The integration of natural language processing enhances the conversational capabilities of virtual assistants, enabling more dynamic and context-aware interactions. Voice interactions provide an alternative and often more convenient mode of engagement, particularly in scenarios where hands-free control is advantageous, contributing to a more accessible and user-friendly operating system experience.

Security and privacy considerations are influencing user experience design in operating systems. With growing concerns about data breaches and privacy violations, operating systems are incorporating transparent and user-centric security features. From clear privacy settings to robust encryption protocols, modern operating systems prioritize user awareness and control over their personal data. Security features are seamlessly integrated into the user experience, providing a balance between safeguarding sensitive information and ensuring that security measures do not impede the usability and accessibility of the operating system.

Continued emphasis on user feedback and iterative design processes is shaping the evolution of operating system interfaces. Operating system developers are increasingly adopting user-centered design methodologies, involving users in the feedback loop through beta programs, user testing, and feedback forums. This iterative approach enables continuous refinement of interfaces based on user input, addressing usability issues, and incorporating user preferences. Operating systems are evolving in response to real-world user experiences, ensuring that design decisions are informed by the diverse needs and perspectives of the user community.

The rise of augmented reality (AR) and mixed reality (MR) is introducing new dimensions to user experience design in operating systems. While AR overlays digital information onto the real world through devices like smart glasses and smartphones, MR seamlessly integrates virtual elements with the physical environment. Operating systems are exploring ways to incorporate AR and MR interfaces, offering users interactive and contextually relevant information in real-time. This trend reflects a shift towards more immersive and spatially aware interfaces, with the potential to transform how users interact with both the digital and physical worlds through their operating systems.

In conclusion, current trends in user experience design for operating systems reflect a holistic approach that encompasses aesthetics, functionality, accessibility, personalization, and security. From minimalist and customizable interfaces to the integration of AI, gesture-based interactions, and cross-platform consistency, operating systems are adapting to the evolving needs and expectations of users. The emphasis on accessibility, privacy, and augmented reality underscores a commitment to inclusivity and the exploration of innovative interfaces. As technology continues to advance, user experience design for operating systems will likely continue evolving, driven by a user-centric ethos and a desire to provide seamless, intuitive, and delightful computing experiences across a diverse range of devices and scenarios.

Chapter 6: Security Measures and Challenges in Operating Systems

Discuss the critical role of security in operating systems.

The critical role of security in operating systems is paramount as these systems serve as the foundational infrastructure for computing devices, managing and controlling hardware resources, executing applications, and facilitating communication between various components. Security in operating systems is multifaceted, encompassing a range of measures designed to protect the integrity, confidentiality, and availability of information and resources. One of the fundamental aspects of operating system security lies in access control mechanisms. Operating systems implement robust user authentication and authorization protocols to ensure that only authorized individuals or processes gain access to specific resources. Passwords, biometric authentication, and multi-factor authentication are employed to verify user identities, while access control lists and permission systems define and regulate the level of access granted to users or processes.

The concept of least privilege is a cornerstone of operating system security, emphasizing the principle that users or processes should have the minimum level of access necessary to perform their tasks. By adhering to the principle of least privilege, operating systems reduce the potential attack surface, limiting the impact of security breaches or unauthorized access. Role-based access control (RBAC) frameworks further enhance access management by assigning permissions based on user roles, streamlining the administration of access policies and ensuring that users only possess the privileges essential to their designated roles.

The secure management of user data and file systems is integral to operating system security. Encryption mechanisms, such as file-level or full-disk encryption, safeguard sensitive data from unauthorized access or tampering. Operating systems implement file permission systems to control user access to files and directories, specifying who can read, write, or execute specific files. Audit trails and logging mechanisms play a vital role in tracking user activities, system events, and potential security incidents. These logs provide valuable insights for security professionals to monitor and analyze the behavior of users and processes, aiding in the detection of anomalous or suspicious activities.

Network security is a critical dimension of operating system security, especially in the context of interconnected computing environments. Firewalls, implemented at the operating system or network level, regulate incoming and outgoing network traffic, acting as a barrier against unauthorized access and potential cyber threats. Intrusion detection and prevention systems (IDPS) are employed to monitor network activities and identify patterns indicative of malicious behavior. Secure communication protocols, such as Transport Layer Security (TLS) and Secure Shell (SSH), ensure the confidentiality and integrity of data transmitted over networks, mitigating the risk of eavesdropping or data manipulation.

The ongoing evolution of operating systems has seen a growing emphasis on security features to counteract the rising sophistication of cyber threats. Vulnerability management is a crucial aspect, with operating system developers regularly releasing updates and patches to address known vulnerabilities. Automatic update mechanisms ensure that users receive the latest security patches promptly, reducing the window of opportunity for potential attackers to exploit weaknesses. Operating systems increasingly incorporate features like address space layout randomization (ASLR) and data execution prevention (DEP) to thwart common exploitation techniques, enhancing the overall resilience of the system against various types of attacks.

Secure boot mechanisms are designed to safeguard the integrity of the boot process, ensuring that only authenticated and unaltered components are loaded during system startup. This protects against the injection of malicious code or unauthorized modifications to the boot sequence, establishing a trusted foundation for the operating system. Trusted Platform Modules (TPMs) or hardware-based security modules further enhance the security posture by providing a secure enclave for cryptographic operations and key storage, safeguarding sensitive information from potential attacks.

Virtualization, a prevalent feature in modern operating systems, introduces additional security considerations. Hypervisors, responsible for managing virtual machines, play a crucial role in ensuring the isolation and security of virtualized environments. Secure virtualization relies on robust hypervisor security, preventing unauthorized access between virtual machines and safeguarding the underlying host system. Features like virtual LANs (VLANs), virtual firewalls, and secure containerization contribute to the secure deployment and management of virtualized resources within the operating system environment.

Malware prevention and detection are imperative aspects of operating system security. Antivirus software, integrated with operating systems or deployed as third-party solutions, scans for and removes malicious software, mitigating the risk of infections. Behavioral analysis and heuristics contribute to proactive threat detection, identifying potential malware based on anomalous patterns of behavior. Sandboxing techniques isolate untrusted processes, limiting their impact on the operating system and preventing the spread of malware. Operating systems also implement secure boot processes to verify the integrity of system files and prevent the execution of compromised or tampered code.

Operating systems play a pivotal role in securing communication and data storage through the implementation of cryptographic protocols. Secure sockets layer (SSL) and its successor TLS secure communication channels over networks, ensuring the confidentiality and integrity of transmitted data. File and disk encryption, such as BitLocker on Windows and FileVault on macOS, protect data at rest, mitigating the risk of unauthorized access to stored information. Cryptographic hashing algorithms are employed to verify the integrity of files and ensure that they have not been tampered with, providing a mechanism for detecting unauthorized modifications.

User awareness and education are integral components of operating system security. Operating systems often incorporate user interfaces and notifications that inform users about potential security risks, such as unsecured connections or outdated software. Education programs within the operating system environment may provide users with guidance on best security practices, password hygiene, and recognizing phishing attempts. By fostering a security-conscious user culture, operating systems contribute to a collaborative approach to cybersecurity, recognizing that users play a crucial role in maintaining the overall security posture.

Containerization technologies, such as Docker and Kubernetes, introduce new paradigms in operating system security by encapsulating applications and their dependencies into isolated containers. Containers enhance security by minimizing the attack surface, isolating applications from the underlying operating system, and facilitating consistent deployment across diverse environments. Operating systems that support containerization technologies prioritize secure container orchestration, access control, and image integrity, ensuring that containerized applications maintain a robust security posture within the operating system ecosystem.

As the Internet of Things (IoT) proliferates, operating systems are adapting to the unique security challenges posed by interconnected devices. Security features such as device authentication, secure communication protocols, and over-the-air (OTA) updates are crucial in securing IoT ecosystems. Operating systems designed for IoT environments prioritize resource efficiency, ensuring that even constrained devices can implement essential security measures. Security in IoT operating systems extends beyond traditional computing devices to encompass a diverse array of connected devices, emphasizing the need for comprehensive security frameworks and standards.

Compliance with industry standards and regulations is a driving force in shaping operating system security practices. Operating systems are developed and configured to adhere to security standards such as Common Criteria, Federal Information Processing Standards (FIPS), and International Organization for Standardization (ISO) specifications. Compliance with these standards ensures that operating systems meet recognized benchmarks for security, providing users and organizations with a level of assurance regarding the robustness of the security features implemented.

In conclusion, the critical role of security in operating systems is foundational to the reliability, integrity, and functionality of computing environments. Operating systems implement a myriad of security measures, encompassing access control, encryption, network security, vulnerability management, and protection against malware. The evolving threat landscape necessitates continuous advancements in security features, with operating systems adapting to emerging technologies such as virtualization, containerization, and the Internet of Things. As the digital ecosystem continues to expand, operating system security remains an ever-evolving discipline, demanding vigilance, innovation, and collaboration to address the dynamic challenges posed by cybersecurity threats.

Discuss methods of user authentication and authorization in operating systems.

User authentication and authorization are critical components of operating system security, ensuring that only authorized individuals or processes gain access to specific resources while maintaining the integrity and confidentiality of the system. Authentication is the process of verifying the identity of a user or entity attempting to access the system, while authorization involves granting or denying access rights and permissions based on the authenticated identity.

One of the most common methods of user authentication in operating systems is the use of usernames and passwords. Users are required to provide a unique username along with a corresponding password during the login process. The system then compares the entered credentials with stored records to authenticate the user. While widely used, passwords are susceptible to various security risks, such as brute force attacks and password cracking. To enhance security, operating systems often enforce password complexity requirements, multi-factor authentication, and account lockout policies to mitigate the risk of unauthorized access.

Multi-factor authentication (MFA) is an authentication method that combines two or more independent factors to verify a user's identity. In addition to traditional passwords, MFA may include factors such as something the user knows (a PIN), something the user has (a smart card or mobile device), or something the user is (biometric authentication like fingerprint or facial recognition). MFA significantly strengthens user authentication by adding an extra layer of security, making it more challenging for attackers to compromise user accounts.

Biometric authentication leverages unique physical or behavioral characteristics of an individual to verify their identity. Common biometric modalities include fingerprint recognition, facial recognition, iris scanning, and voice recognition. Biometric authentication offers a high level of security and user convenience, as it eliminates the need to remember passwords. However, it is essential to address privacy concerns and potential vulnerabilities associated with biometric data storage and processing.

Smart cards and token-based authentication systems are additional methods used in user authentication. Smart cards are physical cards containing an embedded chip that stores user credentials. Users must insert the smart card into a card reader and provide a personal identification number (PIN) to authenticate. Token-based authentication involves the use of physical or virtual tokens, which generate one-time passcodes for user authentication. Time-based One-Time Passwords (TOTPs) generated by authenticator apps on mobile devices fall under this category. These methods add an extra layer of security by requiring possession of a physical device in addition to knowledge-based authentication.

Public key infrastructure (PKI) is a cryptographic approach used for user authentication in secure communication environments. PKI involves the use of public and private key pairs. The public key is shared openly, while the private key is kept secret. When a user attempts to authenticate, the system verifies the user's identity by decrypting a challenge with the user's private key. PKI is commonly used in conjunction with secure protocols like Secure Sockets Layer (SSL) or Transport Layer Security (TLS) for secure communication over networks.

Once a user is authenticated, the next step is authorization, where the system determines the level of access rights and permissions the authenticated user should have. Role-based access control (RBAC) is a prevalent authorization method in operating systems. RBAC assigns users to roles based on their job responsibilities, and each role is associated with specific permissions. This approach simplifies access management, as administrators can assign or revoke permissions by modifying user roles rather than adjusting individual user permissions.

Mandatory access control (MAC) is an authorization model that restricts access based on security labels associated with each user and resource. The system enforces a predefined security policy that determines the access permissions of users. MAC is commonly used in high-security environments, such as government or military systems, where strict control over data access is essential.

Discretionary access control (DAC) allows users to control access to their resources. In a DAC system, users can assign permissions to their files, directories, or objects. While DAC provides flexibility for individual users, it can pose security risks if users grant excessive permissions, leading to potential data breaches or unauthorized access. Careful management and monitoring are necessary to maintain security in a DAC environment.

Attribute-based access control (ABAC) is an authorization model that evaluates a set of attributes associated with the user, the resource, and the environment to make access control decisions. ABAC provides fine-grained control over permissions by considering various contextual factors. For example, a user may be granted access to a document only if they are accessing it from a specific location during business hours. ABAC is highly adaptable and suits dynamic environments where access decisions depend on multiple variables.

In addition to these traditional methods, modern operating systems are incorporating contextual and risk-based authentication and authorization mechanisms. Contextual authentication considers contextual information such as the user's location, device used, and time of access to make informed authentication decisions. Risk-based authentication assesses the level of risk associated with a particular access attempt, triggering additional security measures if the risk is deemed high. These adaptive authentication approaches enhance security by responding dynamically to changing circumstances.

OAuth (Open Authorization) and OpenID Connect are authentication and authorization protocols commonly used in web-based applications and services. OAuth enables secure authorization by allowing a user to grant a third-party application limited access to their resources without sharing their credentials. OpenID Connect builds on OAuth to provide user authentication, allowing users to log in to multiple services using a single set of credentials. These protocols enhance security and user convenience in the context of web-based authentication.

The continuous evolution of user authentication and authorization methods is driven by the need to address emerging security challenges and adapt to changing technological landscapes. Operating systems play a pivotal role in implementing and refining these methods to ensure robust security postures. As threats evolve, user authentication and authorization mechanisms will continue to advance, incorporating innovative technologies and adaptive approaches to safeguard the integrity and confidentiality of computing environments.

Discuss the role of firewalls in protecting operating systems from network-based threats.

Firewalls play a pivotal role in fortifying operating systems against network-based threats, serving as a critical line of defense in the complex landscape of cybersecurity. The primary objective of a firewall is to monitor, filter, and control incoming and outgoing network traffic based on predetermined security rules. By establishing a barrier between a trusted internal network and untrusted external networks, firewalls act as gatekeepers, regulating the flow of data and thwarting potential threats that may exploit vulnerabilities in operating systems.

One of the fundamental functions of firewalls is packet filtering, where they inspect individual data packets based on predefined rules. These rules specify which packets are allowed or denied based on criteria such as source and destination IP addresses, port numbers, and the protocol used. Packet filtering provides a basic yet effective means of blocking unauthorized access attempts and preventing malicious traffic from reaching the operating system. It acts as a filter at the network layer, evaluating each packet and making decisions to either permit or deny its passage through the firewall.

Stateful inspection, an advanced form of packet filtering, enhances the security capabilities of firewalls by maintaining a state table that tracks the state of active connections. Unlike traditional packet filtering, stateful inspection considers the context of a connection, allowing the firewall to make more informed decisions based on the state of the communication. This enables firewalls to discern legitimate responses to outbound requests and helps prevent certain types of attacks, such as session hijacking and network reconnaissance.

Proxy servers, employed by firewalls, act as intermediaries between internal users and external servers. By intercepting requests and responses, proxy servers can inspect and filter content, thereby providing an additional layer of security. They play a crucial role in protecting operating systems by serving as a barrier that shields internal systems from direct exposure to external networks. Proxies can enforce security policies, cache content to enhance performance, and log activities for analysis, contributing to a more secure and controlled network environment.

Network Address Translation (NAT) is another firewall feature that enhances security by modifying network address information in packet headers while in transit. NAT helps conceal the internal IP addresses of devices within a network, presenting a single public IP address to external networks. This obfuscation adds a layer of security by preventing direct exposure of internal network structure and potentially thwarting certain types of attacks that rely on knowledge of internal IP addresses.

Firewalls play a crucial role in preventing unauthorized access to operating systems through the implementation of access control lists (ACLs). These lists specify which devices or users are allowed or denied access to specific resources based on various criteria, including IP addresses, port numbers, and protocols. By configuring ACLs, administrators can establish granular control over network traffic, mitigating the risk of unauthorized access attempts and ensuring that only legitimate connections are permitted.

Deep packet inspection (DPI) is an advanced firewall capability that involves the analysis of the actual content of data packets beyond the packet headers. DPI enables firewalls to inspect the payload of packets for patterns, signatures, or anomalies that may indicate malicious activity. This level of scrutiny allows firewalls to detect and block sophisticated threats, such as malware, intrusion attempts, and data exfiltration, contributing to a more robust defense against network-based attacks.

Intrusion Prevention Systems (IPS) integrated into firewalls add an active layer of defense by identifying and blocking malicious activities in real-time. IPS utilizes a combination of signature-based detection, anomaly detection, and heuristic analysis to identify potential threats. When suspicious activity is detected, the firewall can take immediate action, such as blocking the malicious IP address or dropping specific packets. IPS enhances the proactive nature of firewalls, enabling them to actively prevent potential threats from compromising the security of the operating system.

Virtual Private Networks (VPNs) integrated with firewalls provide secure communication channels over untrusted networks, such as the internet. VPNs employ encryption and tunneling protocols to create a secure and private connection between the user's device and a trusted network. Firewalls play a crucial role in VPN security by enforcing policies, authenticating users, and encrypting/decrypting data as it traverses the network. This ensures that sensitive information remains confidential and secure, even when transmitted over potentially insecure channels.

Firewalls contribute significantly to the protection of operating systems from Distributed Denial of Service (DDoS) attacks, a prevalent form of network-based threat. DDoS attacks aim to overwhelm a target system or network with an excessive volume of traffic, rendering it unavailable to legitimate users. Firewalls can detect and mitigate DDoS attacks by implementing rate limiting, traffic filtering, and other countermeasures. By intelligently managing incoming traffic, firewalls help maintain the availability and performance of the operating system even under the strain of a DDoS onslaught.

Firewalls are instrumental in securing wireless networks, where the absence of physical boundaries makes them susceptible to unauthorized access and eavesdropping. Wireless firewalls implement security measures such as encryption (e.g., WPA2, WPA3), authentication protocols (e.g., WPA3-Enterprise), and intrusion detection mechanisms to safeguard wireless communication. They play a crucial role in preventing unauthorized devices from gaining access to the network and protect against various wireless-specific threats, including man-in-the-middle attacks and rogue access points.

Web Application Firewalls (WAFs) focus on protecting operating systems from threats targeting web applications. WAFs inspect HTTP traffic, analyze requests and responses, and apply security policies to identify and block common web application vulnerabilities. This includes protection against SQL injection, cross-site scripting (XSS), and other injection attacks. By scrutinizing web traffic at the application layer, WAFs add an extra layer of defense, shielding web applications and their underlying operating systems from targeted attacks.

Firewalls also contribute to network segmentation, a strategy that involves dividing a network into distinct segments or subnetworks to enhance security. By isolating different parts of the network, firewalls can control traffic flow between segments, preventing lateral movement of attackers within the network. Network segmentation reduces the attack surface and limits the potential impact of security incidents, providing an additional layer of defense for operating systems.

Logging and auditing capabilities in firewalls play a critical role in post-event analysis, forensics, and compliance. Firewalls generate logs that capture information about network traffic, user activities, and security events. These logs are valuable for monitoring and analyzing network behavior, identifying security incidents, and adhering to regulatory compliance requirements. By maintaining comprehensive logs, firewalls empower administrators to assess the security posture of the operating system, investigate incidents, and implement improvements based on insights gained from historical data.

Firewalls are evolving to address the challenges posed by cloud computing and virtualization. Cloud-based firewalls provide security for virtualized environments and cloud infrastructure by extending traditional firewall capabilities to the cloud. They help control and secure traffic between on-premises systems and cloud-based resources, ensuring consistent security policies across hybrid environments. Additionally, containerized environments benefit from container firewalls that protect applications and their underlying operating systems within isolated containers.

In conclusion, firewalls are indispensable guardians in the realm of cybersecurity, acting as a crucial defense mechanism for operating systems against an array of network-based threats. Through packet filtering, stateful inspection, proxy servers, access control, deep packet inspection, intrusion prevention, VPNs, and other features, firewalls establish a robust perimeter defense. Their ability to adapt to evolving threats, such as DDoS attacks, wireless vulnerabilities, and web application exploits, underscores their significance in fortifying operating systems. As technology advances, firewalls continue to evolve, incorporating innovative capabilities to safeguard operating systems in the ever-changing landscape of cybersecurity.

Discuss strategies for protecting operating systems from malware.

Protecting operating systems from malware is a multifaceted challenge that demands a comprehensive strategy, encompassing proactive measures, vigilant monitoring, and responsive actions. Malware, a term derived from "malicious software," includes a wide array of threats such as viruses, worms, trojans, ransomware, and spyware, all designed to compromise the integrity, confidentiality, and availability of operating systems. Employing a combination of preventive, detective, and corrective strategies is essential to establish a resilient defense against the diverse and evolving landscape of malware.

Preventive measures form the first line of defense in safeguarding operating systems from malware. These measures encompass various strategies, including the use of antivirus software. Antivirus programs employ signature-based detection, heuristic analysis, and behavioral monitoring to identify and neutralize known and potential threats. Regular updates to antivirus databases are crucial to ensure that the software can recognize the latest malware variants. Additionally, endpoint protection solutions that go beyond traditional antivirus, incorporating features such as advanced threat intelligence, machine learning, and sandboxing, offer enhanced protection against sophisticated malware.

Ensuring the timely and comprehensive application of security patches and updates is a fundamental preventive strategy. Operating system vendors regularly release patches to address vulnerabilities that could be exploited by malware. Regular system updates, including patches for the operating system, applications, and firmware, mitigate the risk of exploitation and enhance the overall security posture. Automated patch management solutions streamline the process of deploying updates across large-scale environments, reducing the window of opportunity for attackers to exploit known vulnerabilities.

The practice of secure configuration management plays a vital role in preventing malware infections. Operating systems should be configured with security best practices in mind, disabling unnecessary services, restricting user privileges, and implementing access controls. Security configuration baselines, provided by organizations such as the Center for Internet Security (CIS) or the National Institute of Standards and Technology (NIST), offer guidance on secure system configurations. Regular audits and assessments of system configurations help identify and remediate deviations from the established security baselines, reducing the attack surface and minimizing the likelihood of successful malware attacks.

Network security measures are integral components of the preventive strategy against malware. Firewalls, intrusion prevention systems (IPS), and secure network architectures contribute to the defense against malicious network-based activities. Firewalls monitor and filter incoming and outgoing network traffic, blocking unauthorized access and thwarting potential malware communication. IPS systems analyze network traffic for patterns indicative of malicious behavior, actively preventing intrusion attempts. Implementing secure network segmentation isolates different parts of the network, limiting the lateral movement of malware within the environment.

Email security is a critical aspect of malware prevention, given that email remains a common vector for malware distribution. Email filtering solutions scan incoming emails for malicious attachments, links, and content. Anti-phishing measures, including the detection of phishing emails and the use of email authentication protocols such as DMARC (Domain-based Message Authentication, Reporting, and Conformance), help mitigate the risk of users falling victim to social engineering attacks that often lead to malware infections. Security awareness training for users reinforces the importance of cautious behavior when interacting with emails, reducing the likelihood of inadvertent malware downloads.

Application whitelisting is a preventive strategy that restricts the execution of only approved applications on the operating system. By defining a list of authorized applications, organizations can prevent the execution of unapproved or potentially malicious software. This approach helps mitigate the risk of unauthorized and uncontrolled software installations, which are common vectors for malware infiltration. However, effective application whitelisting requires continuous monitoring and updating to accommodate legitimate software changes and updates.

Detective measures focus on identifying and analyzing potential malware threats that may have evaded preventive measures. Continuous monitoring of system logs, network traffic, and endpoint activities provides insights into anomalous behavior that may indicate the presence of malware. Security Information and Event Management (SIEM) solutions aggregate and analyze log data from various sources, enabling the detection of patterns or signatures associated with malware activities. Intrusion detection systems (IDS) complement preventive measures by actively monitoring network traffic for signs of suspicious behavior, triggering alerts or automated responses when potential threats are detected.

Behavioral analytics and anomaly detection contribute to the detective strategy by identifying deviations from normal system behavior. By establishing baselines for typical user and system activities, organizations can detect unusual patterns that may indicate malware infections or unauthorized access. Machine learning algorithms enhance the capability to recognize subtle anomalies, adapting to evolving malware tactics and evasive techniques. Continuous refinement of behavioral models based on historical data ensures the accuracy and effectiveness of anomaly detection mechanisms.

Endpoint detection and response (EDR) solutions focus on monitoring and responding to activities at the endpoint level, including individual devices and servers. EDR solutions provide real-time visibility into endpoint activities, enabling rapid detection of malicious processes, file changes, or system modifications indicative of malware. Behavioral analysis, threat intelligence integration, and automated response capabilities enhance the effectiveness of EDR solutions in identifying and mitigating malware threats. Integration with broader security frameworks, including SIEM and threat intelligence platforms, facilitates a holistic approach to malware detection and response.

Security information sharing and collaboration within the cybersecurity community contribute to the detective strategy by enhancing threat intelligence. Information sharing platforms, industry collaborations, and threat intelligence feeds provide organizations with timely and relevant data on emerging malware threats, attack techniques, and indicators of compromise (IoCs). By leveraging shared intelligence, organizations can enhance their detection capabilities, proactively adapting defenses to emerging threats and vulnerabilities.

Corrective measures involve responding to identified malware threats to minimize their impact and eradicate the infection. Incident response plans outline the steps to be taken when a malware incident is detected, including isolation of affected systems, analysis of the malware, and remediation. Incident response teams, equipped with the necessary skills and tools, play a crucial role in executing effective response actions. Timely and well-coordinated incident response efforts contribute to containing the spread of malware, reducing downtime, and preventing data breaches.

Endpoint protection and remediation tools aid in the corrective strategy by providing the means to quarantine or remove malware from infected systems. These tools often include features such as real-time threat detection, automated response actions, and the ability to roll back system changes made by malware. Integration with centralized management consoles facilitates the coordination of response efforts across multiple endpoints, streamlining the remediation process.

Data backup and recovery strategies are essential components of the corrective approach to malware incidents. Regularly backing up critical data ensures that organizations can recover from a malware attack with minimal data loss and downtime. Backup solutions should include features such as versioning, encryption, and offsite storage to protect against ransomware attacks that may attempt to encrypt or delete backup data. Regular testing of backup restoration processes validates the reliability of the backup strategy and ensures readiness for effective recovery.

Post-incident analysis and lessons learned form a crucial aspect of corrective measures. Conducting a thorough investigation into the root cause of a malware incident helps organizations understand the attack vectors, vulnerabilities exploited, and the effectiveness of existing security controls. The insights gained from post-incident analysis inform the refinement of security policies, procedures, and preventive measures to better defend against future malware threats.

Regular security awareness training for users is an overarching strategy that spans preventive, detective, and corrective measures. Educating users about the risks associated with malware, social engineering tactics, and safe computing practices empowers them to recognize and avoid potential threats. User awareness contributes to the prevention of malware infections, aids in the detection of suspicious activities, and fosters a collaborative approach to incident response by encouraging users to report security incidents promptly.

In conclusion, protecting operating systems from malware requires a holistic and adaptive strategy that combines preventive, detective, and corrective measures. By implementing robust preventive measures, maintaining vigilant detective capabilities, and executing effective corrective actions, organizations can establish a resilient defense against the diverse and evolving threats posed by malware. The integration of advanced technologies, threat intelligence sharing, and user education contributes to a comprehensive and proactive approach to malware protection in the dynamic landscape of cybersecurity.

Discuss the importance of timely security patching.

Timely security patching is of paramount importance in maintaining the integrity, confidentiality, and availability of computer systems, networks, and applications. Security patches, also known as updates or fixes, are software modifications designed to address vulnerabilities and weaknesses identified in the software's code or configuration. These vulnerabilities, if left unaddressed, can be exploited by malicious actors to compromise the security of the system, leading to unauthorized access, data breaches, and other cybersecurity incidents. The significance of timely security patching lies in its role as a proactive and preventive measure against the ever-evolving landscape of cyber threats.

One of the primary reasons for the importance of timely security patching is the constant emergence of new vulnerabilities. As software is developed, vulnerabilities may inadvertently be introduced into the codebase. Additionally, as cyber threats evolve, attackers continually discover and exploit new vulnerabilities to compromise systems. Timely security patching ensures that software vendors can respond promptly to the discovery of these vulnerabilities, releasing patches to rectify the issues before malicious actors can exploit them. The rapid pace of technological advancements and the increasing sophistication of cyber threats underscore the critical need for organizations to stay ahead of potential vulnerabilities through proactive patch management.

Security patches address a variety of vulnerabilities, ranging from common software bugs to critical security flaws. These vulnerabilities can manifest in different forms, including programming errors, design flaws, or misconfigurations that create opportunities for unauthorized access, privilege escalation, or the execution of malicious code. By applying security patches in a timely manner, organizations can close these security gaps, reducing the attack surface and mitigating the risk of exploitation. Neglecting security patching leaves systems susceptible to known vulnerabilities, effectively providing cyber adversaries with low-hanging fruit for exploitation.

The principle of least privilege, a fundamental tenet of cybersecurity, underscores the importance of timely security patching. Even systems with robust access controls and well-defined user privileges can be compromised if underlying vulnerabilities exist. Security patches often include fixes that enhance access controls, restrict unnecessary privileges, and strengthen authentication mechanisms. By promptly applying these patches, organizations ensure that their systems adhere to the principle of least privilege, limiting the potential impact of security incidents and reducing the likelihood of unauthorized access.

Timely security patching is integral to regulatory compliance and adherence to industry standards. Many regulatory frameworks, such as the General Data Protection Regulation (GDPR), Health Insurance Portability and Accountability Act (HIPAA), and Payment Card Industry Data Security Standard (PCI DSS), require organizations to implement security measures, including patch management, to protect sensitive information and ensure data privacy. Non-compliance with these regulations can result in severe consequences, including legal repercussions, financial penalties, and damage to an organization's reputation. Timely security patching demonstrates a commitment to fulfilling these regulatory obligations, fostering a culture of compliance within the organization.

The interconnected nature of modern IT ecosystems emphasizes the ripple effect of unpatched vulnerabilities across networks. A single unpatched system within a network can serve as a foothold for attackers to move laterally, compromising other systems and escalating their privileges. Timely security patching disrupts this chain of exploitation, preventing the lateral movement of attackers and limiting the potential scope of a security incident. The interconnectedness of networks underscores the collective responsibility of organizations to contribute to the overall security of the digital ecosystem by diligently applying security patches.

The importance of timely security patching extends to the protection of sensitive and confidential data. Vulnerabilities in software can be exploited to gain unauthorized access to databases, compromising the confidentiality of stored information. Security patches often include fixes for vulnerabilities related to data encryption, access controls, and data leakage prevention. Applying these patches promptly safeguards sensitive data, protecting it from unauthorized disclosure and mitigating the risk of data breaches. In an era where data breaches can have severe financial, legal, and reputational consequences, organizations must prioritize the protection of sensitive information through proactive patch management.

Cybersecurity incidents, such as ransomware attacks and data breaches, often exploit known vulnerabilities for initial access. Timely security patching serves as a crucial defense against such incidents by closing the door on common exploitation vectors. Notorious malware strains, like WannaCry and NotPetya, leveraged unpatched vulnerabilities to propagate and wreak havoc on a global scale. The lessons learned from these incidents underscore the imperative for organizations to prioritize the timely application of security patches, as it represents a fundamental defense against the types of exploits commonly employed by cyber adversaries.

The increasing sophistication of cyber threats highlights the dynamic nature of the cybersecurity landscape. Attackers are quick to adapt to new vulnerabilities, making it essential for organizations to be equally agile in their defense mechanisms. Timely security patching aligns with the concept of continuous security improvement, enabling organizations to stay ahead of evolving threats. Regularly updating software and systems ensures that organizations can proactively address emerging vulnerabilities, reducing the window of opportunity for attackers and enhancing the overall resilience of their cybersecurity posture.

Mobile devices, IoT (Internet of Things) devices, and other endpoints are integral components of modern computing environments, and their security is equally critical. Timely security patching extends beyond traditional computing devices to include these diverse endpoints. Mobile operating systems, firmware on IoT devices, and other embedded systems often require regular updates to address vulnerabilities and improve security. Neglecting the security of these endpoints can introduce weak links in the overall security chain, providing attackers with entry points into the broader network. Timely security patching, encompassing all facets of an organization's digital infrastructure, reinforces a comprehensive approach to cybersecurity.

The dynamic nature of software development introduces the need for continuous improvement in security. Software vendors regularly release updates not only to patch vulnerabilities but also to enhance features, improve performance, and address evolving user needs. Timely security patching aligns with the broader concept of software hygiene, ensuring that organizations benefit from the latest security enhancements and optimizations. Organizations that prioritize software hygiene by regularly applying updates position themselves to reap the advantages of a more secure, efficient, and resilient computing environment.

The growing prevalence of supply chain attacks underscores the interconnected nature of the digital ecosystem. Software vendors and service providers are integral components of an organization's supply chain, and their security practices directly impact the security of end-users. Timely security patching reflects a collaborative approach between organizations and their vendors, emphasizing the shared responsibility for cybersecurity. By promptly applying patches provided by software vendors, organizations contribute to a collective defense against potential supply chain vulnerabilities, reinforcing the overall security posture of the digital ecosystem.

In conclusion, the importance of timely security patching cannot be overstated in the context of cybersecurity. Proactive patch management is a fundamental practice that aligns with principles of risk mitigation, compliance, and continuous improvement. By promptly addressing vulnerabilities, organizations fortify their defenses against cyber threats, protect sensitive data, and contribute to the broader security of interconnected networks. In an era where cyber adversaries are persistent and agile, organizations that prioritize timely security patching demonstrate a commitment to resilience, adaptability, and the safeguarding of digital assets.

Explore encryption mechanisms for protecting data at rest and in transit.

Encryption serves as a fundamental pillar of information security, playing a crucial role in safeguarding data at rest and in transit. Protecting sensitive information from unauthorized access and interception is paramount, and encryption provides a robust and effective means to achieve this goal.

Data at rest refers to information stored on physical or digital storage devices, such as hard drives, solid-state drives, or cloud storage. Encrypting data at rest involves transforming the stored information into a format that is unreadable without the appropriate decryption key. This ensures that even if an unauthorized entity gains access to the storage medium, the encrypted data remains incomprehensible and inaccessible. Full disk encryption is a widely used mechanism for securing data at rest, where the entire contents of a storage device, including the operating system and user files, are encrypted. Technologies like BitLocker for Windows, FileVault for macOS, and dm-crypt for Linux exemplify full disk encryption solutions. These technologies employ strong encryption algorithms to protect the confidentiality of stored data, ensuring that only authorized users with the correct decryption key can access the information.

In addition to full disk encryption, organizations often implement file-level encryption to selectively protect specific files or directories. This approach allows for more granular control over encryption policies, enabling organizations to secure only the most sensitive or confidential data. File-level encryption solutions typically provide features such as access controls and user-specific encryption keys, enhancing the overall security of stored information. Moreover, some cloud storage providers offer client-side encryption, where data is encrypted on the client device before being transmitted to the cloud. This ensures that even if the cloud service is compromised, the stored data remains encrypted and unreadable without the corresponding decryption key.

While encryption at rest focuses on securing data stored on physical or digital media, encrypting data in transit addresses the protection of information as it travels across networks. In transit, data is susceptible to interception by malicious entities, making encryption essential for maintaining the confidentiality and integrity of communication. Secure Sockets Layer (SSL) and its successor, Transport Layer Security (TLS), are widely adopted protocols for encrypting data in transit on the internet. These protocols establish a secure communication channel between a client and a server, encrypting the data exchanged during the communication process. SSL/TLS employ cryptographic algorithms and digital certificates to ensure the authenticity of the communicating parties and protect against eavesdropping or tampering.

Virtual Private Networks (VPNs) represent another powerful mechanism for encrypting data in transit, especially in the context of remote access and secure communication between geographically dispersed locations. VPNs create a secure tunnel over the internet, encrypting data as it traverses from the source to the destination. This ensures that even if the data is intercepted during transit, it remains encrypted and unreadable to unauthorized parties. VPNs are widely used for secure remote access to corporate networks and for establishing secure connections between branch offices.

End-to-end encryption (E2EE) is a concept that has gained prominence in recent years, particularly in the context of messaging and communication platforms. With E2EE, the content of messages or communications is encrypted on the sender's device and decrypted only on the recipient's device. This ensures that even the service provider facilitating the communication cannot access the unencrypted content. Popular messaging apps like Signal, WhatsApp, and Telegram implement end-to-end encryption, providing users with a high level of privacy and security in their communications.

Email encryption is another crucial aspect of protecting data in transit, given the pervasive use of email for business and personal communication. Technologies such as Pretty Good Privacy (PGP) and its open-source alternative, GNU Privacy Guard (GPG), enable users to encrypt and digitally sign their email messages. This ensures the confidentiality of the email content and verifies the authenticity of the sender. Additionally, secure email gateways and services often leverage Transport Layer Security (TLS) for encrypting email traffic in transit between mail servers, preventing unauthorized access or tampering during transmission.

The selection of appropriate encryption algorithms is a critical consideration in both data at rest and in transit scenarios. Advanced

Encryption Standard (AES) is widely regarded as a secure and efficient symmetric encryption algorithm for encrypting data. AES supports key lengths of 128, 192, and 256 bits, with longer key lengths providing stronger security. For asymmetric encryption, commonly used algorithms include RSA (Rivest–Shamir–Adleman) and Elliptic Curve Cryptography (ECC). Asymmetric encryption is often employed in key exchange mechanisms, where a secure communication channel is established by exchanging cryptographic keys without transmitting sensitive data.

Key management is an integral aspect of effective encryption implementation. Properly managing encryption keys ensures the security and usability of encrypted data. Symmetric encryption requires the secure distribution and storage of a shared secret key, while asymmetric encryption involves managing public and private key pairs. Key management practices include secure generation, storage, distribution, rotation, and revocation of cryptographic keys. Key escrow mechanisms, where a trusted third party securely stores encryption keys, are sometimes employed to ensure key recovery in case of accidental loss or other unforeseen circumstances.

The advent of quantum computing has raised concerns about the potential compromise of existing encryption algorithms. While current encryption standards remain secure against traditional computers, the emergence of quantum computers with the ability to break widely used encryption algorithms poses a future threat. Post-quantum cryptography research is underway to develop encryption algorithms that can resist attacks from quantum computers. Organizations need to stay abreast of developments in this area and be prepared to transition to quantum-resistant encryption algorithms as they become available.

Despite the evident benefits of encryption, there are challenges and considerations that organizations must navigate. Performance overhead, especially in resource-constrained environments, is a consideration, as encryption and decryption processes can introduce latency. However, advancements in hardware acceleration and optimized encryption algorithms mitigate these concerns. Compatibility and interoperability between different encryption implementations can also pose challenges, necessitating standardized protocols and formats for seamless integration across systems.

In conclusion, encryption stands as a linchpin in the realm of information security, providing a robust mechanism for protecting data at rest and in transit. Whether safeguarding stored information on physical or digital storage media or ensuring the secure transmission of data across networks, encryption plays a pivotal role in maintaining the confidentiality, integrity, and authenticity of information. As technologies evolve, encryption mechanisms continue to adapt to address emerging threats, emphasizing the ongoing importance of encryption in the ever-changing landscape of cybersecurity.

Discuss technologies such as secure boot and trusted computing.

Secure boot and trusted computing are technologies designed to enhance the security and integrity of computing systems, addressing vulnerabilities and threats that can compromise the boot process, operating system, and overall system integrity. These technologies play a pivotal role in establishing a trusted foundation for computing environments, ensuring that only authorized and unaltered components are executed during the system startup process.

Secure boot is a security feature that aims to prevent the execution of unauthorized code during the boot process. It is primarily implemented in the Unified Extensible Firmware Interface (UEFI), the modern successor to the traditional BIOS (Basic Input/Output System). The secure boot process involves the use of digital signatures to verify the integrity and authenticity of each component involved in the boot sequence, including the firmware, bootloader, and operating system kernel. This prevents the loading and execution of malicious or tampered code at the early stages of system initialization. Secure boot relies on the concept of a trusted Root of Trust (RoT), often implemented through a hardware-based mechanism like Trusted Platform Module (TPM), to store and manage cryptographic keys used in the verification process.

Trusted Platform Module (TPM) is a hardware-based security module that provides a secure and isolated environment for storing cryptographic keys, certificates, and other sensitive information. TPM is often integrated into the motherboard of a computing device and works in conjunction with secure boot and other security features. TPM contributes to the establishment of a hardware-based Root of Trust, ensuring the confidentiality and integrity of cryptographic operations. TPM can be utilized to store encryption keys used in disk encryption solutions, such as BitLocker in Windows or dm-crypt in Linux. It also plays a crucial role in attestation processes, where a system's security state is verified and reported to a trusted entity, establishing a foundation for trusted computing.

Trusted Computing is a broader concept that encompasses various technologies and principles aimed at creating a secure and trustworthy computing environment. At its core, trusted computing relies on the establishment of trust in the hardware and software components of a system. In addition to secure boot and TPM, trusted computing involves technologies such as Trusted Execution Environment (TEE), which provides isolated and secure execution environments for sensitive applications. TEEs, often implemented through technologies like Intel SGX (Software Guard Extensions) or ARM TrustZone, enable the execution of code in a secure enclave, isolated from the rest of the system, thereby protecting sensitive computations and data from external interference.

Remote Attestation is a key aspect of trusted computing, allowing a system to prove its trustworthiness to external entities. Through remote attestation, a computing device can generate a cryptographic attestation that verifies its secure boot, configuration, and integrity to a remote entity. This remote entity can be a server, network service, or any other system that requires assurance of the client's security posture. Remote attestation leverages cryptographic mechanisms to ensure the validity of the attestation and enables the establishment of secure and trusted communication channels between devices.

Measured Boot is a process within trusted computing that involves the continuous measurement and logging of the system's boot components. Each stage of the boot process, from the firmware to the operating system kernel, is measured and recorded in a secure manner. The resulting log, often stored in a secure enclave like TPM, serves as an attestation of the system's boot integrity. If any component in the boot chain is compromised or tampered with, the measured boot process can detect these changes and signal a potential security issue.

Intel Boot Guard is a technology designed to enhance secure boot by protecting the system firmware from unauthorized modifications. It relies on a hardware-based root of trust provided by Intel processors to verify the authenticity and integrity of the system firmware during the boot process. If the firmware is found to be unmodified and signed with a valid digital signature, Boot Guard allows the system to proceed with the boot process. This protects against firmware-level attacks and ensures that only authorized firmware is executed on the system.

Trusted Computing Group (TCG) is an industry consortium that develops and promotes open standards for trusted computing and security technologies. TCG has played a significant role in the development of specifications such as Trusted Platform Module (TPM) and Trusted Network Communications (TNC). These specifications provide a standardized framework for implementing trusted computing technologies across different hardware and software platforms, fostering interoperability and compatibility in the deployment of trusted computing solutions.

Intel Software Guard Extensions (SGX) is a technology that enables the creation of secure enclaves within the processor, allowing for the execution of code in an isolated and protected environment. SGX facilitates the development of applications that can run securely even in the presence of a compromised operating system or hypervisor. It ensures the confidentiality and integrity of sensitive computations by protecting them from external interference. SGX is a key component of trusted computing, providing a hardware-based enclave for secure execution and data protection.

Trusted computing technologies are particularly relevant in the context of cloud computing and remote services, where the assurance of system integrity and confidentiality is critical. In cloud environments, attestation mechanisms can be leveraged to verify the security posture of virtual machines or containers before allowing them to join a network or access sensitive data. Trusted computing principles help build trust between entities in a distributed and often untrusted environment, establishing a foundation for secure and reliable interactions.

Challenges in the implementation of trusted computing technologies include the need for standardized practices, compatibility across diverse hardware platforms, and addressing potential privacy concerns. The deployment of trusted computing may also introduce complexities related to key management, attestation policies, and the coordination of security features across heterogeneous systems. Furthermore, the evolving threat landscape requires continuous adaptation and enhancement of trusted computing technologies to address emerging risks and vulnerabilities.

In conclusion, secure boot, Trusted Platform Module (TPM), and trusted computing collectively contribute to the establishment of a secure and trustworthy computing environment. These technologies address vulnerabilities in the boot process, protect cryptographic keys, enable secure execution environments, and facilitate attestation for remote verification. Trusted computing is foundational in building trust in modern computing systems, offering resilience against a variety of threats and ensuring the confidentiality, integrity, and authenticity of sensitive information in both local and cloud-based environments. As the cybersecurity landscape evolves, trusted computing technologies continue to play a crucial role in fortifying the security posture of computing devices and services.

Discuss the role of security auditing and logging in operating systems.

Security auditing and logging constitute integral components of operating system security, serving as crucial mechanisms for monitoring, analyzing, and responding to security events. These practices contribute to the overall cybersecurity posture by providing visibility into system activities, detecting anomalous behavior, and facilitating post-incident analysis. Security auditing involves the systematic examination of security-relevant events, while logging captures and records these events for subsequent analysis and review. Together, they form a dynamic duo in the realm of cybersecurity, offering insights into the security landscape of operating systems.

Auditing encompasses the process of examining events and activities within an operating system to assess compliance with security policies, detect potential security incidents, and facilitate forensic analysis. Operating systems often include built-in auditing capabilities that allow administrators to define and configure which events to monitor. These events may range from user logins and file access to system configuration changes and network activities. Security auditing is instrumental in achieving accountability, as it provides a trail of evidence that can be used to trace actions back to specific users or processes. By capturing details about who did what and when, auditing aids in the identification of security policy violations and malicious activities.

Logging, on the other hand, involves the recording of events and activities in a log file for future reference and analysis. Operating systems maintain various logs, each serving a specific purpose, such as system logs, security logs, and application logs. The security log, in particular, is a focal point for capturing security-related events. Logging is crucial for preserving a historical record of system activities, enabling administrators and security professionals to review events retrospectively. Logs serve as a valuable resource for post-incident analysis, aiding in the identification of the root causes of security incidents, tracking the progression of attacks, and supporting forensic investigations.

The security audit trail created through auditing and logging is invaluable for compliance with regulatory requirements and industry standards. Many regulatory frameworks, such as the Payment Card Industry Data Security Standard (PCI DSS), Health Insurance Portability and Accountability Act (HIPAA), and General Data Protection Regulation (GDPR), mandate the implementation of robust auditing and logging practices. Compliance often involves regularly reviewing and analyzing logs, demonstrating due diligence in monitoring and responding to security events, and maintaining an auditable record of system activities. The audit trail serves as evidence of adherence to security policies and assists organizations in demonstrating compliance during audits or assessments.

User authentication and authorization events are fundamental components of security auditing, providing insights into who accesses the system and what actions they are authorized to perform. By monitoring login attempts, password changes, and privilege escalations, security auditing helps organizations detect unauthorized access and potential credential misuse. Failed login attempts, especially those repeated in quick succession, may indicate brute-force attacks or unauthorized access attempts, triggering alerts for further investigation. In the context of user authorization, auditing tracks changes in user permissions, ensuring that access controls are maintained and any unauthorized privilege changes are promptly identified.

File and resource access auditing is essential for tracking how files, directories, and system resources are accessed, modified, or deleted. Operating systems allow administrators to configure auditing policies to monitor specific file or directory activities, such as reads, writes, and deletions. This level of granularity is vital for identifying suspicious or unauthorized file access patterns, such as unexpected modifications to critical system files or unauthorized attempts to exfiltrate sensitive data. Security auditing in this context provides a layer of defense against insider threats, external attacks, and data breaches by detecting and responding to unauthorized access or manipulation of files and resources.

Configuration changes to the operating system and critical system components are prime targets for security auditing. Alterations to system settings, network configurations, and security policies can have significant security implications. Auditing these changes helps organizations maintain the integrity of their systems and ensures that modifications align with established security baselines. Unauthorized changes to system configurations may indicate attempts to compromise security controls, and auditing facilitates the rapid detection and response to such incidents. By tracking configuration changes, organizations can maintain a secure and compliant operational environment.

Network auditing plays a pivotal role in monitoring network activities and detecting potential security threats. Auditing network events, such as network connections, firewall rule modifications, and network traffic patterns, provides insights into network-based attacks and unauthorized communication. Unusual network traffic, patterns indicative of scanning or reconnaissance, and unexpected changes to firewall rules can be indicative of a security incident. Network auditing is particularly critical for identifying anomalies that may precede or accompany a cyberattack, enabling organizations to respond promptly and mitigate potential risks to their network infrastructure.

Application-level auditing focuses on monitoring events related to specific applications or services running on the operating system. This can include auditing database transactions, web server activities, and application-specific events. Application-level auditing is crucial for identifying abnormal behavior within applications that may indicate security vulnerabilities, unauthorized access, or potential exploitation. For example, auditing database transactions helps organizations track access to sensitive data and detect anomalous queries or data modifications that may signify a security breach. By integrating application-level auditing with overall security monitoring, organizations can gain a comprehensive view of their security landscape.

Security Information and Event Management (SIEM) solutions play a central role in aggregating, correlating, and analyzing logs from various sources, including operating systems. SIEM systems enhance the effectiveness of security auditing and logging by providing real-time visibility into security events and enabling rapid incident response. SIEM solutions automate the process of log analysis, generating alerts for suspicious activities or security incidents. Additionally, SIEM platforms facilitate the creation of dashboards, reports, and visualizations that offer insights into the overall security posture of the operating system. Organizations leverage SIEM solutions to streamline the monitoring and analysis of security events, improving their ability to detect and respond to potential threats.

Continuous monitoring and real-time alerting are critical aspects of effective security auditing and logging. Security incidents often unfold rapidly, requiring organizations to respond promptly to mitigate potential risks. Real-time alerting mechanisms notify security teams of suspicious activities, enabling them to investigate and respond swiftly. Alerts can be triggered based on predefined thresholds, patterns indicative of attacks, or deviations from established baselines. By combining continuous monitoring with automated alerting, organizations enhance their ability to detect and respond to security incidents in a timely manner, reducing the potential impact of security breaches.

Forensic analysis relies heavily on the wealth of information provided by security logs. In the aftermath of a security incident, organizations engage in forensic investigations to understand the scope of the incident, identify the root causes, and gather evidence for potential legal or regulatory proceedings. Security logs serve as a primary source of evidence in forensic analysis, offering a chronological record of events leading up to, during, and after a security incident. Forensic analysts leverage log data to reconstruct timelines, trace the activities of malicious actors, and ascertain the impact on the affected systems. The comprehensive information captured through security auditing and logging is instrumental in conducting thorough forensic investigations.

While security auditing and logging are powerful tools for enhancing the security posture of operating systems, challenges exist in their implementation and management. The sheer volume of log data generated by operating systems can be overwhelming, making it challenging to sift through and identify relevant security events. Efficient log management strategies, including log aggregation, retention policies, and storage optimization, are essential for handling large volumes of log data effectively. Moreover, ensuring the accuracy and integrity of logs is crucial, as tampered or incomplete log data can undermine the reliability of security monitoring and forensic analysis.

Security auditing and logging also pose challenges related to privacy considerations and compliance with data protection regulations. Logs may contain sensitive information, including user credentials, personal identifiers, and confidential data. Organizations must implement measures to safeguard the privacy of individuals whose information is captured in logs. This involves implementing access controls, encryption, and anonymization techniques to protect sensitive log data. Additionally, compliance with data protection regulations, such as GDPR, requires organizations to be transparent about the types of data collected, the purposes of data processing, and the retention periods for log data.

In conclusion, security auditing and logging play a pivotal role in fortifying the security posture of operating systems. These practices provide a systematic and comprehensive approach to monitoring, analyzing, and responding to security events. By examining user activities, network traffic, configuration changes, and application-specific events, security auditing and logging contribute to the detection of anomalies, identification of security incidents, and facilitation of forensic analysis. The integration of Security Information and Event Management (SIEM) solutions enhances the effectiveness of security monitoring, enabling real-time alerting and continuous analysis. While challenges exist in managing the volume of log data and addressing privacy considerations, the benefits of security auditing and logging in enhancing overall cybersecurity resilience are undeniable. As organizations navigate the evolving threat landscape, the proactive implementation of robust security auditing and logging practices remains a cornerstone of effective cybersecurity defense.

Emphasize the role of user awareness in maintaining operating system security.

User awareness stands as a linchpin in maintaining operating system security, playing a pivotal role in fostering a proactive and resilient cybersecurity culture within organizations. Operating systems, as the core software platforms facilitating user interactions with computing devices, are susceptible to various security threats, and the actions of users significantly impact the overall security posture. The dynamic threat landscape, characterized by evolving cyber threats and sophisticated attack vectors, necessitates a comprehensive approach to security that extends beyond technological safeguards. User awareness emerges as a critical component, encompassing the understanding of security best practices, the recognition of potential risks, and the adoption of responsible behaviors to mitigate security threats.

A fundamental aspect of user awareness is the comprehension of common security threats and attack vectors that can target operating systems. Users need to be educated about the diverse range of threats, including malware, phishing, ransomware, and social engineering tactics. Malware, encompassing viruses, trojans, and other malicious software, poses a persistent risk to operating systems, often exploiting vulnerabilities to compromise system integrity. Phishing attacks, where malicious actors attempt to deceive users into divulging sensitive information, are prevalent and can lead to unauthorized access or data breaches. Ransomware, a type of malware that encrypts files and demands payment for decryption, highlights the financial motivations of cybercriminals. Social engineering tactics involve manipulating individuals to divulge confidential information, emphasizing the human element as a potential weak link in the security chain. User awareness programs should comprehensively cover these threats, providing users with the knowledge to recognize and respond effectively to potential security risks.

Phishing attacks, in particular, underscore the importance of user awareness in preventing successful compromises. Users are often targeted through deceptive emails, messages, or websites that appear legitimate but are designed to trick them into revealing sensitive information or installing malicious software. User awareness campaigns should educate users on how to identify phishing attempts by scrutinizing email sender addresses, verifying website URLs, and recognizing common phishing tactics. By instilling a sense of skepticism and caution, users can become a formidable line of defense against phishing attacks, mitigating the risk of falling victim to social engineering tactics.

Understanding the role of passwords in securing operating systems is a foundational aspect of user awareness. Passwords serve as the first line of defense against unauthorized access, and users must be educated on the importance of creating strong, unique passwords. User awareness programs should emphasize the use of complex passwords that include a combination of uppercase and lowercase letters, numbers, and special characters. Additionally, users should be encouraged to avoid using easily guessable information, such as birthdays or common words, and to refrain from using the same password across multiple accounts. Implementing multi-factor authentication (MFA) further enhances security by requiring users to provide additional verification beyond passwords. User awareness initiatives should highlight the significance of MFA as a supplementary layer of protection, enhancing the resilience of operating systems against unauthorized access.

Regular software updates and patch management represent critical aspects of operating system security, and user awareness plays a pivotal role in ensuring timely updates. Users should be educated on the importance of applying software updates promptly, as updates often include security patches that address known vulnerabilities. Many cyberattacks exploit outdated software to gain unauthorized access or execute malicious code. User awareness programs should emphasize the role of software updates in fortifying the operating system against potential exploits, and users should be empowered to recognize and respond to update prompts promptly. Cultivating a culture of proactive update management contributes to the overall resilience of operating systems, reducing the risk of exploitation through known vulnerabilities.

The significance of user privileges and access controls cannot be overstated in maintaining operating system security. Users should be aware of the principle of least privilege, which advocates for providing individuals with the minimum level of access required to perform their tasks. Unrestricted administrative privileges can expose operating systems to elevated security risks, as malicious actors who gain control over an account with administrative privileges can potentially compromise the entire system. User awareness initiatives should educate users on the potential consequences of excessive privileges, promoting responsible use and adherence to access control policies. By understanding the implications of user privileges, individuals contribute to the creation of a secure operating environment that aligns with the principle of least privilege.

User awareness extends beyond technical considerations to encompass the protection of sensitive information and data. Users should be educated on the importance of safeguarding sensitive data, including personal information, intellectual property, and confidential documents. Security practices such as data encryption, secure file storage, and adherence to data protection policies contribute to the overall protection of sensitive information. Additionally, user awareness programs should emphasize the risks associated with removable media, such as USB drives, and caution users against unauthorized data transfers. By instilling a sense of responsibility for data protection, user awareness becomes a proactive defense against data breaches and unauthorized access to sensitive information.

Social engineering attacks, which exploit human psychology to manipulate individuals into divulging confidential information, highlight the critical role of user awareness in recognizing and resisting manipulation. Users should be educated on common social engineering tactics, such as pretexting, baiting, and quid pro quo, and be equipped with strategies to identify and thwart such attempts. Security awareness programs should emphasize the importance of verifying the identity of individuals requesting sensitive information and caution against sharing confidential details over the phone or through unsolicited communications. By fostering a heightened awareness of social engineering tactics, users become a formidable barrier against manipulation, reducing the likelihood of falling victim to deceptive schemes.

In the context of endpoint security, user awareness plays a crucial role in the recognition of indicators of compromise (IoCs) and potential security incidents. Users should be trained to identify unusual system behavior, unexpected error messages, or suspicious pop-ups that may indicate a security threat. Reporting mechanisms and incident response procedures should be clearly communicated to users, empowering them to promptly escalate potential security incidents to the appropriate authorities. By cultivating a sense of vigilance and responsiveness among users, organizations enhance their ability to detect and mitigate security incidents in their early stages, minimizing potential damage and disruption.

User awareness also extends to remote work scenarios, where the boundaries between personal and professional computing environments may blur. Remote workers should be educated on the importance of applying security best practices in their home offices, including the use of secure Wi-Fi networks, the implementation of virtual private networks (VPNs) for secure communication, and the adoption of endpoint security measures. Security awareness programs should address the unique challenges of remote work, emphasizing the need for heightened vigilance and adherence to security protocols in diverse computing environments. By extending user awareness to encompass remote work scenarios, organizations enhance their overall cybersecurity resilience in the face of evolving work paradigms.

Organizations can leverage simulated phishing exercises as part of their user awareness programs to provide hands-on experience and reinforce the principles of phishing detection. Simulated phishing campaigns allow organizations to assess the effectiveness of their user awareness initiatives by gauging users' responses to simulated phishing attempts. These exercises contribute to a continuous cycle of improvement, enabling organizations to tailor their awareness programs based on observed user behavior and responses. By incorporating simulated phishing exercises, organizations create a proactive and interactive learning environment that reinforces user awareness and prepares individuals to navigate real-world phishing threats effectively.

In conclusion, user awareness stands as a cornerstone in maintaining operating system security, transcending technical safeguards to empower individuals with the knowledge and behaviors necessary to mitigate security risks. From recognizing common security threats and adopting secure password practices to understanding the importance of software updates and adherence to access control policies, user awareness encompasses a spectrum of principles that collectively contribute to a resilient cybersecurity culture. By cultivating a heightened sense of responsibility, vigilance, and proactive engagement among users, organizations strengthen their overall security posture and create a human-centric defense against the dynamic and evolving landscape of cybersecurity threats. As technology continues to advance, user awareness remains a timeless and indispensable element in the ongoing effort to maintain the security and integrity of operating systems.

Discuss common challenges and complexities in securing operating systems.

Securing operating systems presents a multifaceted challenge characterized by a myriad of complexities stemming from the evolving threat landscape, diverse system architectures, and the need to balance security with usability. One of the enduring challenges is the constant proliferation of sophisticated malware and exploits targeting operating systems. Malicious actors exploit vulnerabilities in operating systems to gain unauthorized access, compromise system integrity, and execute malicious code. The race between security researchers and cybercriminals to discover and patch vulnerabilities adds a layer of complexity, as organizations must maintain a proactive stance in updating and patching systems to mitigate the risk of exploitation.

The heterogeneity of operating systems in use across diverse computing environments introduces a significant challenge in achieving uniform security standards. Organizations often manage a mix of operating systems, including Windows, macOS, Linux, and various mobile operating systems. Each platform has its own security mechanisms, vulnerabilities, and best practices, necessitating a nuanced and adaptive approach to security management. This diversity complicates efforts to implement consistent security policies, conduct unified security monitoring, and streamline incident response. Organizations must navigate the intricacies of securing a heterogeneous operating system landscape, striving to establish a cohesive security posture that addresses the unique attributes of each platform.

Another challenge in securing operating systems is the delicate balance between security and usability. Stringent security measures, such as complex authentication requirements and restrictive access controls, can impede user productivity and lead to user resistance. Conversely, overly permissive security configurations may introduce vulnerabilities that can be exploited by malicious actors. Striking the right balance involves understanding the operational needs of users, aligning security measures with organizational goals, and implementing user-friendly security practices. The challenge lies in designing security solutions that enhance protection without hindering user workflows, fostering a security culture that is embraced rather than resisted.

The prevalence of legacy systems poses a persistent challenge in operating system security. Many organizations continue to rely on outdated operating systems due to compatibility issues, legacy applications, or budget constraints. Legacy systems may lack support for modern security features and receive limited or no security updates, rendering them vulnerable to exploits and attacks. Securing legacy systems requires a strategic approach, including risk assessments, compensatory controls, and, when feasible, migration to more secure platforms. The coexistence of legacy and modern systems introduces complexities in maintaining a unified security posture, demanding continuous efforts to manage and mitigate associated risks.

Mobile devices, integral components of modern computing, introduce a unique set of challenges in operating system security. Mobile operating systems, such as Android and iOS, are targeted by a variety of mobile-specific threats, including malicious apps, mobile malware, and attacks exploiting device vulnerabilities. The diverse app ecosystems and the prevalence of Bring Your Own Device (BYOD) policies amplify the challenge of securing mobile devices. Organizations must navigate the complexities of mobile security, implementing measures such as mobile device management (MDM), app whitelisting, and secure containerization to safeguard sensitive data and ensure the integrity of mobile operating systems.

Cloud computing, with its transformative impact on IT infrastructure, introduces new challenges in operating system security. Cloud environments often leverage virtualization and containerization technologies, adding layers of abstraction that impact traditional security paradigms. Securing virtualized operating systems requires specialized approaches, including hypervisor security, virtual machine (VM) isolation, and secure container orchestration. Additionally, shared responsibility models in cloud computing necessitate collaboration between cloud service providers and organizations to ensure a cohesive security strategy. The dynamic nature of cloud environments, with on-demand resource provisioning and elastic scaling, adds complexity to security monitoring, incident detection, and response.

Access control complexities pose a significant challenge in securing operating systems, especially in large organizations with diverse user roles and access requirements. Striking a balance between granting users the necessary permissions to perform their duties and limiting privileges to reduce the attack surface is a delicate task. Role-based access control (RBAC) and least privilege principles aim to address these challenges by assigning permissions based on job roles and restricting access to the minimum necessary for users to perform their tasks. However, the dynamic nature of organizational structures, changes in job roles, and evolving access requirements introduce ongoing complexities in access control management. Regular reviews, audits, and adjustments are crucial for maintaining an effective and secure access control framework.

Endpoint security, encompassing the security of individual devices within a network, introduces complexities due to the diversity of endpoints and the evolving nature of threats. Securing endpoints involves protecting devices such as desktops, laptops, servers, and IoT devices, each with its own security considerations. Endpoint security solutions must address vulnerabilities, detect and prevent malware, and enforce security policies. The rise of remote work further complicates endpoint security, as organizations must extend security measures to devices outside traditional network perimeters. Balancing the need for comprehensive endpoint security with considerations for device performance, user experience, and remote accessibility presents an ongoing challenge.

Intrusion detection and prevention in operating systems are essential for identifying and mitigating security threats. However, the sheer volume of data generated by system logs, network traffic, and security events poses a challenge in distinguishing genuine security incidents from regular system activities. The complexity lies in deploying effective intrusion detection and prevention systems that can correlate diverse data sources, analyze patterns indicative of malicious behavior, and generate actionable alerts. Tuning these systems to minimize false positives without overlooking genuine threats requires continuous refinement and adaptation to the evolving threat landscape.

The global nature of cyber threats introduces geopolitical complexities in securing operating systems. Nation-state actors, cyber-criminal groups, and hacktivists operate on an international scale, leveraging sophisticated tactics to target organizations and governments. The attribution of cyber attacks, the coordination of international cybersecurity efforts, and the development of effective global cybersecurity policies are complex endeavors. Operating systems are exposed to threats that transcend borders, and securing them requires collaboration between nations, public-private partnerships, and a collective commitment to addressing cybersecurity challenges at a global scale.

Education and awareness are crucial elements in the security landscape, but they also present challenges in ensuring that users and IT professionals stay abreast of the evolving threat landscape and best practices. Continuous training and awareness programs are essential to equip users with the knowledge to recognize and respond to security threats. However, the fast-paced nature of cybersecurity, the emergence of new attack vectors, and the need for ongoing education make it challenging to maintain a consistently high level of awareness across organizations. Overcoming this challenge involves the development of dynamic, engaging, and regularly updated training programs that address the latest threats and empower users to become active participants in the organization's security posture.

Vendor management complexities add an additional layer of challenge in securing operating systems, particularly when relying on third-party software, components, or services. Organizations often integrate a multitude of software and hardware solutions from various vendors, each with its own security considerations. The challenge lies in assessing the security posture of third-party vendors, ensuring that they adhere to robust security practices, and mitigating potential risks associated with vulnerabilities in vendor-supplied products. Effective vendor management requires due diligence in evaluating security controls, establishing contractual security obligations, and maintaining continuous communication to address emerging security concerns.

In conclusion, securing operating systems presents a myriad of challenges and complexities that require a holistic and adaptive approach. From the persistent threat of evolving malware to the intricacies of managing diverse operating system environments, organizations must navigate a dynamic landscape. Balancing security with usability, addressing legacy systems, securing mobile and cloud environments, and managing access controls are ongoing challenges that demand strategic planning and continuous improvement. The complexities in vendor management, the global nature of cyber threats, and the need for effective education and awareness further underscore the multifaceted nature of operating system security. As technology continues to advance and threats evolve, organizations must remain vigilant, proactive, and collaborative to effectively secure their operating systems in the face of diverse and dynamic cybersecurity challenges.

Chapter 7: Operating Systems in the Mobile Era: From Smartphones to IoT

Define mobile operating systems and their role in powering smartphones and mobile devices.

Mobile operating systems form the bedrock of the modern digital landscape, playing a pivotal role in powering smartphones and a myriad of mobile devices. A mobile operating system (OS) is a specialized software platform designed to manage and facilitate the functioning of mobile devices, providing a framework for hardware interactions, application execution, and user interface interactions. The evolution of mobile operating systems has been closely intertwined with the rapid advancements in smartphone technology, shaping the user experience and capabilities of these ubiquitous devices.

At the core of a mobile operating system is the imperative to optimize performance, resource utilization, and power efficiency to cater to the constraints of mobile devices. One of the earliest and most influential mobile operating systems is Symbian, developed by Symbian Ltd. and later managed by the Symbian Foundation. Initially designed for PDAs and later adapted for smartphones, Symbian dominated the mobile OS market in the early 2000s. It introduced features like multitasking, customizable user interfaces, and support for third-party applications, setting the stage for the era of smartphones.

The advent of the iPhone in 2007 marked a seismic shift in the mobile landscape with the introduction of Apple's iOS. A proprietary mobile operating system developed exclusively for Apple's mobile devices, iOS revolutionized the smartphone experience with its touch-based interface, intuitive gestures, and the App Store ecosystem. iOS emphasized seamless integration between hardware and software, delivering a consistent and visually appealing user interface that set new standards for user experience in the mobile industry.

Concurrently, the open-source nature of the Android operating system, developed by the Open Handset Alliance led by Google, introduced a new paradigm of accessibility and customization. Android quickly emerged as a dominant force, powering a diverse range of devices from various manufacturers. The open nature of Android allowed device manufacturers to customize the OS to suit their hardware specifications, fostering a broad ecosystem of smartphones with varying features and price points. The Android Market, later rebranded as Google Play, became a vast repository of applications, contributing to the platform's popularity and adaptability.

Microsoft entered the mobile OS arena with Windows Mobile, offering a user-friendly interface and integration with Microsoft's ecosystem of productivity tools. However, Windows Mobile faced challenges in keeping pace with the rapidly evolving mobile landscape, leading to the introduction of Windows Phone in 2010. Windows Phone featured a distinctive tiled interface known as Metro, providing a fresh visual approach to mobile interactions. Despite its innovative design, Windows Phone struggled to gain significant market share, eventually leading to Microsoft's shift towards integrating mobile functionality into Windows 10.

As the mobile operating system landscape continued to evolve, BlackBerry OS, known for its secure communication features and physical keyboards, faced challenges in adapting to the touch-centric paradigm popularized by iOS and Android. BlackBerry OS eventually gave way to BlackBerry 10, an attempt to modernize the platform, but it failed to regain widespread consumer appeal.

The emergence of the Internet of Things (IoT) and the proliferation of connected devices led to the development of mobile operating systems beyond traditional smartphones. Tizen, an open-source operating system initiated by the Linux Foundation and championed by Samsung, found application in smart TVs, wearables, and other IoT devices. Similarly, KaiOS, a lightweight mobile operating system, gained traction in feature phones and devices aimed at bridging the digital divide in emerging markets.

In recent years, the mobile operating system landscape has witnessed the evolution of iOS and Android as the primary contenders in the smartphone market. iOS continues to be the exclusive operating system for Apple's iPhone and iPad devices, maintaining a cohesive user experience across the Apple ecosystem. Android, being an open-source platform, powers a vast array of smartphones from various manufacturers, offering diversity in hardware configurations, price points, and features.

Both iOS and Android have evolved with each iteration, introducing new features, enhancing security, and optimizing performance. iOS, known for its stringent control over hardware-software integration, has focused on delivering a premium and secure user experience. Android, with its emphasis on openness and customization, has implemented features such as Project Treble to streamline the software update process and enhance device longevity.

The mobile operating system landscape also witnessed the emergence of HarmonyOS, developed by Huawei as a multi-device operating system designed to unify experiences across smartphones, tablets, smart TVs, and other connected devices. HarmonyOS aims to provide a seamless and consistent user experience while supporting a diverse range of hardware.

The role of mobile operating systems extends beyond the core functionalities of smartphones to encompass a vast ecosystem of mobile applications. App stores, such as Apple's App Store and Google Play, serve as hubs for downloading and updating applications that enhance the capabilities of mobile devices. The app ecosystem has become a dynamic marketplace for developers, offering opportunities to innovate, reach global audiences, and monetize their creations.

Mobile operating systems also play a crucial role in shaping the security landscape of smartphones. Both iOS and Android have implemented security measures such as app sandboxing, secure boot processes, and biometric authentication to protect user data and ensure the integrity of the device. Regular software updates, often delivered over-the-air, address vulnerabilities and enhance the overall security posture of mobile devices.

The integration of mobile operating systems with cloud services has become a defining feature of the modern mobile experience. Features such as cloud backups, synchronization of settings and data, and seamless transitions between devices contribute to a cohesive and connected user experience. Mobile operating systems have evolved into integral components of broader ecosystems, connecting users across devices and services.

As mobile devices continue to evolve, mobile operating systems are expected to play a crucial role in supporting emerging technologies. The advent of 5G connectivity, augmented reality (AR), virtual reality (VR), and foldable displays presents new challenges and opportunities for mobile operating systems to optimize performance, enhance user experiences, and enable innovative applications.

In conclusion, mobile operating systems serve as the foundation of the contemporary digital era, powering the smartphones and mobile devices that have become indispensable in daily life. The evolution of mobile operating systems, from the early days of Symbian to the dominance of iOS and Android, reflects the dynamic interplay between hardware advancements, user experience design, and the ever-expanding ecosystem of mobile applications. These operating systems have not only transformed how we communicate, work, and entertain ourselves but have also become key enablers of connectivity, security, and innovation in the mobile landscape. The ongoing evolution of mobile operating systems is poised to shape the future of mobile technology, influencing how we interact with digital devices and navigate the interconnected world of tomorrow.

Trace the evolution of mobile operating systems from early handheld devices to smartphones.

The evolution of mobile operating systems from early handheld devices to smartphones is a captivating journey that mirrors the transformative trajectory of mobile technology. The story begins with the nascent days of mobile computing, where handheld devices were primarily designed for specific tasks and lacked the sophisticated operating systems we know today. In the late 20th century, devices like the Psion Organiser series and early Palm PDAs (Personal Digital Assistants) introduced the concept of handheld computing, featuring basic applications such as calendars, contacts, and notes. However, these devices were limited in their capabilities, running on proprietary operating systems with rudimentary functionalities.

The watershed moment in the evolution of mobile operating systems occurred with the introduction of the Simon Personal Communicator, often regarded as the first smartphone. Developed by IBM engineer Frank Canova Jr. and released in 1994, the Simon combined the features of a mobile phone with PDA functionalities. Its operating system, though basic by today's standards, represented a pioneering step towards the convergence of communication and computing. The Simon's touchscreen interface and the ability to make calls, send faxes, and manage contacts laid the groundwork for the multifunctional smartphones that would emerge in subsequent years.

The late 1990s witnessed the rise of Palm OS, a significant player in the early mobile operating system landscape. Palm OS powered the popular Palm Pilot series, offering a user-friendly interface and a suite of productivity applications. Palm OS devices became synonymous with handheld computing, showcasing the potential for mobile devices to extend beyond basic tasks. However, these devices were primarily PDAs with cellular capabilities rather than dedicated smartphones.

As the new millennium dawned, Nokia's Symbian OS emerged as a dominant force in mobile operating systems. Symbian, jointly developed by Nokia, Ericsson, Motorola, and Psion, became the foundation for a wide range of smartphones, including Nokia's iconic Communicator series. Symbian introduced features like multitasking, customizable home screens, and support for third-party applications, laying the groundwork for the smartphone era. The Nokia 9210 Communicator, released in 2000, exemplified the convergence of communication and computing with its QWERTY keyboard, color display, and the ability to run third-party applications.

While Symbian was making strides in Europe and Asia, a new player emerged in the United States that would redefine the smartphone landscape. In 2007, Apple unveiled the first iPhone, a device that revolutionized the concept of mobile computing. Running on the proprietary iOS, the iPhone introduced a touch-based interface, the App Store ecosystem, and a level of design sophistication that set a new standard for smartphones. iOS, with its seamless integration between hardware and software, transformed the user experience and propelled the iPhone to iconic status.

The success of the iPhone spurred intense competition, prompting other companies to reassess their mobile operating systems and design principles. Google entered the fray with Android, an open-source operating system developed by the Open Handset Alliance. Released in 2008, Android quickly gained traction for its flexibility, customization options, and support for a diverse range of devices. Android's adoption by various manufacturers contributed to the proliferation of smartphones with varying form factors, features, and price points.

The rivalry between iOS and Android defined the smartphone landscape in the following years, with each platform pushing the boundaries of innovation. iOS continued to refine its user interface, introduce new features, and expand its ecosystem with devices like the iPad. Android, with its regular updates and iterations named after desserts, evolved into a powerful and versatile platform. The Android Market, later rebranded as Google Play, became a bustling marketplace for applications, fostering a vibrant developer community.

Microsoft entered the smartphone arena with Windows Mobile, offering an operating system that aimed to integrate seamlessly with Windows desktop environments. However, Windows Mobile faced challenges in keeping pace with the rapid advancements in user expectations and the app ecosystem. In response, Microsoft introduced Windows Phone in 2010, featuring a distinctive tiled interface known as Metro. Despite its innovative design and user-centric approach, Windows Phone struggled to gain significant market share against the dominance of iOS and Android.

As the smartphone market matured, BlackBerry OS became synonymous with secure communication and enterprise use. BlackBerry devices, with their physical keyboards and robust security features, gained popularity among business professionals. However, BlackBerry faced challenges in adapting to the touch-centric paradigm popularized by iOS and Android. The introduction of BlackBerry 10 in 2013 aimed to modernize the platform, but it failed to regain widespread consumer appeal.

The evolution of mobile operating systems extended beyond smartphones to include other connected devices. Apple's iOS expanded to power the iPad and later the Apple Watch, creating a seamless ecosystem across devices. Google's Android diversified into various form factors, including tablets, smart TVs, and wearables.

The concept of a unified ecosystem became increasingly relevant, with users expecting a cohesive experience across their devices.

In the quest for a seamless multi-device experience, Huawei introduced HarmonyOS in 2019. HarmonyOS, designed as a multi-device operating system, aimed to provide a unified user experience across smartphones, tablets, smart TVs, and IoT devices. Huawei's vision was to create a flexible and adaptable platform that could transcend the limitations of individual device categories.

The concept of app ecosystems became a defining feature of mobile operating systems, influencing user preferences and brand loyalty. The App Store and Google Play, as well as alternative app markets, became central hubs for downloading and updating applications. The proliferation of apps transformed smartphones into versatile tools for communication, productivity, entertainment, and more.

The integration of cloud services became another hallmark of modern mobile operating systems. Features like cloud backups, synchronization of settings and data, and seamless transitions between devices contributed to a connected and cohesive user experience. The ability to access content and information across devices reinforced the idea of a continuous and integrated digital experience.

The advancement of mobile operating systems also intersected with the rollout of high-speed mobile networks. The transition from 3G to 4G and, subsequently, the deployment of 5G connectivity brought about new possibilities for mobile experiences. Faster data speeds, lower latency, and increased network capacity opened doors to augmented reality (AR), virtual reality (VR), and enhanced multimedia experiences.

In recent years, the mobile operating system landscape has witnessed the ongoing dominance of iOS and Android in the smartphone market. iOS, known for its closed ecosystem and emphasis on privacy and security, continues to power Apple's iPhone and iPad devices. Android, with its open-source nature and widespread adoption, remains the go-to platform for a diverse range of manufacturers and devices.

The evolution of mobile operating systems reflects not only technological advancements but also shifts in user behaviors, preferences, and societal expectations. From the early days of handheld devices with limited capabilities to the era of smartphones that serve as integral parts of our daily lives, the journey of mobile operating systems is a testament to the dynamic interplay between innovation, competition, and user-centric design. As we stand on the cusp of new technological frontiers, the evolution of mobile operating systems continues to shape the way we connect, communicate, and interact in the digital age.

Explore the architecture of smartphones and how mobile operating systems integrate with hardware.

The architecture of smartphones represents a sophisticated amalgamation of hardware and software components, meticulously designed to deliver a seamless user experience. At its core, a smartphone comprises several key hardware elements, with the central processing unit (CPU) standing as the proverbial brain. CPUs in modern smartphones are typically multi-core processors, exhibiting varying degrees of performance and power efficiency. Accompanying the CPU is the system-on-a-chip (SoC), an integrated circuit that consolidates various functions, including the CPU, graphics processing unit (GPU), memory management, and connectivity modules, thereby enhancing overall efficiency.

Memory, a critical component, is divided into RAM (Random Access Memory) for short-term data storage and internal storage for long-term data retention. The latter is often flash-based, ensuring rapid access times and data persistence. The display, a crucial user interface, is usually an organic light-emitting diode (OLED) or liquid crystal display (LCD) screen, characterized by high resolution and vibrant color reproduction. Touchscreens, often capacitive, facilitate user interaction by converting touch gestures into digital signals.

Mobile operating systems (OS) serve as the software foundation, seamlessly integrating with the smartphone's hardware to orchestrate its various functions. Two dominant players, Android and iOS, employ distinct architectures but share a common objective of optimizing hardware utilization. Android, an open-source OS developed by Google, is renowned for its versatility and compatibility with a myriad of devices. Its architecture includes the Linux kernel, responsible for core system operations, and a middleware layer facilitating communication between applications and the kernel.

iOS, the proprietary operating system developed by Apple, exhibits a more closed architecture, exclusively tailored for Apple devices. It encompasses a Unix-based foundation, providing a stable and secure environment. Both Android and iOS leverage a user interface framework, with Android utilizing XML-based layouts and iOS employing Interface Builder for designing intuitive interfaces.

The interaction between the OS and hardware is facilitated by device drivers, software components that enable communication between the OS and specific hardware peripherals. These drivers act as intermediaries, translating high-level OS commands into instructions that the hardware can execute. The kernel, residing at the core of the OS, plays a pivotal role in managing resources, executing processes, and maintaining system integrity.

Communication protocols, such as Bluetooth, Wi-Fi, and cellular connectivity standards like 4G and 5G, are integral to smartphones, enabling seamless data exchange between devices and networks. These protocols are supported by dedicated hardware modules, including radios and antennas, ensuring reliable and efficient wireless communication.

Power management is a critical aspect of smartphone architecture, given the limited energy capacity of batteries. Advanced power management units regulate the distribution of power to various components, optimizing energy consumption and prolonging battery life. Additionally, operating systems incorporate power-saving features and algorithms to intelligently manage background processes and device sleep states.

Sensors, including accelerometers, gyroscopes, proximity sensors, and ambient light sensors, enhance the smartphone's functionality by providing input for various applications. These sensors contribute to screen orientation adjustments, gaming experiences, and energy-efficient display brightness control.

Security is a paramount concern in smartphone architecture. Both hardware and software collaborate to safeguard user data and protect against unauthorized access. Secure boot processes, biometric authentication (such as fingerprint scanners and facial recognition), and encryption mechanisms ensure the confidentiality and integrity of user information.

The evolution of smartphones has witnessed the integration of artificial intelligence (AI) into their architecture. AI accelerators, specialized hardware designed for AI computations, enhance performance in tasks such as image recognition, language processing, and virtual assistants. Operating systems leverage AI algorithms for predictive text input, image enhancement, and adaptive battery management.

In conclusion, the architecture of smartphones is a nuanced interplay between sophisticated hardware components and intricately designed operating systems. The synergy between CPU, memory, display, connectivity modules, and sensors forms the backbone of the hardware, while mobile operating systems provide the intelligent interface to harness this hardware potential. The continuous advancement in both hardware and software domains ensures that smartphones remain at the forefront of technological innovation, providing users with increasingly powerful, versatile, and secure devices.

Discuss the app-centric nature of mobile operating systems.

The app-centric nature of mobile operating systems constitutes a foundational paradigm that has fundamentally transformed how users interact with their smartphones. At the heart of this architecture is the concept of mobile applications, small software programs designed to perform specific tasks, ranging from communication and productivity to entertainment and utility. Mobile operating systems, exemplified by giants like Android and iOS, have evolved to prioritize and optimize the user experience around these applications.

The app-centric nature is perhaps most evident in the graphical user interface (GUI) of mobile operating systems. Home screens are organized as a collection of app icons, each representing a distinct application installed on the device. Users navigate through these icons, tapping to launch apps and interact with their features. This design paradigm simplifies accessibility, allowing users to intuitively locate and use applications without delving into complex directory structures.

App stores are central to the app-centric nature of mobile operating systems. Google Play Store for Android and Apple's App Store for iOS serve as centralized hubs where users can discover, download, and update applications. These platforms provide a curated environment that ensures a level of security and quality control, assuring users that the apps they install adhere to certain standards. App stores have also become economic ecosystems, enabling developers to distribute and monetize their creations while offering users a vast array of choices.

The versatility of mobile applications is another key aspect of the app-centric paradigm. Whether it's social media, productivity tools, gaming, or specialized utilities, the diverse range of apps caters to nearly every conceivable need. This diversity is fostered by the development frameworks provided by mobile operating systems, allowing developers to create applications using standardized tools and languages.

Moreover, the app-centric nature has led to a dynamic and competitive app development landscape. Developers constantly innovate and iterate to deliver new functionalities and improved user experiences. This has resulted in a continuous cycle of app updates, ensuring that users benefit from the latest features, security patches, and performance enhancements. Mobile operating systems facilitate this process by providing robust frameworks and developer tools, fostering a community of creative minds pushing the boundaries of what smartphones can achieve.

Mobile operating systems prioritize multitasking capabilities, allowing users to seamlessly switch between multiple applications. This multitasking support enables users to run several apps simultaneously, enhancing efficiency and enabling a smoother workflow. Background processes and push notifications ensure that users stay connected and informed, even when not actively using a particular application.

Inter-app communication is another dimension of the app-centric nature. Mobile operating systems provide mechanisms, such as application programming interfaces (APIs), to enable apps to interact with each other. This allows for features like sharing content between apps, using data generated in one app within another, and creating a cohesive user experience that transcends individual application boundaries.

The app-centric paradigm extends beyond the core operating system to influence device manufacturers and hardware specifications. Devices are often designed with the app ecosystem in mind, featuring hardware configurations that optimize app performance. From powerful processors and ample RAM to high-resolution displays and advanced cameras, these specifications aim to enhance the user experience across a wide range of applications.

While the app-centric nature brings unprecedented convenience and functionality, it also raises challenges. Issues such as app discoverability, app quality assurance, and potential security vulnerabilities are considerations that mobile operating systems continually address. The app-centric model also necessitates effective resource management to ensure optimal performance, particularly as the complexity and capabilities of applications continue to grow.

In conclusion, the app-centric nature of mobile operating systems has redefined how users engage with their smartphones. This paradigm places applications at the forefront of the user experience, shaping the design principles of graphical interfaces, app stores, and multitasking capabilities. The dynamic and competitive landscape of app development, coupled with the continuous evolution of hardware specifications, ensures that mobile operating systems remain at the forefront of technological innovation, delivering a rich and diverse ecosystem of applications that cater to the varied needs of users worldwide.

Discuss the design principles of user interfaces in mobile operating systems.

The design principles of user interfaces (UI) in mobile operating systems represent a pivotal aspect of the overall user experience, shaping how individuals interact with their devices on a daily basis. At the core of these principles lies the pursuit of simplicity, an ethos that strives to streamline user interactions and minimize cognitive load. Simplicity is manifested in the clean and intuitive layout of graphical elements, with a focus on decluttered screens and easily comprehensible navigation. By reducing complexity, mobile UI design enhances accessibility for users of varying technological proficiency, fostering a more inclusive and user-friendly environment.

Consistency is another fundamental design principle that underlies the coherence of mobile operating system interfaces. Consistency ensures a uniform visual language and interaction patterns across different applications and system components, promoting a sense of familiarity for users. Icons, navigation gestures, and color schemes maintain consistency, allowing users to seamlessly transition between various apps without encountering abrupt shifts in design conventions. This principle contributes to a cohesive user experience, facilitating ease of use and reducing the learning curve associated with new applications.

Efficiency in user interaction is a key consideration in UI design for mobile operating systems. Designers aim to optimize workflows by minimizing the number of steps required to accomplish tasks. This involves strategically placing frequently used features within easy reach, employing intuitive gestures for navigation, and implementing shortcuts to expedite common actions. The pursuit of efficiency extends to responsiveness, with fluid animations and swift transitions contributing to a sense of immediacy and responsiveness, reinforcing a positive user perception.

Mobile UI design is deeply rooted in the principle of feedback, which involves providing users with clear and immediate responses to their actions. Visual and haptic feedback mechanisms convey acknowledgment of user input, ensuring that interactions feel tangible and responsive. From button presses to gestures, users rely on feedback cues to confirm the successful execution of their commands, enhancing the overall sense of control and confidence in the system.

Visual hierarchy is a design principle that guides users' attention to the most important elements on the screen. Through the strategic use of size, color, contrast, and typography, designers create a visual hierarchy that guides users through the interface in a logical and intuitive manner. This principle ensures that essential information and interactive elements stand out, facilitating efficient information processing and navigation. By establishing a clear visual hierarchy, mobile UI design empowers users to quickly grasp the structure of content and prioritize their focus accordingly.

Accessibility is a foundational principle that underscores the importance of designing interfaces that cater to users with diverse needs and abilities. Mobile operating systems incorporate features such as adjustable font sizes, screen readers, and voice commands to ensure inclusivity. The design also considers color contrast and legibility, accommodating users with visual impairments. Accessibility principles not only enhance the usability of mobile interfaces for all users but also align with ethical considerations, promoting digital inclusivity.

The concept of affordance plays a crucial role in mobile UI design by ensuring that on-screen elements communicate their intended functionality. Affordances are visual cues that suggest how users should interact with an element. For instance, buttons should appear tactile, inviting users to tap, while sliders should imply drag-and-drop interactions. By incorporating clear and intuitive affordances, mobile UI design minimizes the need for explicit instructions, enabling users to instinctively understand how to navigate and interact with the interface.

Mobile UI design also emphasizes the importance of user feedback and iterative refinement. Designers leverage user testing, feedback loops, and analytics to continuously refine and enhance the user interface based on real-world usage patterns and user preferences. This iterative approach enables designers to adapt to evolving user expectations, technological advancements, and emerging trends, ensuring that the interface remains relevant and effective over time.

Personalization is a contemporary design principle that acknowledges the diverse preferences and habits of users. Mobile operating systems offer customization options, allowing users to personalize their home screens, app layouts, and even system-wide themes. This principle recognizes the importance of tailoring the user experience to individual preferences, enhancing user engagement and satisfaction.

In conclusion, the design principles of user interfaces in mobile operating systems reflect a holistic approach that prioritizes simplicity, consistency, efficiency, feedback, visual hierarchy, accessibility, affordance, user feedback, and personalization. These principles collectively contribute to the creation of interfaces that are not only aesthetically pleasing but also highly functional and user-centric. As mobile technology continues to advance, these design principles will undoubtedly evolve to meet the ever-changing expectations of users, ensuring that mobile interfaces remain at the forefront of usability and innovation.

Discuss security challenges specific to mobile operating systems.

Security challenges specific to mobile operating systems represent an intricate and ever-evolving landscape, where the ubiquity of smartphones has made them prime targets for various cyber threats. One prominent challenge lies in the diverse ecosystem of mobile devices and operating systems. Unlike the relatively homogenous environment of desktop computers, the mobile landscape encompasses a myriad of devices running different versions of operating systems, often customized by manufacturers or network carriers. This diversity introduces complexities in ensuring consistent security updates and patches, leaving a sizable portion of devices vulnerable to known exploits.

App store security is another critical concern, as mobile users primarily obtain applications from centralized repositories such as Google Play Store for Android and the App Store for iOS. While these platforms implement stringent app review processes, malicious applications occasionally slip through the cracks, posing threats to user privacy and device integrity. The phenomenon of "app cloning" or counterfeit apps further exacerbates this challenge, as users may inadvertently download malicious replicas of legitimate applications, unknowingly exposing themselves to security risks.

Mobile malware represents a persistent and evolving threat that specifically targets vulnerabilities in mobile operating systems. Malicious software, including trojans, ransomware, and spyware, seeks to exploit vulnerabilities in operating systems or applications to compromise user data, financial information, or even take control of the device. The dynamic nature of the mobile landscape, with frequent operating system updates and the introduction of new features, requires a proactive and adaptive approach to combat emerging malware threats.

The prevalence of mobile phishing attacks adds another layer of complexity to the security landscape. Cybercriminals employ sophisticated techniques to deceive users into divulging sensitive information, such as login credentials or financial details. Mobile phishing often involves deceptive emails, text messages, or fraudulent websites designed to mimic legitimate platforms, exploiting users' trust and familiarity with mobile interfaces. Educating users about phishing risks and implementing robust anti-phishing measures within mobile operating systems are essential components of mitigating this security challenge.

The inherent nature of mobile devices, frequently connected to various networks and utilizing diverse communication protocols, exposes them to network-based attacks. Man-in-the-middle attacks, where an attacker intercepts and potentially alters communication between two parties, are of particular concern in mobile environments. Public Wi-Fi networks, commonly used by mobile users, present additional vulnerabilities, as attackers can exploit unsecured connections to eavesdrop on sensitive data transmissions. Implementing secure communication protocols, such as HTTPS, and promoting user awareness about the risks associated with public Wi-Fi are crucial steps in addressing network-based security challenges.

The issue of device theft or loss poses a unique security challenge for mobile operating systems. Beyond the immediate loss of the physical device, the potential compromise of sensitive data and unauthorized access to personal information become significant concerns. Mobile operating systems incorporate features such as remote lock, wipe, and tracking functionalities to mitigate these risks. However, user awareness and adoption of these security measures remain essential, emphasizing the need for effective communication and education regarding device security practices.

Biometric authentication, while enhancing the overall security posture of mobile devices, introduces its own set of challenges. The reliance on fingerprint sensors, facial recognition, or other biometric methods necessitates robust protection mechanisms to safeguard the biometric data stored on the device. Additionally, the potential for biometric data interception or spoofing raises concerns about the overall effectiveness of these authentication methods. Striking a balance between user convenience and robust security measures is a constant challenge in the evolution of biometric authentication within mobile operating systems.

The concept of mobile payment security is gaining prominence with the increasing adoption of digital wallets and mobile payment solutions. While these technologies offer convenience and efficiency, they also attract the attention of cybercriminals seeking to exploit vulnerabilities in payment processes. Security challenges include the potential compromise of payment credentials, unauthorized transactions, and the security of Near Field Communication (NFC) technology used in contactless payments. Ensuring the encryption of payment data, implementing secure authentication mechanisms, and collaborating with financial institutions to detect and prevent fraudulent activities are integral aspects of addressing these challenges.

The intersection of mobile devices with Internet of Things (IoT) ecosystems introduces additional security complexities. Mobile operating systems often serve as the control interfaces for IoT devices, creating a potential attack vector for cybercriminals aiming to compromise interconnected systems. Vulnerabilities in IoT devices, coupled with insufficient security measures in mobile operating systems, could lead to unauthorized access, data breaches, or even the manipulation of physical IoT devices. A comprehensive security framework must encompass both mobile operating systems and IoT devices to mitigate these evolving challenges.

User privacy concerns represent an overarching theme in the security landscape of mobile operating systems. The extensive collection of user data, ranging from location information and browsing habits to personal preferences and contact lists, raises ethical and regulatory considerations. Mobile operating systems must strike a delicate balance between providing personalized services and protecting user privacy. Increasing scrutiny from regulatory bodies worldwide has led to the implementation of measures such as enhanced user consent mechanisms, transparent data practices, and stricter controls over data access by third-party applications.

In conclusion, the security challenges specific to mobile operating systems underscore the dynamic and multifaceted nature of the contemporary threat landscape. The diverse ecosystem of devices, the proliferation of mobile malware, the sophistication of phishing attacks, network vulnerabilities, device theft, biometric authentication concerns, mobile payment security, IoT integration, and user privacy considerations collectively demand a comprehensive and adaptive approach to mobile security. As technology continues to advance, collaboration between industry stakeholders, ongoing research and development, and user education will play pivotal roles in addressing and mitigating these challenges, ensuring the continued trust and resilience of mobile operating systems.

Explore the role of operating systems in the context of IoT devices.

The role of operating systems in the context of Internet of Things (IoT) devices is pivotal, serving as the underlying software infrastructure that enables the seamless integration, management, and functionality of a diverse array of interconnected devices. IoT, at its core, involves the interconnection of physical objects embedded with sensors, actuators, and communication capabilities, and operating systems play a crucial role in orchestrating these components to create a cohesive and intelligent ecosystem.

One fundamental aspect of the role of operating systems in IoT devices is resource management. Unlike traditional computing devices, many IoT devices operate with constrained resources, including limited processing power, memory, and energy. Operating systems designed for IoT must efficiently allocate these resources to ensure optimal performance and longevity of the devices. This resource optimization is particularly critical for battery-powered IoT devices, where energy-efficient operations play a vital role in prolonging battery life.

In the context of IoT, operating systems often need to support a wide range of hardware architectures and communication protocols. IoT ecosystems comprise devices with diverse functionalities, ranging from simple sensors to complex actuators. The operating system acts as an abstraction layer, allowing developers to create applications that can run seamlessly across various IoT devices, regardless of their specific hardware specifications. This abstraction facilitates interoperability within the IoT ecosystem, enabling devices from different manufacturers to work together harmoniously.

Security is a paramount concern in the IoT landscape, given the potential consequences of unauthorized access, data breaches, and manipulation of connected devices. Operating systems for IoT devices must incorporate robust security measures, including secure boot processes, encryption of communication channels, and mechanisms for secure storage of sensitive data. These security features are essential to safeguard against cyber threats and ensure the integrity and confidentiality of data transmitted and processed within the IoT network.

Interconnectivity is a defining characteristic of IoT, and operating systems play a central role in managing communication between devices. Protocols such as MQTT (Message Queuing Telemetry Transport) and CoAP (Constrained Application Protocol) are commonly used in IoT operating systems to facilitate efficient and lightweight communication between devices. The operating system acts as the mediator, enabling devices to exchange data, status updates, and commands, thereby fostering the collaborative functionality of the IoT ecosystem.

The scalability of operating systems is paramount in the context of IoT, where the number of connected devices can range from a few to potentially millions. Scalable operating systems can efficiently handle the growing complexity of IoT deployments, supporting the addition of new devices without compromising overall performance. This scalability is crucial for the expansion of IoT applications in various domains, including smart cities, industrial automation, healthcare, and agriculture.

Real-time capabilities are often essential in IoT applications where timely and accurate responses are critical. Operating systems designed for real-time processing ensure that IoT devices can meet stringent timing requirements, making them suitable for applications such as industrial automation, autonomous vehicles, and healthcare monitoring. Real-time operating systems (RTOS) provide deterministic behavior, ensuring that tasks are executed within predefined time constraints, contributing to the reliability and predictability of IoT systems.

The role of operating systems extends to facilitating over-the-air (OTA) updates for IoT devices. Given the distributed nature of IoT deployments, updating device firmware or software manually can be impractical. Operating systems with built-in support for OTA updates enable seamless and secure delivery of patches, bug fixes, and new features, ensuring that IoT devices remain up-to-date with the latest improvements and security enhancements.

Edge computing, an essential component of many IoT architectures, involves processing data closer to the source, reducing latency and conserving bandwidth. Operating systems designed for edge computing enable IoT devices to perform local data processing and analysis, minimizing the need for constant communication with centralized servers. This decentralized approach enhances the efficiency and responsiveness of IoT applications, particularly in scenarios where low-latency responses are crucial.

The role of operating systems in IoT extends beyond the device level to include gateway devices that serve as intermediaries between IoT devices and cloud services. These gateways often run sophisticated operating systems capable of managing multiple communication protocols, processing data locally, and facilitating secure connections between IoT devices and cloud platforms. Operating systems for gateways play a crucial role in aggregating and transmitting data from diverse IoT endpoints to cloud services for further analysis and storage.

In the context of industrial IoT (IIoT), operating systems play a vital role in enabling the convergence of operational technology (OT) and information technology (IT). Operating systems designed for IIoT must accommodate the unique requirements of industrial environments, including real-time control systems, robust security measures, and compatibility with legacy industrial protocols. These specialized operating systems contribute to the integration of IIoT solutions, enhancing efficiency, productivity, and automation in industrial settings.

The development of IoT applications often involves programming languages and frameworks that cater to the constraints of resource-limited devices. Operating systems must provide support for these development environments, fostering the creation of applications that can run efficiently on IoT devices. Additionally, operating systems for IoT should offer tools and libraries that simplify the development process, accelerating the time-to-market for IoT solutions.

As the IoT landscape evolves, the role of operating systems is closely intertwined with the ongoing development of standards and protocols. Standardization efforts aim to ensure interoperability, security, and consistency across diverse IoT ecosystems. Operating systems that adhere to established standards contribute to the creation of a cohesive and well-defined IoT framework, enabling seamless integration and collaboration among devices from different vendors.

In conclusion, the role of operating systems in the context of IoT devices is multifaceted and integral to the functionality, security, and scalability of interconnected systems. Operating systems for IoT must address the challenges of resource constraints, support diverse hardware architectures, ensure robust security measures, facilitate efficient communication, enable real-time capabilities, and adapt to the evolving landscape of IoT applications. The continuous evolution of operating systems in tandem with the dynamic requirements of IoT will play a crucial role in shaping the future of interconnected and intelligent devices across various domains.

Discuss how operating systems power wearable devices.

The powering of wearable devices is intricately tied to the role of operating systems, marking a convergence of miniaturized computing, sensor technology, and user-centric design. Wearables, ranging from smartwatches and fitness trackers to augmented reality glasses, have gained prominence as personal companions that seamlessly integrate into users' daily lives. At the heart of these devices is the operating system, a critical software layer that orchestrates hardware components, enables applications, and shapes the overall user experience.

One of the fundamental functions of operating systems in wearables is resource management. Given the inherently constrained nature of wearable devices in terms of processing power, memory, and battery life, operating systems play a crucial role in efficiently allocating and utilizing these resources. Wearable operating systems must strike a delicate balance between delivering optimal performance and ensuring energy efficiency to extend battery life, a particularly critical consideration given the limited physical space available for battery capacity in wearables.

User interface design is a key aspect of wearable operating systems, as these devices often feature compact displays and touch-sensitive surfaces. The operating system must provide an intuitive and user-friendly interface that accommodates the reduced screen real estate while ensuring ease of navigation and interaction. Gesture controls, voice commands, and innovative input methods become integral components of wearable user interfaces, all managed and facilitated by the operating system to enhance the user experience.

The seamless integration of sensors is a hallmark of wearable devices, enabling functionalities such as activity tracking, heart rate monitoring, and environmental sensing. Wearable operating systems must support a diverse array of sensors and manage their data streams effectively. From accelerometers and gyroscopes to heart rate monitors and GPS modules, these sensors contribute to the rich tapestry of information that wearables utilize to provide users with actionable insights and personalized experiences.

Connectivity is a pivotal aspect of wearable operating systems, enabling wearables to communicate with other devices, sync data with cloud services, and receive real-time updates. Bluetooth and Wi-Fi connectivity are commonplace in wearables, and the operating system must handle the intricacies of pairing, data transfer, and network interactions. Wearables often serve as extensions of smartphones, and operating systems facilitate the seamless integration of these devices into broader connected ecosystems.

Operating systems for wearables must prioritize real-time capabilities, particularly in devices designed for health and fitness tracking or augmented reality experiences. The ability to process and respond to data with low latency is critical for applications that require immediate user feedback, such as step counting, gesture recognition, or augmented reality overlays. Real-time operating systems (RTOS) or features that ensure timely execution of tasks contribute to the responsiveness and effectiveness of wearables in dynamic scenarios.

Wearable operating systems are integral to ensuring data security and privacy. Given the intimate nature of wearables, which often track health metrics and store personal information, robust security measures are paramount. Encryption of data, secure authentication mechanisms, and protection against unauthorized access are crucial aspects of wearable operating systems. As wearables continue to evolve into essential tools for health monitoring and daily life, maintaining user trust through stringent security practices is imperative.

Customization and personalization are key considerations in the design of wearable operating systems. Wearables cater to diverse user preferences and lifestyles, and the operating system must accommodate these variations. From customizable watch faces and app layouts to personalized health and fitness goals, wearables aim to provide users with a tailored experience. The operating system serves as the foundation for implementing these customization features, allowing users to configure their wearables to align with their individual needs and preferences.

The app ecosystem is a vibrant component of wearable operating systems, offering a diverse range of applications tailored for the unique capabilities of wearables. Whether it's fitness apps, productivity tools, or notifications from messaging services, wearables extend their functionality through a curated selection of applications.

The operating system manages the installation, execution, and interaction with these apps, ensuring a cohesive and integrated experience for users.

Updates and maintenance are critical aspects of wearable operating systems, ensuring that devices remain current with the latest features, security patches, and improvements. Over-the-air (OTA) updates are a common mechanism by which wearable operating systems deliver these enhancements without requiring manual intervention from users. The ability to seamlessly update the operating system and applications contributes to the longevity and relevance of wearables in an ever-evolving technological landscape.

The role of artificial intelligence (AI) is increasingly prominent in wearable operating systems. AI algorithms enable wearables to analyze and interpret sensor data, providing insights into user behavior, health trends, and contextual information. From smartwatches that offer predictive text responses to fitness trackers that adapt workout recommendations based on user performance, AI-driven features enhance the capabilities and intelligence of wearables, enriching the overall user experience.

Interoperability is a critical consideration for wearable operating systems, especially as wearables often complement other devices in users' lives. Whether it's syncing health data with a smartphone or integrating with smart home systems, wearables need to seamlessly interact with various platforms and devices. Standardization efforts and support for common communication protocols enable wearables to function harmoniously within broader ecosystems, fostering a cohesive and interconnected user experience.

The evolution of wearables extends beyond traditional form factors, with innovations such as smart clothing, smart eyewear, and even implantable devices entering the landscape. Wearable operating systems must adapt to diverse hardware configurations, accommodating the unique challenges posed by unconventional device designs. The flexibility to support a wide range of wearable types reflects the adaptability and scalability of operating systems in this dynamic and rapidly evolving domain.

In conclusion, the role of operating systems in powering wearable devices is multi-faceted, encompassing resource management, user interface design, sensor integration, connectivity, real-time capabilities, security, customization, app ecosystems, updates, AI integration, interoperability, and adaptability to diverse form factors. Operating systems serve as the foundational layer that enables wearables to deliver a seamless and intelligent user experience, whether it's tracking health metrics, providing timely notifications, or enhancing daily productivity. As wearables continue to advance, the role of operating systems will remain central in shaping the future of these devices and their integration into our connected lives.

Explore how mobile operating systems extend to tablets and hybrid devices.

The extension of mobile operating systems to tablets and hybrid devices represents a paradigm shift in the computing landscape, blurring the lines between traditional personal computers and portable, touch-enabled devices. Mobile operating systems, initially designed for smartphones, have undergone substantial evolution to accommodate the larger form factors and diverse functionalities of tablets and hybrid devices, such as 2-in-1 laptops and convertible tablets. This evolution reflects the increasing demand for versatile computing experiences that seamlessly transition between productivity, entertainment, and portability.

At the core of the extension of mobile operating systems is the adaptation to larger screens. Tablets, with their expansive displays, necessitate user interfaces that capitalize on the additional real estate. Mobile operating systems, such as Android and iOS, have undergone interface optimizations to leverage the larger canvas, allowing for more comprehensive multitasking, enhanced content consumption, and improved navigation. The fluidity of touch gestures, initially tailored for smartphones, has been refined to accommodate the nuances of touch interaction on larger tablet screens, providing users with a more immersive and intuitive experience.

The expansion to tablets brings forth the challenge of optimizing applications for diverse screen sizes. Mobile operating systems have introduced frameworks and guidelines for developers to create responsive and adaptive applications that seamlessly scale across different form factors. This ensures that users can enjoy a consistent experience whether they are interacting with an app on a compact smartphone or a larger tablet. The adaptability of mobile operating systems to varying screen sizes contributes to the versatility of tablets and enhances their appeal for both productivity and entertainment purposes.

The convergence of mobile operating systems with tablets extends beyond mere screen size considerations; it encompasses the integration of productivity features traditionally associated with personal computers. The introduction of multitasking interfaces, split-screen views, and improved file management systems are examples of how mobile operating systems have evolved to meet the demands of users seeking enhanced productivity on tablets. These features enable users to perform tasks such as document editing, content creation, and research more efficiently, positioning tablets as viable alternatives for certain professional workflows.

Hybrid devices, combining the features of both tablets and laptops, have gained prominence in the market. Mobile operating systems have adapted to the hybrid form factor by incorporating features that cater to the dual nature of these devices. For instance, the introduction of keyboard and trackpad support in mobile operating systems like iPadOS and Android has transformed tablets into versatile 2-in-1 devices, blurring the boundaries between tablets and traditional laptops. This integration allows users to seamlessly switch between touch-based interactions and traditional input methods, offering flexibility in how they approach various tasks.

The expansion to tablets has also prompted advancements in stylus or pen input support within mobile operating systems. Drawing inspiration from the stylus-centric features of professional graphics tablets, mobile operating systems have incorporated functionalities that enhance creative expression and note-taking on tablets. Features like pressure sensitivity, palm rejection, and advanced gesture recognition contribute to a more natural and immersive stylus experience, appealing to artists, designers, and professionals seeking a portable and versatile creative tool.

The integration of tablet-specific features within mobile operating systems extends to device management and security. As tablets are often shared devices within households or organizations, mobile operating systems have introduced features like multi-user support and robust user authentication mechanisms. These features enable personalized user experiences for multiple individuals sharing a single tablet, while ensuring secure access to sensitive data. Device management functionalities, such as remote wipe and security policies, add an additional layer of control for organizations deploying tablets in enterprise settings.

Mobile operating systems have embraced the potential of tablets as educational tools. The adaptability of these systems to the education sector is evident in features like digital textbooks, collaborative learning applications, and classroom management tools. Educational content providers and developers have capitalized on the tablet ecosystem, creating interactive and engaging learning experiences that leverage the mobility, touch interactivity, and multimedia capabilities of tablets. Mobile operating systems play a pivotal role in fostering a digital learning environment that goes beyond traditional educational paradigms.

The seamless integration of mobile operating systems with tablets has also impacted the entertainment industry. The larger screens and enhanced multimedia capabilities of tablets offer an immersive platform for consuming content such as movies, TV shows, and games. Mobile operating systems provide app developers with tools to optimize their offerings for tablet displays, ensuring a captivating and enjoyable user experience. The proliferation of streaming services, gaming platforms, and interactive content has been facilitated by the adaptability of mobile operating systems to the tablet form factor.

In the realm of healthcare, the extension of mobile operating systems to tablets has facilitated the development of applications that enhance patient care, medical research, and health monitoring. Tablets serve as versatile tools for healthcare professionals, allowing them to access electronic health records, view medical imaging, and engage in telemedicine. The touch-enabled interface of tablets, coupled with the power of mobile operating systems, has led to the creation of innovative healthcare solutions that improve efficiency, accuracy, and patient outcomes.

Accessibility features within mobile operating systems have also played a significant role in extending the usability of tablets to a broader audience, including individuals with diverse abilities. Features such as screen readers, voice commands, and magnification tools empower users with visual or motor impairments to navigate and interact with tablets. The commitment to accessibility aligns with the inclusive design principles that prioritize making technology accessible to users with varying needs, ensuring that the benefits of tablets are available to all.

The extension of mobile operating systems to tablets has not been limited to consumer-oriented devices; it has also influenced the rugged tablet market. Industries such as logistics, manufacturing, and field services have adopted rugged tablets equipped with mobile operating systems for their durability, portability, and adaptability to challenging environments. These ruggedized tablets, running on mobile operating systems, provide reliable solutions for professionals working in harsh conditions, where traditional computers may be impractical.

As tablets continue to evolve, the synergy between mobile operating systems and these devices remains dynamic. The collaborative efforts of hardware manufacturers, application developers, and operating system providers have contributed to a diverse ecosystem of tablets catering to various use cases and user preferences. The extension of mobile operating systems to tablets has not only broadened the scope of these systems but has also redefined how users approach computing, emphasizing flexibility, mobility, and the convergence of productivity and entertainment in a singular device.

Discuss current and future trends in mobile operating systems.

The current landscape of mobile operating systems is characterized by a dynamic interplay of technological advancements, user expectations, and industry competition, shaping the present and laying the groundwork for future trends. One prominent trend is the continual evolution of user interfaces, with an emphasis on enhancing user experiences across devices. Both Android and iOS have embraced gestures, contextual menus, and streamlined navigation paradigms, reflecting a shift towards more intuitive and seamless interactions. The pursuit of a unified user experience across smartphones, tablets, and hybrid devices signifies a departure from rigid design conventions, fostering a more cohesive and adaptable interface that caters to the diverse needs of users.

Another prevailing trend is the emphasis on privacy and security within mobile operating systems. In response to heightened concerns about data breaches and unauthorized access, both Android and iOS have implemented robust privacy features. These include granular app permissions, enhanced encryption protocols, and privacy indicators to inform users about data access by apps. The evolving regulatory landscape, such as the implementation of GDPR in Europe, has prompted mobile operating systems to prioritize user privacy, giving individuals more control over their data and raising the bar for app developers in terms of transparency and responsible data handling practices.

The integration of artificial intelligence (AI) and machine learning (ML) into mobile operating systems represents a transformative trend with far-reaching implications. Both Android and iOS leverage AI and ML algorithms to enhance various aspects of the user experience, from predictive text suggestions and voice recognition to personalized recommendations in applications. As AI capabilities continue to advance, mobile operating systems are expected to further integrate smart features, such as context-aware assistance, intelligent automation, and even more sophisticated predictive functionalities that anticipate user needs based on behavioral patterns.

The advent of 5G technology is reshaping the capabilities of mobile operating systems, ushering in an era of faster data speeds, lower latency, and increased network capacity. Both Android and iOS are adapting to harness the potential of 5G, enabling new possibilities for real-time communication, augmented reality (AR), and immersive multimedia experiences. The enhanced connectivity facilitated by 5G is expected to influence the development of applications, with a focus on leveraging the low-latency network for emerging technologies like cloud gaming, remote collaboration, and high-bandwidth content streaming.

Cross-platform compatibility and interoperability have emerged as key trends, reflecting a growing desire for seamless integration between different devices and ecosystems. Both Android and iOS are exploring avenues to facilitate cross-device experiences, allowing users to transition seamlessly between smartphones, tablets, laptops, and other connected devices. Initiatives such as Apple's Continuity and Google's efforts in creating a unified app platform for both Android and Chrome OS exemplify the industry's push towards a more integrated and harmonious ecosystem.

Continuing the trend of sustainability and environmental consciousness, mobile operating systems are incorporating features to monitor and manage device usage, with an emphasis on reducing electronic waste and energy consumption. Both Android and iOS have introduced tools that provide insights into screen time, app usage, and notifications, empowering users to make informed decisions about their digital habits. As sustainability becomes an increasingly important consideration, mobile operating systems are likely to adopt more measures aimed at promoting responsible device usage and minimizing environmental impact.

The rise of foldable and flexible display technologies is shaping the future of mobile operating systems, introducing new possibilities for device form factors and user interactions. Both Android and iOS are adapting to accommodate these innovations, with features that seamlessly transition between different display configurations and orientations. The potential for foldable devices to bridge the gap between smartphones and tablets has prompted mobile operating systems to optimize their interfaces for a variety of screen sizes and aspect ratios, presenting new challenges and opportunities for app developers and designers.

Mobile operating systems are also witnessing a trend towards increased customization and personalization, empowering users to tailor their devices to suit their preferences. Both Android and iOS have introduced features that allow users to customize home screen layouts, select widgets, and personalize the overall look and feel of their devices. This trend is expected to evolve further, with an emphasis on providing users with more control over the appearance and functionality of their mobile interfaces, fostering a sense of ownership and individuality.

The evolution of augmented reality (AR) and virtual reality (VR) is influencing the development of mobile operating systems, with a focus on creating immersive and interactive experiences. Both Android and iOS have integrated AR capabilities into their frameworks, enabling developers to create applications that overlay digital content onto the real world. The potential for AR to enhance navigation, gaming, education, and social interactions is driving innovation in mobile operating systems, with ongoing efforts to optimize performance and expand AR capabilities across a broader range of devices.

As the Internet of Things (IoT) ecosystem continues to expand, mobile operating systems are poised to play a pivotal role in orchestrating the connectivity and interoperability of diverse IoT devices. Both Android and iOS are exploring ways to integrate IoT functionalities into their frameworks, allowing users to control smart home devices, access IoT data, and seamlessly interact with connected environments. The convergence of mobile operating systems with IoT reflects a broader trend towards creating cohesive and interconnected digital experiences that span various facets of users' lives.

Looking ahead, the future of mobile operating systems is likely to be shaped by a convergence of these trends, driven by ongoing technological advancements, user expectations, and the broader digital landscape. The seamless integration of AI, the continued evolution of user interfaces, enhanced privacy measures, the impact of 5G, sustainability considerations, cross-platform compatibility, flexible displays, customization options, AR/VR developments, and the growing influence of IoT collectively contribute to the trajectory of mobile operating systems. As the industry navigates these trends, the user-centric approach and adaptability of mobile operating systems will remain crucial in delivering innovative and meaningful experiences that resonate with an ever-evolving user base.

Chapter 8: Future Horizons: Innovations and Trends in Operating Systems

Discuss the dynamic nature of technology and its impact on the future of operating systems.

The dynamic nature of technology, marked by rapid advancements and continuous innovation, profoundly influences the future trajectory of operating systems. This dynamism is inherent in the relentless pace of hardware evolution, the proliferation of novel computing paradigms, and the ever-expanding landscape of user expectations. As hardware components become more powerful and diverse, operating systems must adapt to harness their capabilities fully. The relentless increase in processing power, memory capacity, and storage capabilities sets the stage for operating systems to leverage these resources efficiently, enabling more sophisticated applications, seamless multitasking, and enhanced user experiences.

One of the key dynamics shaping the future of operating systems is the ongoing evolution of user interfaces. The traditional graphical user interfaces (GUIs) are continually refined to accommodate emerging technologies and changing user preferences. The rise of touch-based interfaces, gestural controls, and voice commands has redefined the way users interact with devices. Operating systems are compelled to embrace these changes, ensuring that interfaces remain intuitive, accessible, and adaptable across diverse devices, including smartphones, tablets, laptops, and emerging form factors. The dynamic nature of user interfaces reflects the ongoing quest for a more natural and immersive user experience.

The integration of artificial intelligence (AI) and machine learning (ML) represents a transformative force that profoundly influences the future of operating systems. As AI algorithms become more sophisticated, operating systems are evolving to incorporate intelligent features that enhance user interactions, predict user behavior, and automate tasks. AI-driven personal assistants, contextual awareness, and predictive capabilities are becoming integral components of modern operating systems. This dynamic integration of AI not only refines the user experience but also opens avenues for more efficient resource management, security enhancements, and adaptive computing.

The impact of the Internet of Things (IoT) on the dynamic nature of operating systems is unmistakable. As the IoT ecosystem expands, operating systems must evolve to manage the increasing complexity of interconnected devices. The seamless integration and communication between diverse IoT devices demand operating systems that can orchestrate these interactions efficiently. The dynamic challenge lies in providing a cohesive user experience across a spectrum of IoT devices, ranging from smart home appliances to industrial sensors. The future of operating systems will likely involve a continued emphasis on interoperability, security, and the ability to adapt to the evolving landscape of IoT technologies.

The emergence of 5G technology introduces a new dimension to the dynamic landscape of operating systems. The higher data speeds, lower latency, and increased network capacity afforded by 5G have implications for how operating systems handle communication, data transfer, and real-time interactions. The dynamic nature of 5G networks prompts operating systems to optimize for enhanced connectivity, enabling applications that leverage the full potential of low-latency communication. This dynamic shift is expected to influence the development of applications, services, and user experiences that capitalize on the transformative capabilities of 5G.

Security remains a paramount concern in the dynamic evolution of technology, and operating systems play a pivotal role in addressing emerging threats. The dynamic landscape of cybersecurity involves an ongoing cat-and-mouse game between malicious actors and the defenders of digital systems. Operating systems must adapt to incorporate robust security measures, including encryption, secure boot processes, and advanced authentication methods. The dynamic nature of cyber threats requires operating systems to stay ahead of evolving attack vectors, leveraging proactive security measures and timely updates to mitigate potential vulnerabilities.

The dynamic nature of technology is exemplified by the evolution of computing paradigms, with edge computing and cloud computing playing increasingly prominent roles. Operating systems must adapt to the distributed nature of computing, where processing tasks occur both at the device level (edge) and in centralized cloud infrastructures. The dynamic interplay between edge and cloud computing necessitates operating systems that seamlessly manage workloads, data synchronization, and security across these diverse computing environments. This dynamic shift has implications for application development, resource optimization, and the overall architecture of operating systems.

The dynamic landscape of technology extends to the realm of augmented reality (AR) and virtual reality (VR). As AR and VR technologies mature, operating systems must incorporate features that facilitate immersive experiences, spatial computing, and seamless integration with AR/VR hardware. The dynamic challenge lies in optimizing operating systems for the resource-intensive demands of AR/VR applications, ensuring low-latency interactions, and providing a platform for developers to create compelling virtual experiences. The integration of AR and VR into the fabric of operating systems reflects the dynamic evolution of digital interactions and user engagement.

The sustainability imperative is another dynamic aspect influencing the future of operating systems. As environmental considerations gain prominence, operating systems are expected to incorporate features that promote energy efficiency, responsible resource usage, and reduced electronic waste. The dynamic nature of sustainability involves optimizing power consumption, implementing intelligent resource allocation, and encouraging eco-friendly practices among users. Operating systems play a crucial role in shaping the sustainable computing landscape, aligning with the broader societal shift towards environmentally conscious technology.

The dynamic interplay between open-source and proprietary models contributes to the evolution of operating systems. The dynamic nature of open-source development fosters collaboration, innovation, and community-driven enhancements. Operating systems that embrace open-source principles benefit from a diverse ecosystem of contributors, rapid updates, and transparency. Conversely, proprietary operating systems must navigate the dynamic landscape of intellectual property, market competition, and proprietary software ecosystems. The future of operating systems may witness a continued convergence of these models, with a dynamic interplay between open-source components and proprietary innovations.

The dynamic nature of user expectations, fueled by evolving lifestyles, cultural shifts, and emerging technologies, is a driving force shaping the future of operating systems. Users increasingly demand seamless integration between devices, personalized experiences, and a balance between convenience and privacy. Operating systems must dynamically adapt to these changing expectations, offering features that cater to individual preferences, prioritize user control over data, and provide a consistent experience across a spectrum of devices. The dynamic nature of user-centric design underscores the ongoing evolution of operating systems in response to the ever-shifting landscape of user needs and preferences.

In conclusion, the dynamic nature of technology manifests in the continuous evolution of operating systems, driven by advancements in hardware, the integration of AI, the rise of IoT, the deployment of 5G, cybersecurity challenges, computing paradigms, AR/VR technologies, sustainability imperatives, open-source dynamics, and evolving user expectations. The future of operating systems lies in their ability to navigate this dynamic landscape, embracing innovation, adapting to emerging trends, and providing a foundation for the next wave of transformative digital experiences. The dynamic interplay between technological progress and the evolving role of operating systems is a testament to the resilience and adaptability of these fundamental components in the digital era.

Discuss the integration of artificial intelligence (AI) in operating systems.

The integration of artificial intelligence (AI) into operating systems represents a transformative shift, reshaping the way computers interact with users, manage resources, and deliver personalized experiences. At its core, AI in operating systems introduces a layer of intelligence that enables systems to learn, adapt, and make decisions based on data-driven insights. This integration is evident in various facets of operating systems, influencing everything from user interfaces and automation to security and resource optimization.

User interfaces have undergone a profound transformation through the infusion of AI in operating systems. The advent of virtual assistants, such as Siri on iOS and Google Assistant on Android, exemplifies how AI can enhance user interactions. These virtual assistants leverage natural language processing (NLP) and machine learning algorithms to understand and respond to user commands, providing a conversational and context-aware interface. The dynamic nature of AI-driven interfaces allows users to perform tasks, get information, and even control smart home devices through voice commands, contributing to a more intuitive and accessible user experience.

Automation is a cornerstone of AI integration in operating systems, streamlining routine tasks and enhancing overall efficiency.

Operating systems leverage AI algorithms to automate processes like software updates, file organization, and system maintenance. For instance, predictive text suggestions, autocorrect features, and intelligent keyboard algorithms on mobile operating systems showcase how AI enhances user input and reduces manual effort. The dynamic nature of automation driven by AI extends to predictive analytics, where operating systems anticipate user needs and automate responses, ultimately saving time and enhancing productivity.

Security is a paramount concern in the digital landscape, and AI plays a pivotal role in fortifying operating systems against evolving cyber threats. AI-driven security features include behavior analysis, anomaly detection, and threat intelligence integration. Operating systems equipped with AI can detect patterns of malicious activity, identify potential security breaches, and respond in real-time to mitigate risks. The dynamic nature of cybersecurity demands continuous adaptation, and AI in operating systems provides the agility to stay ahead of emerging threats through proactive measures, threat modeling, and rapid response mechanisms.

Resource optimization is a critical aspect of AI integration in operating systems, especially in environments with diverse hardware configurations. AI algorithms analyze usage patterns, prioritize frequently used applications, and allocate resources dynamically to enhance overall system performance. This dynamic resource management ensures that computing power, memory, and storage are efficiently utilized, leading to improved responsiveness and a more seamless user experience. Operating systems with AI-driven resource optimization contribute to the adaptability required for handling the varying demands of modern applications and workflows.

The integration of AI in operating systems has also influenced the evolution of recommendation systems. These systems leverage machine learning algorithms to analyze user behavior, preferences, and historical data to offer personalized recommendations. Whether suggesting apps, content, or settings, AI-driven recommendation systems contribute to a tailored user experience. The dynamic nature of these recommendation systems involves continuous learning and adaptation, ensuring that the suggestions align with users' evolving preferences and activities.

In the realm of data management, AI in operating systems facilitates intelligent organization, search, and retrieval. Operating systems employ AI algorithms to categorize files, predict user actions, and offer context-aware search results. For instance, features like Apple's Siri Suggestions on iOS use AI to predict which apps a user might need at a particular time or location. The dynamic nature of AI-driven data management extends to content indexing, allowing users to find files more efficiently based on contextual relevance and usage patterns.

AI integration has also extended to the realm of accessibility features, enhancing the inclusivity of operating systems. AI-driven technologies, such as image recognition and text-to-speech capabilities, empower users with visual or motor impairments. Operating systems leverage AI to provide voice commands, screen readers, and other assistive technologies, creating a more inclusive computing environment. The dynamic nature of AI-driven accessibility features involves continuous refinement to cater to the diverse needs of users with varying abilities.

The advent of edge computing has further expanded the role of AI in operating systems. Edge devices, such as smartphones, IoT devices, and edge servers, benefit from AI capabilities that enable real-time processing and decision-making at the device level. Operating systems designed for edge computing leverage AI algorithms for tasks like image recognition, natural language processing, and sensor data analysis. This dynamic integration of AI at the edge contributes to low-latency interactions, reduced dependency on centralized cloud services, and enhanced responsiveness in diverse application scenarios.

AI-driven personalization is a hallmark of modern operating systems, shaping user experiences based on individual preferences, behaviors, and contexts. From personalized content recommendations to adaptive user interfaces, operating systems leverage AI to create tailored experiences. The dynamic nature of personalization involves continuous learning, as AI algorithms adapt to changing user preferences and accommodate new patterns of usage. Operating systems that prioritize personalization contribute to a more engaging and user-centric computing environment.

The development of AI frameworks and toolkits has facilitated the creation of AI-powered applications within operating systems. Developers can harness machine learning capabilities to build applications that utilize speech recognition, image analysis, natural language understanding, and other AI-driven functionalities. The dynamic nature of AI application development involves ongoing innovation, as developers explore new ways to integrate AI into various aspects of operating system functionality and user-facing applications.

In the future, the integration of AI in operating systems is poised to witness further advancements and refinements. The dynamic landscape of AI research and development will likely contribute to more sophisticated algorithms, improved learning models, and enhanced capabilities in natural language understanding and contextual awareness. As AI technologies continue to mature, operating systems will play a pivotal role in harnessing these advancements to deliver more intelligent, adaptive, and user-centric computing experiences. The dynamic interplay between AI and operating systems is emblematic of the ongoing evolution in technology, where innovation and adaptation converge to shape the future of digital interactions.

Explore the role of operating systems in edge computing environments.

The role of operating systems in edge computing environments is pivotal, reflecting a paradigm shift in how computing resources are distributed, managed, and leveraged at the edge of the network. Edge computing involves the processing of data closer to the source of generation, minimizing latency and optimizing real-time decision-making. In this context, operating systems serve as the foundational layer that orchestrates the myriad of devices, sensors, and computing nodes at the edge, ensuring seamless coordination, efficient resource allocation, and a cohesive computing environment.

One of the primary roles of operating systems in edge computing is to manage the diverse array of devices and sensors that constitute the edge ecosystem. These devices can range from sensors embedded in industrial machinery to IoT devices in smart homes. Operating systems provide a unified framework that enables these devices to communicate, share data, and collaborate in real-time. The dynamic nature of edge environments, with devices coming online or going offline, demands adaptive and responsive operating systems that can accommodate the heterogeneity of hardware and software configurations.

Resource optimization is a critical aspect of operating systems in edge computing. Given the often constrained nature of edge devices in terms of processing power, memory, and storage, operating systems must efficiently allocate resources to meet the demands of applications and services running at the edge. Dynamic resource management becomes crucial, with operating systems adapting to fluctuations in workloads, prioritizing critical tasks, and ensuring optimal performance. The ability to balance resource usage while maintaining low latency is fundamental to the success of edge computing applications, and operating systems play a central role in achieving this balance.

Real-time processing is a key requirement in many edge computing scenarios, particularly those involving critical applications such as industrial automation, autonomous vehicles, and healthcare monitoring. Operating systems in edge environments must support real-time capabilities, ensuring that time-sensitive tasks can be executed with minimal latency. Real-time operating systems (RTOS) or features integrated into general-purpose operating systems are essential for handling tasks that require immediate processing, such as sensor data analysis, control systems, and rapid decision-making in dynamic environments.

Security is a paramount concern in edge computing, where data is processed and stored closer to the source. Operating systems must implement robust security measures to protect sensitive information, especially in scenarios like healthcare, finance, and industrial control. Encryption, secure boot processes, and secure communication protocols are integral components of operating systems in edge environments. Additionally, operating systems play a role in managing access control, ensuring that only authorized entities can interact with edge devices and systems. The dynamic nature of security threats necessitates continuous updates and adaptive security mechanisms within operating systems to counter emerging risks effectively.

Connectivity is a central theme in edge computing, and operating systems facilitate the seamless integration of edge devices into broader network infrastructures. Whether through wired connections or wireless protocols like Wi-Fi, Bluetooth, or 5G, operating systems manage the intricacies of device connectivity. Edge computing often involves a mesh of interconnected devices, and operating systems must handle issues such as device discovery, network configurations, and efficient data routing. The dynamic nature of edge environments, with devices moving within a network or joining/leaving dynamically, requires operating systems to adapt to changes in network topology while maintaining reliable and low-latency connectivity.

Distributed computing in edge environments relies on the ability of operating systems to enable collaborative processing and decision-making across multiple edge nodes. Operating systems provide the framework for managing distributed applications, orchestrating communication between nodes, and ensuring data consistency. The dynamic nature of distributed edge computing, with nodes coming in and out of operation, demands fault-tolerant mechanisms and efficient data synchronization. Operating systems play a crucial role in implementing distributed algorithms, ensuring that edge devices can collectively process data, make decisions, and respond to events in a coordinated fashion.

Containerization has emerged as a key technology in edge computing, and operating systems play a significant role in supporting containerized applications. Container orchestration platforms like Kubernetes have been adapted to function in edge environments, and operating systems must provide the necessary support for container runtimes. The dynamic nature of edge computing, with the deployment and scaling of containerized applications across diverse edge nodes, requires operating systems to handle container lifecycles, resource isolation, and efficient deployment mechanisms. The ability to seamlessly integrate containers into edge environments enhances flexibility, scalability, and ease of application management.

Edge computing often involves the integration of artificial intelligence (AI) and machine learning (ML) at the edge to enable real-time decision-making based on data analysis. Operating systems play a role in supporting AI frameworks, providing the necessary runtime environments for executing AI/ML models on edge devices. The dynamic nature of AI processing at the edge demands operating systems that can handle the computational requirements of inferencing, adapt to varying model sizes, and optimize energy consumption. Operating systems must support edge-specific AI workloads while ensuring interoperability with edge devices' diverse hardware architectures.

The lifecycle management of applications and services is a significant responsibility of operating systems in edge computing environments. Edge nodes may host a variety of applications with different requirements, ranging from simple IoT device management tasks to complex data analytics and AI workloads. Operating systems must facilitate the deployment, updating, and removal of applications in a seamless and dynamic manner. Container orchestration, over-the-air (OTA) updates, and application lifecycle management features are essential components that allow operating systems to adapt to the evolving application landscape at the edge.

Data storage and management in edge computing environments pose unique challenges that operating systems must address. Edge devices may generate vast amounts of data, and operating systems must implement efficient storage solutions that balance the need for local data processing with the requirements for data aggregation and offloading. The dynamic nature of edge data, with varying levels of importance and sensitivity, demands adaptive data storage and retrieval mechanisms. Operating systems play a role in implementing edge storage policies, ensuring that data is managed effectively based on contextual factors, storage constraints, and data lifecycle requirements.

Interoperability is a critical aspect of edge computing, where devices from different manufacturers and with diverse functionalities must seamlessly work together. Operating systems must support standard communication protocols, data formats, and device management frameworks to foster interoperability. The dynamic nature of edge ecosystems, with the continuous addition of new devices and services, requires operating systems to adapt to evolving standards and support a diverse range of interfaces. Interoperability at the operating system level ensures that edge computing environments can accommodate a broad spectrum of devices and applications.

Energy efficiency is a crucial consideration in edge computing, particularly for battery-powered devices and IoT sensors. Operating systems must implement power management features to optimize energy consumption, extend device battery life, and minimize the environmental impact. The dynamic nature of energy requirements in edge environments, where devices may operate in various power states based on workload demands, necessitates adaptive power management strategies. Operating systems play a role in coordinating power policies, adjusting device performance levels, and implementing energy-efficient mechanisms to strike a balance between performance and energy conservation.

The role of operating systems in edge computing extends to facilitating the development of edge-specific applications. Edge computing environments often require applications that can harness the unique capabilities of edge devices, such as low-latency processing, real-time decision-making, and proximity-based interactions. Operating systems provide the necessary programming interfaces, development frameworks, and runtime environments for developers to create applications tailored for edge scenarios. The dynamic nature of edge application development involves continuous innovation, adaptation to emerging technologies, and the integration of new features and functionalities into the application ecosystem.

In conclusion, the role of operating systems in edge computing environments is multifaceted and crucial to the success of distributed, real-time, and context-aware computing at the edge of the network. Operating systems provide the foundational framework for managing devices, optimizing resources, ensuring security, enabling connectivity

, supporting distributed computing, handling containerization, integrating AI, managing application lifecycles, implementing efficient data storage, fostering interoperability, optimizing energy consumption, and facilitating edge-specific application development. The dynamic nature of edge computing, with its diverse and evolving requirements, underscores the adaptive and responsive capabilities that operating systems must exhibit to enable the seamless integration of edge devices into the broader computing landscape. Operating systems serve as the linchpin that harmonizes the complexities of edge computing, offering a cohesive and efficient platform for the next wave of computing innovation.

Discuss the potential integration of blockchain technology in operating systems.

The potential integration of blockchain technology into operating systems marks a paradigm shift in the way computing systems handle data, transactions, and security. Blockchain, originally designed as the decentralized ledger technology underpinning cryptocurrencies like Bitcoin, has evolved beyond its financial roots to offer a decentralized and tamper-resistant framework with wide-ranging applications. As operating systems form the core infrastructure of computing devices, the integration of blockchain introduces a new layer of transparency, security, and trust, potentially reshaping the landscape of data management and system interactions.

One of the primary aspects of blockchain integration in operating systems is the enhancement of security. Blockchain's decentralized and cryptographic nature makes it inherently resistant to unauthorized alterations or tampering. By implementing blockchain at the operating system level, the integrity of critical system files, configurations, and updates can be assured. This dynamic security model significantly mitigates the risk of malware attacks, unauthorized modifications, and ensures the authenticity of the operating system's components. The distributed and consensus-driven nature of blockchain technology introduces a novel approach to securing the foundational elements of computing systems, fostering trust in the integrity of the operating environment.

Blockchain's potential impact extends to the domain of secure identity management within operating systems. The decentralized and immutable nature of blockchain allows for the creation of secure and verifiable digital identities. Integrating blockchain into operating systems could enable users to have a self-sovereign identity, where personal information is cryptographically secured on the blockchain. This dynamic identity management paradigm reduces the reliance on centralized authorities, providing users with greater control over their digital personas while enhancing privacy and reducing the risk of identity theft. Operating systems that integrate blockchain-based identity solutions contribute to a more secure and user-centric computing environment.

The potential for blockchain integration in operating systems becomes particularly evident in the realm of software distribution and updates. Blockchain's distributed ledger can be leveraged to create a transparent and auditable record of software versions, releases, and updates. This dynamic approach to version control ensures that the provenance of software components is traceable, mitigating the risk of malicious modifications or unauthorized alterations during the distribution process. Blockchain-based software distribution mechanisms enhance the trustworthiness of updates, providing users with verifiable information about the origin, authenticity, and integrity of the software being installed on their systems.

Smart contracts, self-executing agreements with the terms of the contract directly written into code, represent another facet of blockchain technology that holds potential for integration into operating systems. By embedding smart contract functionality, operating systems can automate and secure various processes, such as licensing agreements, digital rights management, and user permissions. The dynamic nature of smart contracts facilitates the creation of self-executing, trustless agreements that operate without the need for intermediaries. This integration not only streamlines administrative processes but also enhances the transparency and efficiency of interactions within the operating system environment.

Decentralized storage is an area where blockchain integration in operating systems could revolutionize data management. Traditional operating systems rely on centralized storage solutions, often controlled by a single entity. Blockchain, particularly in combination with decentralized file systems, enables the creation of distributed storage networks. This dynamic storage paradigm allows users to contribute their unused storage space to a network, creating a decentralized and resilient storage infrastructure. Operating systems integrated with blockchain-based storage solutions offer increased data redundancy, improved fault tolerance, and the potential for a more equitable and decentralized data storage ecosystem.

The integration of blockchain technology in operating systems also has implications for the Internet of Things (IoT) landscape. With the increasing proliferation of IoT devices, security and trust become paramount concerns. Blockchain's decentralized and tamper-resistant characteristics offer a robust solution for securing the interactions and data exchanges within IoT ecosystems. Operating systems designed for IoT devices can leverage blockchain to establish trust among devices, authenticate data transactions, and ensure the integrity of sensor data. This dynamic approach to securing IoT interactions enhances the overall reliability and security of connected systems.

Blockchain's potential to redefine digital ownership and provenance is another aspect with implications for content creators and consumers within operating systems. Through the integration of blockchain, operating systems can support digital asset ownership through non-fungible tokens (NFTs). Content creators, such as artists, musicians, and writers, can tokenize their work on a blockchain, providing a verifiable and immutable record of ownership. Operating systems that support NFTs enable users to securely manage, transfer, and prove ownership of digital assets, fostering a dynamic ecosystem where creators have greater control over their intellectual property.

The potential for blockchain integration in operating systems extends to the realm of supply chain management. Operating systems can leverage blockchain to create transparent and traceable supply chains, enhancing the provenance of products and materials. This dynamic approach ensures that every step of the supply chain is recorded on an immutable ledger, offering stakeholders visibility into the production, distribution, and delivery of goods. The integration of blockchain in operating systems contributes to a more accountable and resilient supply chain ecosystem, with applications ranging from verifying the authenticity of products to streamlining logistics.

Blockchain technology's potential to revolutionize data privacy and consent management is a critical consideration for its integration into operating systems. By leveraging blockchain's decentralized and cryptographic features, operating systems can empower users with greater control over their personal data. Users could maintain ownership of their data, grant specific permissions through smart contracts, and audit how their information is utilized. The dynamic nature of blockchain-based data privacy solutions aligns with the growing emphasis on user-centric data control and consent management, providing a robust framework within operating systems for safeguarding user privacy.

Interoperability is a key consideration in the integration of blockchain technology into operating systems, particularly in heterogeneous computing environments. Blockchain's decentralized nature allows for interoperability between different systems, platforms, and applications. Operating systems that facilitate interoperability through blockchain can enable seamless communication and data exchange between devices and networks with varying architectures. This dynamic interoperability fosters an ecosystem where diverse technologies can coexist, collaborate, and share data securely, contributing to a more interconnected and flexible computing environment.

Energy efficiency is a critical consideration in the integration of blockchain technology into operating systems. Traditional blockchain consensus mechanisms, such as proof-of-work (PoW), are resource-intensive and energy-consuming. The dynamic nature of blockchain integration in operating systems necessitates the exploration and implementation of more energy-efficient consensus mechanisms, such as proof-of-stake (PoS) or delegated proof-of-stake (DPoS). Operating systems must strike a balance between the security and energy efficiency of blockchain protocols, especially in resource-constrained environments like mobile devices or edge computing nodes.

Governance models within blockchain networks also present considerations for the integration of blockchain technology into operating systems. Decentralized autonomous organizations (DAOs), enabled by blockchain, introduce dynamic governance structures that rely on community-driven decision-making. Operating systems integrated with blockchain may need to adapt to or support these governance models, allowing users to participate in decision-making processes related to the evolution of the operating system itself. This dynamic approach to governance aligns with the principles of decentralization and community-driven development that characterize blockchain ecosystems.

The potential integration of blockchain technology into operating systems is not without its challenges. Scalability, latency, regulatory considerations, and the environmental impact of energy-intensive consensus mechanisms are factors that need to be carefully addressed. The dynamic nature of blockchain technology requires ongoing innovation and adaptation to meet the evolving needs of operating systems in diverse computing environments. As the technology matures and industry standards emerge, operating systems that successfully integrate blockchain have the potential to redefine how data, transactions, and trust are managed in the digital era. The dynamic interplay between blockchain and operating systems reflects a transformative journey toward decentralized, secure, and transparent computing ecosystems.

Explore the impact of quantum computing on operating system design.

The impending advent of quantum computing heralds a transformative era in the landscape of computational capabilities, posing profound implications for the design and functionality of operating systems. Unlike classical computers that use bits to represent information as either 0 or 1, quantum computers leverage quantum bits or qubits, which can exist in multiple states simultaneously due to the principles of superposition and entanglement. This dynamic shift in computational principles necessitates a reimagining of traditional operating systems to harness the unique advantages and address the challenges posed by quantum computing.

Quantum computers have the potential to revolutionize certain computational tasks by performing complex calculations exponentially faster than classical computers. This dynamic enhancement in processing power opens avenues for tackling problems in cryptography, optimization, simulation, and machine learning that were previously considered computationally intractable. Operating systems, in response to the dynamic capabilities of quantum computing, must be equipped to exploit these advantages efficiently. Quantum algorithms, designed for specific computational tasks, may necessitate adaptations in the way operating systems handle and schedule tasks to fully leverage the transformative potential of quantum computation.

The fundamental shift introduced by quantum computing extends to the realm of security, particularly in the domain of cryptography. Classical cryptographic protocols, which rely on the complexity of certain mathematical problems for security, could be rendered vulnerable to quantum algorithms like Shor's algorithm. Operating systems need to dynamically adapt to this quantum threat landscape by integrating post-quantum cryptographic algorithms that resist quantum attacks. The dynamic nature of quantum-resistant cryptography involves ongoing research and standardization efforts to ensure the long-term security of operating systems in a quantum computing era.

The concept of quantum entanglement introduces a unique challenge and opportunity for operating systems in the context of quantum communication. Quantum entanglement enables the instantaneous correlation of quantum states between particles, providing a means for secure communication channels through quantum key distribution (QKD). Operating systems must dynamically integrate support for QKD to enable secure quantum communication between devices. The dynamic nature of quantum communication demands robust protocols, seamless key distribution mechanisms, and integration with classical communication infrastructure to ensure the coexistence of quantum and classical communication channels within the operating system framework.

Quantum computers operate under the constraints of quantum coherence, where the fragile quantum states are susceptible to errors caused by environmental interactions and decoherence. Quantum error correction techniques, such as those based on quantum error-correcting codes like the surface code, are vital for preserving the integrity of quantum information. Operating systems must dynamically manage the complexities of quantum error correction, implementing protocols for fault-tolerant quantum computation. The dynamic nature of quantum error correction involves adapting to the unique challenges posed by quantum hardware, optimizing resource utilization, and ensuring the reliability of quantum computations within the operating system environment.

Quantum parallelism, a fundamental concept in quantum computing, allows quantum algorithms to explore multiple computational paths simultaneously. This dynamic aspect of quantum algorithms introduces new considerations for the scheduling and optimization of computational tasks within operating systems. Quantum parallelism challenges traditional notions of task execution and resource allocation, requiring operating systems to dynamically adapt scheduling policies and optimize the utilization of quantum resources. The dynamic nature of quantum parallelism involves exploring novel approaches to task scheduling, load balancing, and resource allocation to harness the full potential of quantum computation.

Quantum supremacy, the point at which quantum computers surpass classical computers in performing certain tasks, introduces a dynamic shift in the hierarchy of computational capabilities. Operating systems must dynamically navigate this transition, incorporating mechanisms to identify quantum-enabled applications and allocate resources efficiently between classical and quantum tasks. The dynamic nature of quantum supremacy involves redefining benchmarks, performance metrics, and system-level optimizations within operating systems to accommodate the coexistence of classical and quantum computing paradigms.

Quantum-inspired algorithms, which leverage quantum principles to enhance classical computation, represent a dynamic bridge between classical and quantum computing. Operating systems need to dynamically support the integration of quantum-inspired algorithms into classical workflows, offering a seamless environment for developers to leverage quantum-inspired optimization, machine learning, and simulation techniques. The dynamic nature of quantum-inspired computing involves exploring synergies between classical and quantum approaches, enabling operating systems to act as flexible platforms that can harness the strengths of both paradigms.

The development of quantum hardware, including superconducting qubits, trapped ions, and topological qubits, introduces a dynamic range of considerations for operating systems. Quantum computers exhibit unique characteristics, such as sensitivity to temperature fluctuations and the need for extremely low-noise environments. Operating systems must dynamically manage the intricacies of quantum hardware, optimizing for stability, calibration, and error mitigation. The dynamic nature of quantum hardware involves addressing challenges related to hardware-software co-design, ensuring compatibility with diverse quantum architectures, and adapting to the evolving landscape of quantum technology.

Quantum cloud computing, where quantum computing resources are made available as a service over the cloud, introduces a dynamic shift in the way operating systems interact with quantum processors. Operating systems must dynamically integrate with quantum cloud platforms, managing the allocation, scheduling, and execution of quantum tasks. The dynamic nature of quantum cloud computing involves addressing latency considerations, data privacy concerns, and optimizing the orchestration of classical and quantum workflows within the operating system environment. Quantum cloud services present a dynamic opportunity for operating systems to extend their reach into the quantum realm, fostering a hybrid computing ecosystem.

The dynamic nature of quantum software development introduces challenges and opportunities for operating systems in providing robust development environments for quantum programming. Quantum programming languages, such as Qiskit, Cirq, and Quipper, enable developers to express quantum algorithms and applications. Operating systems must dynamically support these quantum programming languages, offering integrated development environments (IDEs), debugging tools, and simulation capabilities. The dynamic nature of quantum software development involves adapting to the unique requirements of quantum programming, supporting the exploration of quantum algorithms, and facilitating a seamless transition between classical and quantum software components.

Quantum machine learning, a burgeoning field that leverages quantum computing to enhance classical machine learning algorithms, introduces dynamic considerations for operating systems. Quantum machine learning algorithms, such as quantum neural networks and quantum support vector machines, require specialized support within operating systems for training, inference, and optimization. The dynamic nature of quantum machine learning involves exploring the integration of quantum computing into classical machine learning frameworks, enabling operating systems to facilitate the development of hybrid machine learning models that leverage both classical and quantum resources.

The potential impact of quantum computing on the field of artificial intelligence (AI) introduces dynamic considerations for operating systems. Quantum algorithms, such as quantum machine learning and quantum-enhanced optimization, have the potential to accelerate certain AI tasks. Operating systems must dynamically adapt to this paradigm shift, providing frameworks for integrating quantum-enhanced AI algorithms into existing AI workflows. The dynamic nature of quantum-enhanced AI involves optimizing the interaction between classical and quantum components within operating systems, enabling the development of AI models that harness the unique advantages of quantum computation.

Quantum sensing and imaging technologies, which leverage quantum principles for enhanced precision in measurements, introduce dynamic challenges and opportunities for operating systems. Quantum sensors, such as atomic clocks and quantum magnetometers, demand specialized interfaces within operating systems for data acquisition, calibration, and real-time processing. The dynamic nature of quantum sensing involves adapting operating systems to the requirements of quantum sensor networks, optimizing for low-latency data processing, and integrating quantum-enhanced sensing capabilities into broader applications.

In conclusion, the impending era of quantum computing poses dynamic challenges and opportunities for the design and functionality of operating systems. From managing the intricacies of quantum hardware and optimizing quantum algorithms to navigating the transition to quantum supremacy and facilitating the coexistence of classical and quantum computing paradigms, operating systems play a pivotal role in shaping the quantum computing landscape. The dynamic nature of quantum computing requires operating systems to be adaptive, resilient, and innovative, fostering an ecosystem where classical and quantum technologies synergize to unlock new frontiers in computation, communication, and problem-solving. Operating systems stand at the forefront of this dynamic quantum revolution, poised to redefine the boundaries of what is computationally possible in the quantum era.

Discuss the concept of ephemeral operating systems that adapt to user behavior.

The concept of ephemeral operating systems represents a groundbreaking paradigm in the evolution of computing environments, introducing a dynamic and adaptive approach that tailors the operating system's behavior to the unique patterns and preferences of individual users. Unlike traditional operating systems with static configurations and predefined settings, ephemeral operating systems embrace a fluidity that mirrors the dynamic nature of user behavior. This paradigm shift is rooted in the recognition that users' computing needs, preferences, and workflows are constantly evolving, necessitating an operating system that can seamlessly adapt in real-time to provide a personalized and responsive user experience.

At the core of ephemeral operating systems is the idea of user-centric computing, where the operating system dynamically adjusts its configuration, interface, and functionality based on an ongoing analysis of user behavior. This dynamic adaptation involves continuously monitoring how users interact with their devices, the applications they use, the files they access, and the settings they prefer. By leveraging machine learning algorithms and artificial intelligence, ephemeral operating systems can discern patterns, infer user preferences, and predict future actions. This dynamic analysis enables the operating system to proactively adjust its features and presentation to align with users' evolving needs.

The ephemeral operating system's adaptability is particularly evident in its user interface design. Traditional operating systems often employ static graphical user interfaces (GUIs) that remain consistent over time. In contrast, ephemeral operating systems introduce a dynamic and context-aware interface that evolves based on user interactions. For instance, frequently used applications, files, or settings may be dynamically prioritized or highlighted, while less frequently accessed elements may be de-emphasized. This adaptability extends to the arrangement of icons, the organization of menus, and the overall layout of the interface, ensuring that the operating system is continuously optimized for user efficiency and satisfaction.

Ephemeral operating systems also excel in the realm of context-aware computing. By continuously analyzing user behavior, these operating systems develop an understanding of the context in which computing tasks are performed. This includes factors such as the time of day, location, device type, and connectivity status. Leveraging this contextual awareness, ephemeral operating systems dynamically adjust system settings, display preferences, and network configurations to align with the user's environment. For example, the operating system might automatically enable a power-saving mode when the user is on battery power, adjust screen brightness based on ambient lighting conditions, or prioritize offline functionalities when connectivity is limited.

Security and privacy are integral aspects of ephemeral operating systems. The dynamic nature of these operating systems allows for real-time adaptation to emerging security threats and user privacy preferences. Through continuous monitoring of user behavior, the operating system can detect anomalies or suspicious activities, triggering immediate responses such as heightened security protocols, alerts, or user authentication checks. Furthermore, ephemeral operating systems empower users with granular control over their privacy settings, allowing them to dynamically adjust the level of data sharing, telemetry, and personalized recommendations based on their comfort level and evolving privacy concerns.

The concept of ephemeral operating systems extends beyond personal computers to encompass a variety of devices within the Internet of Things (IoT) ecosystem. In the context of IoT, where devices range from smart home appliances to wearable gadgets, the adaptability of operating systems becomes even more critical. Ephemeral operating systems in IoT devices can dynamically adjust their functionalities based on user preferences, environmental conditions, and the interactions between interconnected devices. For instance, a smart home operating system might learn the user's daily routine, adjusting lighting, temperature, and security settings accordingly, creating a seamless and personalized living experience.

Collaboration and multitasking are areas where ephemeral operating systems demonstrate their dynamic capabilities. Traditional operating systems often provide static multitasking environments with fixed window management systems. Ephemeral operating systems, on the other hand, dynamically adapt to user workflows by intelligently predicting the applications and tasks users are likely to switch between. For instance, if a user regularly transitions from email to a specific project management tool during certain times of the day, the operating system may proactively arrange windows, pre-load applications, or suggest relevant shortcuts to streamline the transition. This dynamic approach enhances user productivity and fosters a more intuitive computing experience.

Ephemeral operating systems also embrace the concept of anticipatory computing, where the operating system proactively predicts user needs and prepares for them in advance. Through continuous analysis of user behavior, the operating system can anticipate upcoming tasks, preferred applications, and frequently accessed files. For example, if a user typically starts working on a specific project every Monday morning, the ephemeral operating system might preload relevant documents, open the necessary applications, and configure the display settings accordingly, creating a seamless and anticipatory user experience.

The adaptability of ephemeral operating systems extends to software updates and maintenance. Traditional operating systems often require users to manually initiate software updates, leading to potential delays in applying critical security patches or feature enhancements. Ephemeral operating systems adopt a dynamic approach to updates by intelligently scheduling them during periods of low user activity or when the device is idle. This ensures that updates are applied seamlessly, minimizing disruptions to user workflows. Additionally, the operating system can learn from user preferences, such as preferred update times or the importance of certain applications, to tailor the update process accordingly.

Ephemeral operating systems excel in the domain of personalized assistance and virtual companionship. By integrating virtual assistants powered by natural language processing and machine learning, these operating systems become dynamic companions that understand user queries, preferences, and conversational nuances. The virtual assistant evolves alongside the user, adapting to changes in vocabulary, communication style, and context. This dynamic interaction extends beyond simple command-based tasks, enabling users to engage in natural conversations, receive personalized recommendations, and access information in a manner that aligns with their evolving preferences.

User empowerment is a central theme in ephemeral operating systems, where customization and control are prioritized. Through dynamic interfaces, users can easily tailor the appearance, arrangement, and functionalities of their operating environment. The operating system actively seeks user feedback and preferences, providing options for customization based on individual workflows, aesthetic preferences, and accessibility requirements. This dynamic customization fosters a sense of ownership and personalization, empowering users to create computing environments that resonate with their unique needs and preferences.

Ephemeral operating systems also introduce a new dimension to user learning and skill development. By continuously monitoring user interactions, the operating system can identify areas where users may benefit from additional guidance or tutorials. This dynamic learning approach involves providing contextual assistance, hints, or interactive tutorials based on the user's current tasks. For instance, if a user frequently uses a specific software feature but hasn't explored a related advanced functionality, the operating system might dynamically present tips, shortcuts, or video tutorials to enhance the user's proficiency. This dynamic learning environment contributes to an ongoing cycle of user skill development within the operating system.

The dynamic nature of ephemeral operating systems has implications for device resource management and optimization. Traditional operating systems often rely on static resource allocation strategies, which may lead to suboptimal performance in dynamic computing environments. Ephemeral operating systems leverage real-time analytics to dynamically allocate resources based on the user's current activities, prioritizing the applications and tasks that are most relevant at any given moment. This dynamic resource management ensures optimal performance, responsiveness, and energy efficiency, aligning the allocation of CPU, memory, and storage resources with the user's evolving computing needs.

Ephemeral operating systems also play a pivotal role in fostering collaborative computing environments. In scenarios where multiple users interact with a shared device or collaborate on projects, the operating system dynamically adjusts its configurations to accommodate diverse user preferences and workflows. This includes adapting user interfaces, file access permissions, and collaboration tools based on the identities and roles of the users involved. The dynamic nature of collaborative computing within ephemeral operating systems ensures a seamless and inclusive experience, where the operating environment adapts to the nuances of group interactions and fosters a collaborative workflow.

The concept of ephemeral operating systems aligns with the broader trends of edge computing and distributed computing architectures. In edge computing, where computing resources are distributed closer to the data source, ephemeral operating systems dynamically optimize their configurations based on the characteristics of edge devices, network conditions, and the types of data being processed. This dynamic adaptation ensures efficient and context-aware computing at the edge, enhancing the overall responsiveness and reliability of edge computing environments. Similarly, in distributed computing architectures, ephemeral operating systems dynamically coordinate and adapt to the collaborative processing and data sharing across multiple nodes, ensuring a cohesive and optimized computing experience.

The evolving landscape of technology and user expectations underscores the importance of continuous innovation in operating system design. Ephemeral operating systems represent a bold step towards a more adaptive, user-centric, and anticipatory computing paradigm. By dynamically tailoring the computing environment to individual users' behavior, preferences, and context, ephemeral operating systems transcend the limitations of traditional static operating systems, offering a vision of computing that is not just functional but deeply intuitive, personalized, and responsive to the ever-changing needs of users in the digital era.

Explore innovations in human-computer interaction within operating systems.

In the ever-evolving landscape of technology, innovations in human-computer interaction (HCI) within operating systems have played a pivotal role in shaping the way users engage with their digital environments. These innovations encompass a wide array of advancements, from intuitive graphical user interfaces (GUIs) to touch-based interactions, voice commands, gesture recognition, and beyond. One of the transformative innovations lies in the evolution of natural language processing (NLP) and voice recognition technologies. Operating systems equipped with advanced NLP capabilities enable users to interact with their devices through spoken language, issuing commands, dictating text, and engaging in conversational interactions. This innovation not only enhances accessibility for users with diverse abilities but also fosters a more natural and seamless form of communication between humans and computers, redefining the user experience within the operating system.

The integration of touch-based interactions has been a groundbreaking innovation in HCI within operating systems. Touchscreens, prevalent in smartphones and tablets, have become ubiquitous, fundamentally altering the way users interact with their devices. Operating systems have adapted to support gestures, taps, swipes, and pinch-to-zoom actions, providing an intuitive and tactile interface. Multi-touch capabilities further enhance the user experience, allowing for simultaneous interactions with multiple points on the screen. This innovation has extended to traditional computing environments, with operating systems for laptops and desktops incorporating touch functionality, creating a unified and cohesive user experience across diverse form factors.

Gesture recognition represents another dimension of HCI innovation, enabling users to interact with operating systems through hand and body movements. Cameras and sensors embedded in devices detect gestures, translating them into commands or actions within the operating system. This innovation has found applications in gaming, virtual reality (VR), and augmented reality (AR), offering users an immersive and interactive computing experience. Operating systems that seamlessly integrate gesture recognition capabilities provide users with an additional layer of control and engagement, opening avenues for creative and novel interactions beyond traditional input methods.

The concept of augmented reality has introduced innovative HCI paradigms within operating systems, merging the digital and physical worlds. Operating systems equipped with AR capabilities overlay digital information onto the user's real-world environment, creating an enriched and interactive experience. This innovation finds applications in navigation, education, gaming, and various industries. Users can interact with virtual elements superimposed on their surroundings, blurring the lines between the physical and digital realms. Operating systems that embrace AR redefine the way users perceive and interact with information, fostering a dynamic and context-aware computing environment.

Innovations in stylus-based interactions have contributed to the resurgence of digital pen input within operating systems. Devices equipped with stylus support offer users a precise and expressive input method, enabling tasks such as note-taking, drawing, and graphic design. Operating systems that optimize for stylus input provide features like pressure sensitivity, tilt recognition, and palm rejection, offering a versatile and natural writing or drawing experience. This innovation caters to creative professionals, students, and anyone seeking a more tactile and nuanced form of interaction within the digital realm.

Eye-tracking technology represents a cutting-edge innovation in HCI, allowing users to control their devices through eye movements. Operating systems that integrate eye-tracking capabilities enable users to navigate interfaces, scroll through content, and interact with applications using gaze-based commands. This innovation holds particular significance for accessibility, providing an alternative input method for individuals with mobility challenges. Furthermore, eye-tracking enhances the overall user experience by introducing a dynamic and responsive interaction paradigm, where the operating system adapts to the user's visual focus and intentions.

The advent of virtual assistants and AI-driven interactions has reshaped the HCI landscape within operating systems. Virtual assistants, powered by natural language understanding and machine learning algorithms, serve as intelligent interfaces that comprehend user queries, execute commands, and provide contextual information. Operating systems that integrate virtual assistants offer users a dynamic and conversational means of interacting with their devices. This innovation extends beyond simple command-based interactions, enabling users to engage in natural conversations, receive personalized recommendations, and access information in a manner that aligns with their preferences and habits.

Biometric authentication represents a crucial innovation in HCI, enhancing security and user convenience within operating systems. Fingerprint recognition, facial recognition, and iris scanning technologies have become integral features in modern operating systems, allowing users to unlock devices, authorize transactions, and access sensitive information through biometric verification. This innovation not only streamlines the authentication process but also contributes to a more secure computing environment. Operating systems that seamlessly integrate biometric authentication prioritize user convenience while ensuring robust security protocols.

The evolution of haptic feedback technology has introduced a tactile dimension to HCI within operating systems. Haptic feedback, delivered through vibrations or tactile sensations, provides users with sensory cues that enhance the interactive experience. Operating systems leverage haptic feedback for various purposes, such as confirming user inputs, simulating physical interactions, and providing feedback in response to on-screen events. This innovation contributes to a more immersive and responsive user experience, adding a tangible layer to digital interactions and creating a sense of tactility within the operating system environment.

Dynamic adaptive interfaces represent an innovative approach to HCI within operating systems, where the user interface evolves based on contextual factors, user behavior, and preferences. Operating systems equipped with adaptive interfaces continuously analyze user interactions, learning patterns and adjusting the display, layout, and functionalities accordingly. This innovation ensures that the operating system remains responsive to the user's evolving needs, providing a personalized and context-aware computing environment. Adaptive interfaces contribute to a more intuitive and efficient user experience, where the operating system anticipates user actions and dynamically adapts to optimize workflow and productivity.

In the realm of accessibility, innovations in HCI within operating systems have made significant strides toward inclusivity. Accessibility features, such as screen readers, magnification tools, and voice commands, empower users with diverse abilities to interact with their devices effectively. Operating systems that prioritize accessibility ensure that users with visual, auditory, motor, or cognitive impairments can navigate, communicate, and perform tasks seamlessly. This innovation reflects a commitment to creating technology that is inclusive and addresses the diverse needs of users across the spectrum of abilities.

The integration of emotion recognition technology is an emerging innovation that adds a nuanced layer to HCI within operating systems. By analyzing facial expressions, vocal intonations, and physiological cues, operating systems can infer the user's emotional state. This information can be leveraged to tailor the user experience, providing empathetic responses, adjusting interface elements based on mood, or offering supportive interactions. While still in its early stages, emotion-aware HCI holds the potential to create more emotionally intelligent operating systems that dynamically respond to the user's emotional context.

Collaborative computing and shared interfaces represent an innovative direction in HCI within operating systems, especially in the context of remote work and virtual collaboration. Operating systems equipped with collaborative features enable users to share screens, work on documents simultaneously, and engage in real-time interactions with colleagues or collaborators. This innovation transforms the operating system into a dynamic platform for collaborative work, fostering seamless communication and productivity in distributed or virtual team environments.

The concept of zero UI (User Interface) is an avant-garde innovation that envisions a computing experience where interactions are intuitive, ambient, and seamlessly integrated into the user's environment. Operating systems embracing zero UI prioritize minimizing explicit user inputs, relying on context-aware computing, sensor technologies, and AI-driven automation to anticipate and fulfill user needs. This innovation aims to create a more natural and unobtrusive interaction paradigm, where the operating system fades into the background, and computing becomes an integral part of the user's everyday activities.

The advent of mixed reality (MR) and spatial computing introduces a transformative dimension to HCI within operating systems. MR combines elements of both virtual and augmented reality, allowing users to interact with digital content in three-dimensional space. Operating systems that support MR offer users immersive and interactive experiences, where digital objects seamlessly coexist with the physical environment. This innovation opens new possibilities for gaming, design, education, and collaborative work, redefining the boundaries between the digital and physical realms within the operating system ecosystem.

As technology continues to advance, innovations in HCI within operating systems will likely continue to push boundaries and redefine the ways in which users engage with their devices. Whether through advancements in natural language processing, the integration of emerging technologies like emotion recognition, or the evolution of adaptive interfaces, the trajectory of HCI within operating systems reflects a dynamic pursuit of creating more intuitive, inclusive, and immersive computing experiences for users in the digital age.

Discuss the role of operating systems in promoting sustainability and green computing.

Operating systems play a pivotal role in promoting sustainability and green computing by influencing various aspects of computer hardware and software, as well as user behavior. One fundamental way in which operating systems contribute to sustainability is through power management features. These features optimize the use of energy resources by dynamically adjusting the power consumption of hardware components such as the CPU, display, and storage devices. Through advanced power management algorithms, operating systems can intelligently scale the performance of hardware components based on the system's workload, leading to significant energy savings.

Furthermore, operating systems facilitate the implementation of energy-efficient hardware technologies by providing support for features like sleep modes, hibernation, and wake-on-LAN. Sleep modes enable computers to enter a low-power state when not in use, conserving energy without compromising the user's ability to quickly resume tasks. Hibernation allows the system to save its current state to the disk and power down entirely, reducing energy consumption during extended periods of inactivity. Wake-on-LAN features enable remote activation of a computer, promoting energy efficiency by allowing users to power on systems only when necessary.

In addition to power management, operating systems contribute to sustainability through resource allocation and utilization. Virtualization, a key feature in modern operating systems, enables the creation of virtual machines that share physical resources, leading to better resource utilization and reduced hardware requirements. This not only optimizes energy consumption but also minimizes electronic waste by extending the lifespan of existing hardware. Operating systems also facilitate the implementation of containerization technologies, allowing for efficient packaging and deployment of software applications with minimal impact on system resources.

The concept of green computing extends beyond energy efficiency to address electronic waste and the lifecycle of computing devices. Operating systems can play a role in promoting sustainable practices by encouraging the development of modular and upgradeable hardware. This, in turn, facilitates the reuse and repurposing of components, reducing the environmental impact associated with the disposal of electronic waste. Operating systems can support user-friendly interfaces for hardware upgrades, making it easier for individuals and organizations to extend the lifespan of their computing equipment.

Moreover, operating systems influence user behavior and awareness regarding sustainable computing practices. Through user interfaces, notifications, and educational initiatives, operating systems can inform users about the environmental impact of their computing activities. This may include providing insights into energy consumption, carbon footprint, and the benefits of adopting eco-friendly computing habits. By raising awareness and promoting responsible use, operating systems can empower users to make informed decisions that contribute to a more sustainable computing ecosystem.

Security is another crucial aspect where operating systems play a role in sustainability. A secure system is less prone to vulnerabilities and cyberattacks, which can have environmental consequences. Cybersecurity incidents often lead to data breaches, system disruptions, and the need for extensive system repairs or replacements. By incorporating robust security measures, operating systems can help prevent these incidents, reducing the overall environmental impact associated with the resources required to address and recover from security breaches.

Furthermore, operating systems can support the development and integration of energy-efficient software applications. Through software development frameworks and guidelines, operating systems can encourage programmers to optimize their code for energy efficiency. This may involve techniques such as code profiling, resource-efficient algorithms, and minimizing unnecessary computations. By fostering a culture of energy-aware software development, operating systems contribute to the creation of applications that consume fewer resources and operate more sustainably.

Cloud computing, a prevalent paradigm in contemporary computing, is closely tied to operating systems and has implications for sustainability. Operating systems designed for cloud environments can leverage technologies such as server virtualization, load balancing, and resource pooling to enhance the overall efficiency of data centers. This, in turn, reduces the environmental impact of large-scale computing infrastructure by optimizing resource utilization, minimizing energy consumption, and promoting a more sustainable approach to delivering computing services.

In conclusion, operating systems play a multifaceted role in promoting sustainability and green computing. Through power management features, resource allocation strategies, support for energy-efficient hardware technologies, and influencing user behavior, operating systems contribute to energy savings, electronic waste reduction, and overall environmental responsibility. The integration of security measures, support for modular hardware designs, and encouragement of energy-efficient software development further enhance the positive impact of operating systems on sustainability. As the computing landscape continues to evolve, the role of operating systems in shaping a more environmentally conscious and sustainable future remains integral to the broader goals of responsible technology use.

Discuss how operating systems integrate with augmented and virtual reality environments.

Operating systems play a crucial role in the seamless integration of augmented reality (AR) and virtual reality (VR) environments, providing the foundational framework that enables these immersive technologies to function cohesively with various hardware components and applications. One of the primary functions of operating systems in AR and VR is to manage the communication between the underlying hardware and the immersive experiences being delivered to users. This involves coordinating the input from sensors, cameras, and other peripherals to accurately track the user's movements and provide real-time feedback, creating an immersive and interactive environment.

In AR environments, where virtual elements are overlaid onto the real world, operating systems must handle the integration of digital content with the physical surroundings. This includes tasks such as spatial mapping, object recognition, and gesture tracking, all of which require sophisticated algorithms and close coordination with hardware components like cameras and sensors. Operating systems designed for AR, such as Google's Android ARCore or Apple's ARKit, provide developers with the tools and APIs needed to create AR applications that seamlessly interact with the user's environment.

In the realm of VR, where users are fully immersed in a computer-generated environment, operating systems play a fundamental role in managing the hardware resources to deliver a smooth and responsive experience. VR operating systems, like Oculus Home for Oculus devices or SteamVR for various VR platforms, are designed to prioritize low-latency communication between the VR headset and associated peripherals, ensuring that user movements are accurately reflected in the virtual world. These operating systems also facilitate the integration of VR controllers and haptic feedback devices, enhancing the overall sense of presence and interaction within the virtual environment.

Device compatibility is a critical aspect of AR and VR integration, and operating systems act as a bridge between the hardware and software layers to ensure seamless communication. Operating systems need to support a wide range of devices, including headsets, motion controllers, and spatial sensors, by providing standardized drivers and APIs. This ensures that developers can create applications that work across various AR and VR hardware platforms without needing to rewrite code for each specific device. Compatibility efforts often involve collaboration between operating system developers and hardware manufacturers to establish industry standards that promote interoperability.

Moreover, the performance demands of AR and VR require operating systems to prioritize and allocate resources efficiently. This includes optimizing graphics rendering, managing memory usage, and ensuring minimal latency in data processing. Operating systems in AR and VR environments implement techniques like real-time scheduling, graphics acceleration, and hardware abstraction layers to streamline resource utilization and deliver a responsive and immersive user experience. These optimizations are particularly crucial in preventing motion sickness and discomfort, common challenges in virtual reality experiences.

Security is another critical aspect of AR and VR integration with operating systems. As these technologies often involve the use of cameras and sensors to capture the user's environment, privacy concerns arise. Operating systems must implement robust security measures to protect user data, prevent unauthorized access to sensors, and ensure secure communication between the virtual and real worlds. Addressing these security challenges is essential to fostering user trust and encouraging widespread adoption of AR and VR technologies.

Furthermore, operating systems in AR and VR environments facilitate the distribution and management of applications through dedicated app stores or platforms. These app stores serve as centralized hubs for users to discover, download, and update AR and VR applications. Operating systems manage the installation and uninstallation processes, handle software updates, and ensure compatibility with the evolving hardware landscape. This centralized approach not only enhances user convenience but also allows developers to reach a broader audience with their AR and VR creations.

Interoperability is a key consideration in the integration of AR and VR with operating systems. The ability of these immersive technologies to seamlessly work with other applications and services enhances their utility. Operating systems provide APIs and frameworks that enable developers to integrate AR and VR functionalities into existing software, creating a more interconnected and versatile computing environment. This integration can extend to collaboration tools, gaming platforms, education applications, and various other domains, amplifying the impact of AR and VR on diverse industries.

The development of AR and VR ecosystems is closely tied to the ongoing advancements in operating systems. As these technologies continue to evolve, operating systems must adapt to accommodate new features, hardware innovations, and user expectations. Operating system updates often include enhancements specifically tailored to improve AR and VR experiences, such as better support for hand tracking, improved spatial awareness, and increased graphics capabilities. This iterative process ensures that operating systems remain at the forefront of technological innovation, driving the continued growth of AR and VR applications.

In conclusion, operating systems serve as the linchpin in the integration of augmented and virtual reality environments, orchestrating the complex interplay between hardware, software, and user experiences. From managing sensor input to optimizing resource utilization, ensuring device compatibility, addressing security concerns, and fostering interoperability, operating systems play a pivotal role in shaping the landscape of AR and VR technologies. As these immersive technologies become increasingly prevalent in various industries, the symbiotic relationship between operating systems and AR/VR will continue to drive innovation, redefine user interactions, and shape the future of computing.

Discuss the concept of collaborative and decentralized operating systems.

Collaborative and decentralized operating systems represent a paradigm shift in the traditional approach to computing, challenging the centralized model of control and introducing new concepts that prioritize collaboration, distributed decision-making, and resilience. In a collaborative operating system, the emphasis is on enabling multiple users to work together seamlessly, fostering cooperative interactions among diverse entities within a computing environment. Unlike traditional systems, where a single user typically controls the operation of a machine, collaborative operating systems support concurrent access by multiple users, allowing them to share resources, exchange information, and collectively contribute to a shared computing experience.

Decentralized operating systems, on the other hand, extend the principles of collaboration to the management and control of the underlying infrastructure. In a decentralized system, there is no single point of control; instead, decision-making authority is distributed across the network. This approach is in stark contrast to the centralized models employed by traditional operating systems, where a central server or controller governs the actions of connected devices. Decentralized operating systems aim to create a more flexible, resilient, and scalable architecture by distributing control and decision-making responsibilities among multiple nodes.

One fundamental aspect of collaborative and decentralized operating systems is the shift towards peer-to-peer (P2P) communication models. In a P2P network, each node has equal status, and participants can both contribute to and consume resources within the network. This contrasts with client-server models, where a central server holds authority and clients are dependent on it for services. Collaborative and decentralized systems leverage P2P architectures to enable efficient resource sharing, fault tolerance, and improved scalability. This approach not only empowers individual users but also enhances the overall robustness of the system by eliminating single points of failure.

Collaborative operating systems often feature shared workspaces and real-time collaboration tools, facilitating synchronous and asynchronous interactions among users. Shared documents, collaborative editing, and instant messaging are common functionalities in these systems, allowing users to work together on projects regardless of their physical location. This collaborative ethos extends beyond document editing to encompass various applications, fostering a sense of community and collective productivity. Decentralized operating systems, by distributing control across multiple nodes, aim to eliminate the vulnerabilities associated with centralized points of control, such as server outages or targeted attacks. This distributed approach enhances system resilience, as the failure of individual nodes does not necessarily disrupt the entire system. Moreover, decentralized systems often leverage consensus algorithms and blockchain technology to ensure trust and integrity in a distributed environment, enabling secure and tamper-resistant transactions and interactions.

The concept of collaborative and decentralized operating systems is closely linked to the evolving landscape of the Internet and the emergence of Web 3.0. In Web 3.0, the emphasis is on decentralized, user-centric, and privacy-preserving architectures. Collaborative operating systems contribute to this vision by providing tools and platforms that empower users to control their data, collaborate with others without intermediaries, and participate in decentralized ecosystems. The rise of blockchain technology plays a significant role in these developments, providing a secure and transparent foundation for decentralized applications and services.

Security and privacy are critical considerations in collaborative and decentralized operating systems. The distributed nature of these systems introduces new challenges, such as securing communication channels, ensuring data integrity, and protecting user identities. Cryptographic techniques and secure communication protocols become integral components to address these challenges. Privacy-preserving features, including anonymization and end-to-end encryption, are incorporated to safeguard user data in collaborative environments. Decentralized identity systems and blockchain-based authentication mechanisms are explored to give users control over their digital identities while mitigating the risks associated with centralized authentication systems.

Open-source development models often align with the principles of collaborative and decentralized operating systems. The collaborative nature of open-source projects encourages a distributed approach to software development, where contributors from diverse backgrounds and locations collaborate to improve and extend software functionalities. Decentralized decision-making within open-source communities allows for a more inclusive and democratic development process, fostering innovation and adaptability. The transparency inherent in open-source projects aligns with the principles of decentralization, as the source code is accessible to all, and the development process is open to scrutiny.

The Internet of Things (IoT) is another domain where collaborative and decentralized operating systems find relevance. As IoT ecosystems grow, the need for scalable and resilient operating systems becomes evident. Collaborative operating systems enable devices to interact seamlessly, sharing data and coordinating actions. Decentralized architectures enhance the security and reliability of IoT networks by eliminating single points of control, reducing the impact of potential security breaches or device failures.

The concept of edge computing, where computing resources are distributed closer to the data source, also aligns with the principles of collaborative and decentralized operating systems. Edge computing leverages decentralized architectures to reduce latency, improve responsiveness, and enhance the overall efficiency of distributed systems. Collaborative operating systems play a crucial role in enabling seamless collaboration and communication between edge devices, ensuring that the benefits of edge computing are fully realized.

Challenges exist in the adoption of collaborative and decentralized operating systems. Transitioning from traditional, centralized models requires overcoming technical, cultural, and organizational barriers. Standardization efforts are essential to ensure interoperability and compatibility between diverse systems and platforms. Additionally, educating users and organizations about the advantages and best practices of collaborative and decentralized approaches is crucial for widespread adoption.

In conclusion, collaborative and decentralized operating systems represent a transformative approach to computing, redefining the way users interact with technology and shaping the future of distributed systems. By embracing principles such as peer-to-peer communication, decentralized decision-making, and user empowerment, these operating systems contribute to a more inclusive, resilient, and scalable computing environment. As technology continues to evolve, the collaborative and decentralized paradigm serves as a catalyst for innovation, fostering the development of systems that prioritize user collaboration, privacy, and control in an interconnected and distributed world.

****

www.ingramcontent.com/pod-product-compliance
Lightning Source LLC
Chambersburg PA
CBHW060036260726
48658CB00004B/1078